The Spi

The
Spiral of Silence

Public Opinion – Our Social Skin

Elisabeth Noelle-Neumann

SECOND EDITION

The University of Chicago Press
Chicago and London

**To all of my students in Mainz and Chicago
who have worked on the *Spiral of Silence***

The University of Chicago Press, Chicago 60637
The University of Chicago Press, Ltd., London
© 1984, 1993 by The University of Chicago
All rights reserved. Second edition published 1993
Printed in the United States of America
02 01 00 99 98 97 96 95   5 4 3 2
ISBN: 0-226-58935-8 (cloth)   0-226-58936-6 (paper)

The first edition of this book was originally published in German under the title
Die Schweigespirale: Öffentliche Meinung—unsere soziale Haut, © R. Piper &
Co. Verlag, München 1980. Subsequent editions © 1982, 1989, 1991 by Verlag
Ullstein GmbH, Frankfurt am Main–Berlin.

Library of Congress Cataloging-in-Publication Data
Noelle-Neumann, Elisabeth, 1916–
    [Schweigespirale. English]
    The spiral of silence : public opinion, our social skin /
Elisabeth Noelle-Neumann. – 2nd ed.
        p.   cm.
    Includes bibliographical references and index.
    1. Public opinion. 2. Public opinion–Germany (West) I. Title.
    1. Public opinion. 2. Public opinion—Germany. I. Title
HM261.N55713 1993
303.3'8–dc20   93-15484
                                                          CIP

⊗The paper used in this publication meets the minimum requirements of the
American National Standard for Information Sciences—Permanence of Paper for
Printed Library Materials, ANSI Z39.48-1984.

Contents

Introduction to the Second American Edition

*T*he new edition of this book retains most of the material, with minor adjustments, of the 1984 edition. Three new chapters have been added to summarize ongoing research, new findings, and new developments since 1984.

Since the early 1980s we have become aware of a much longer history of the concept of public opinion than was at first believed. It has been found to date back in time almost two thousand years. In a letter to Atticus dated 50 B.C., Cicero apologizes for a mistake by pointing out that he was simply following public opinion— *publicam opinionem*. Characters representing "public" and "opinion" appearing together have been found in Chinese texts of the fourth century A.D.

The effectiveness of public opinion as a powerful force capable of resolving conflicts, toppling governments, and oppressing individuals who resist until the "dead member falls from the social body" has been uncovered in more and more new areas: in the stories of the Bible and in Homer, in the unwritten laws of antiquity, in fairy tales as well as in the present. In recent years, history has taught us a great lesson in public opinion through the breakdown of Marxism in Eastern Europe. Aristotle maintained that a king who loses the support of his people is no longer a king. No longer a king, no longer a dictator, no longer a ruler. Seeing these rulers deposed in Eastern Europe, we are reminded of some words of Goethe: "And you can say that you witnessed it."

If we understand the force of public opinion, we shall not delude ourselves that we can be "good" citizens, completely independent of the pressure of public opinion. And we shall be slower to judge others who, at certain times and under certain circumstances, must come to terms with public opinion.

Allensbach/Germany, August 1992   E.N.N.

Introduction to the First
American Edition

*T*he ballet was by Gian Carlo Menotti. It was performed on a Sunday at International House on the University of Chicago campus. I had heard about it from Cris Miller, a doctoral candidate in English literature at the university, during our daily round of conversation to improve my English. In addition to having directed the ballet with a friend, she had agreed to sing in the chorus and to take a dancing role. Of course I attended the performance.

This was in the spring of 1980, when I was teaching at the University of Chicago for the second time as a visiting professor of political science. What is it that brings this ballet to mind now? The last thing I expected when I went to the performance was to be given a lesson in public opinion. Yet this is exactly what happened. At the same time it was more. The critic who later reviewed the performance in the *Chicago Maroon*, the student paper, wrote that tears came to his eyes. I must admit that I had the same experience. But I would like to tell the story of the ballet, to show what I mean.

Somewhere, possibly in Italy, there is a small town with honest citizens and a count and a countess of local lineage. Outside of the town, in a castle on a hill, lives a strange man who has the oddest ideas. He never ceases to give people cause for amazement; perhaps it would be more appropriate to say that they are partly amazed and partly annoyed by him, while at all times keeping their distance.

One Sunday this man appears in town leading a unicorn by a chain. People can only shake their heads about him. A little later, however, the count and countess are also seen in town leading a unicorn by a chain. This is the signal for everyone in town to get a unicorn.

Another Sunday, the strange man in the castle suddenly appears with a gorgon. People ask him what has become of the unicorn. The man tells them he was tired of the unicorn and decided to pepper and grill him. Everyone is shocked. But when the count and the countess also appear with a gorgon, shocked surprise turns to envy, and all at once gorgons are the rage.

On the third Sunday, the man in the castle turns up with a manticore and tells the people the gorgon was slaughtered. At first the townsfolk are scandalized. But then everything follows the usual course: the count and the countess secretly dispose of their gorgon, the townsfolk follow suit, and all at once the manticore is in vogue.

Time passes; the strange man in the castle is not seen anymore. People are sure the manticore has been slaughtered too. The townspeople form a committee to put an end to these crimes and march on the castle. They enter the castle, but are brought up short by what they see. They find the strange man dying in the company of his three animals—the unicorn, the gorgon, and the manticore. The unicorn represents the dreams of his youth, the gorgon his middle age, and the manticore his old age.

The townspeople discarded his ideas as quickly as they had taken them up; they were just passing whims. For the strange man in the castle, however, they represented the essence of his life. Gian Carlo Menotti titles his ballet: *The Unicorn, the Gorgon, and the Manticore*; or, *The Three Sundays of a Poet*. I would like to explain why I think it could also have been titled "Public Opinion."

We all take the poet's side. Even the *Chicago Maroon* critic wept. The poet represents our image of man as strong, independent, imaginative. And we are all familiar with the count and the countess—superficial trend-setters who have no ideas of their own but want to be leaders wherever they go. Those we despise most, however, are the people who go along with the crowd, first making fun of a person because he is different from them but then absorbing any new fashion and finally giving themselves the air of moral authority.

This is one point of view, and it is the way strange people from the castle, loners, artists, and scholars have always felt.

Now I would like to take the side of the count and the countess and the townspeople. I claim that in siding with the poet we deny our own social nature. We do not even think about the effort it takes for people who live in a social unit to keep a community together. We act as if being in possession of a common rich historical and cultural tradition and of institutions protected by the law did not require a constant effort of adjustment and even "conformity" if that possession is to be kept alive and if we are to remain capable of acting and making decisions on a community level.

There are many indications that we do not want to recognize our social nature, which forces us to conform.

John Locke talks about the law of opinion, the law of reputation, the law of fashion, which is heeded more than any divine law or any law of the state; this is because the individual will immediately be made to suffer for any violation of the law of fashion by losing the sympathy and esteem of his social environment. But there seems to have been little interest over the course of time in exploring the reasons why such behavior is vital if a social community is to survive. Instead, everything connected with fashion takes on a negative quality: fashionable, the follies of fashion, a whim of fashion. Leading the unicorn, the gorgon, and the manticore on a chain is just a way of keeping up with fashion.

We act as if unaware of our social nature. While the topic of imitation has received scholarly attention ever since the French sociologist Gabriel Tarde wrote of it, imitative behavior has been explained almost exclusively as a result of the motivation to learn: the transfer of experience as a way of finding the right solution for oneself more efficiently. This motive does, admittedly, often prompt imitative behavior, but the motive of not wanting to be isolated, to be on the fringes, seems to be much stronger. People "dread isolation more than error," Tocqueville wrote when he wanted to explain why no one in France defended the church anymore toward the end of the eighteenth century. Tocqueville's description of the "spiral of silence" was as precise as a botanist's. Today it can be proved that even when people see plainly that something is wrong, they will keep quiet if public opinion (opinions and behavior that can be exhibited in public without fear of isolation) and, hence, the consensus as to what constitutes good taste and the morally correct opinion speaks against them.

I side with the count and the countess because the poet's ideas would never have been disseminated without them; they are the moderators, the opinion leaders society needs, much as journalists often are today. And the townspeople, the people who go along with the crowd—what do we know about their feelings, their dreams? What do we know about what they are like inside? In public, they don't want to suffer isolation; not one person in ten thousand is callous enough not to care if the social environment withholds its approval, states John Locke. How could you continue to walk around with a unicorn if no one else were walking around with a unicorn anymore? Let's try to imagine a society that consists strictly of loners, of strange men from the castle. A society such as this, lacking either social nature or the fear of isolation, is plainly an impossibility. We may not feel sympathy for man's social nature, but we should try to understand it so as not to be unfair to the people who go along with the crowd.

This is more or less the way I tried to interpret the ballet to my students the following day.

It is almost impossible to say how many ideas, insights, and opportunities for discussions I owe to my stays in Chicago, to the conversations with colleagues, students, and friends. The story of the ballet may serve to illustrate this too. When my students protested, their comments were also instructive: They thought, for example, that I did not pay sufficient attention to the relationship between public opinion and private opinion, to what the individual says in public and what he says or thinks in private. There may be cultural distinctions here—different cultures having different ways of dealing with conflicts between a dominant public opinion and private convictions. In certain cultures, people may have an easier time speaking with a forked tongue; if this is so, the relationship between public and private opinion constitutes a serious problem for survey research, most particularly a problem of methodology. I suspect that there is a strong tendency in Germany for the individual to make the inside and the outside, publicly expressed opinion and private opinion, agree with each other. This frequently requires a great deal of self-persuasion because we are not accustomed to adjusting our private and public attitudes to each other on a purely superficial level.

There are probably also cultural differences in our willingness to accept the social nature of man without a feeling of contempt. The Japanese, for example, do not feel that giving the views of the social environment their due indicates weakness, whereas most Germans, according to Allensbach surveys, have long been saying, "I don't care what anyone else says." Overall, however, the similarities in the role of public opinion at different times and in different places seem by far to outweigh the differences.

Cris Miller, who directed and sang and danced in the ballet by Gian Carlo Menotti and is now assistant professor of English literature at Pomona College in Claremont, California, edited the entire English translation of the book. My colleague Gordon Whiting, professor of communication research at Brigham Young University in Utah, prepared a preliminary draft of the translation while a visiting professor at the Institut für Publizistik of the University of

Mainz in West Germany, with some assistance from the three staff members of the English department of the Institut für Demoskopie Allensbach—Wolfgang Koschnick, head of the department; Mary Siwinski; and Maria Marzahl. Mihaly Csikszentmihalyi, professor of behavioral sciences at the University of Chicago, who is equally familiar with German and English, thoroughly checked and edited the manuscript once more, and, lastly, he and I edited the final version together. I do not know how to thank these friends and colleagues, who are so busy with their own scholarly work, for all they did to ensure the success of the translation.

Chicago, Spring 1983   E.N.N.

1 The Hypothesis of Silence

*F*or the election eve of 1965, the second German television network (ZDF) came up with a new idea: an election party in Bonn's Beethoven Hall. There was a stage review, dinner, several dance orchestras, guests sitting at long banquet tables—the house was packed. To the right, up front, just below the stage, a small podium with a blackboard had been set up. There, a notary public was scheduled to open two letters received two days before, one from the Allensbach Institute and one from EMNID—two competing survey research organizations. The heads of the two organizations would then be invited to enter their predictions about the outcome of the election in the grid already drawn on the blackboard. Over the hubbub, the noise of chairs scraping, the sounds of eating and drinking, I wrote on the board: "Christian Democratic Union / Christian Social Union 49.5%, Social Democratic Party 38.5% . . ." At that moment a cry broke out from hundreds of people behind me and swelled to a thunderous roar. As if suddenly deafened, I completed my entries: "Free Democratic Party 8.0%, Other parties, 4.0%"* The hall seethed with outrage, and the publisher of the weekly *Die Zeit*, Gerd Bucerius, shouted to me: "Elisabeth, how can I defend you now!"

Had my Allensbach Institute been deliberately deceiving the public for months, telling people that the election was neck to neck? Just two days earlier, *Die Zeit* had printed an interview with me under the headline "I would not be at all surprised if the Social Democrats won" (Leonhardt 1965). Later that same evening, as the official election results moved closer to the Allensbach predictions, a Christian Democratic politician gave television viewers to understand, chuckling as he did, that he, of course, had understood the actual situation all along but had been smart enough to keep it to himself—"All's fair in love and war . . ." The quotation in *Die Zeit* was accurate; I had said that. The interview, however, had lain in the editor's files for more than two weeks. At the start of September it had looked like a dead heat. What the people assembled in the

*The Christian Democratic Union is the more conservative of the major German parties. The Christian Social Union is the Christian Democrats' sister party in Bavaria. The Social Democratic Party of Germany represents the left in the spectrum of German politics. The Free Democratic Party (or Liberals) is more middle-of-the-road compared to the two major parties.

Figure 1

The Election Year Puzzle of 1965

Voting intentions remained almost unchanged for many months, indicating a neck-and-neck race between the CDU/CSU and the SPD. At the same time, however, the notion that the CDU/CSU was going to win spread among voters. How did that come about? At the end we find a bandwagon effect in the direction of the expected winner of the election.

Voting intention: CDU/CSU ████████   SPD ▨▨▨▨▨▨▨▨
Expectation: Who will win the election?
CDU/CSU will win ████████   SPD will win ▤▤▤▤

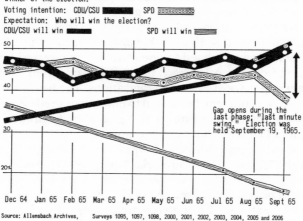

Dec 64 Jan 65 Feb 65 Mar 65 Apr 65 May 65 Jun 65 Jul 65 Aug 65 Sept 65

Source: Allensbach Archives,   Surveys 1095, 1097, 1098, 2000, 2001, 2002, 2003, 2004, 2005 and 2006

Beethoven Hall got to see was what we, to our amazement, had seen appear on our desks in Allensbach three days before the election but had not been able to publish, since to have done so then would have appeared as a massive attempt to influence the outcome of the election by starting a bandwagon effect in favor of the Christian Democrats. What had occurred had been recognized and named centuries earlier, but was still not understood: the power of public opinion. Under its pressure, hundreds of thousands—no, actually millions of voters—had taken part in what was later called a "last minute swing." At the last minute they had gone along with the crowd, swelling the Christian Democratic ranks from a position of equality with the other major party to what official election returns recorded as a lead of more than 8 percent (fig. 1).*

Knowledge lags far behind measurement

Although we did not realize it in 1965, we had in our hands even then the key to this dramatic change in the electorate's intentions. In an article about public opinion appearing in 1968 in the *International Encyclopedia of the Social Sciences*, W. Phillips Davison, professor of communications research and journalism at Co-

---

*In figs. 1–5, 11–17, and 22, CDU/CSU stands for Christian Democratic Union; SPD for Social Democratic Party; and FDP for Free Democratic Party (liberals).

lumbia University in New York, wrote: "Knowledge about the internal structure of public opinions, nevertheless, is still limited and lags far behind measurement" (Davison 1968, 192). That was exactly our situation in 1965; we had measured a lot more than we understood. Thus, while from December 1964 until almost the day of the election in September 1965, the two major parties were locked in a dead heat in terms of the number who intended to vote for them—and these figures were published regularly in the magazine *Stern*—another set of data showed steady and completely independent movement; the question went like this: "Of course nobody can know, but what do you think: who is going to win the election?" In December the number of those expecting the Christian Democrats to win and the number expecting the Social Democrats to win was about even, although the Social Democrats had a slight edge. Then the estimates began to change direction, and the expectation of a Christian Democratic victory rose relentlessly while expectation of a Social Democratic victory decreased. By July 1965, the Christian Democrats were well in the lead, and the expectation of their victory reached almost 50 percent by August. It was as though the measurements of how the electorate intended to vote and which party they expected to win had been taken on different planets. And then, right at the end, people jumped on the bandwagon. As if caught in a current, 3–4 percent of the voters were swept in the direction of the general expectation of who was going to win.

Every piece of research begins with a puzzle

We remained puzzled: How could expectations of who was going to win the election change so completely in the face of constant voter intentions? Not until 1972, when a federal election was called on short notice and there was a campaign period of only a few weeks—not a particularly appropriate election for our purposes—did we set up our survey machinery, with a specially designed questionnaire to gather the kinds of observations we needed. We had already formulated the hypothesis we were to use and had presented it at the International Congress of Psychology held in Tokyo in the summer of 1972 (Noelle-Neumann 1973).

As it happened, the election campaign of 1972 developed just like that of 1965. The two major parties were neck-to-neck when the question of voting intention was asked; meanwhile, the expectation that the Social Democratic Party was going to win grew from week to week like a separate, independent reality, with only one setback. Then, right at the end, again there was a "last minute

Figure 2

The Phenomenon of 1965 Repeats Itself in 1972

While voting intentions remain constant—a neck-and-neck race between the CDU/CSU and the SPD—the climate of opinion changes: expectation of a win declines for the CDU/CSU while it increases for the SPD. Finally, there is the bandwagon effect in the direction of the growing expectation of winning.

Voting intention: CDU/CSU ■■■■   SPD [◎◎◎]
Expectation: Who will win the election?
CDU/CSU will win ■■■■   SPD will win ▭▭▭

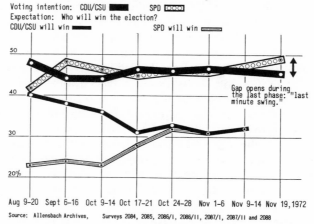

Aug 9–20 Sept 6–16 Oct 9–14 Oct 17–21 Oct 24–28 Nov 1–6 Nov 9–14 Nov 19,1972

Source: Allensbach Archives,   Surveys 2084, 2085, 2086/I, 2086/II, 2087/I, 2087/II and 2088

swing"; people jumped on the bandwagon of the expected winner, this time the Social Democratic Party (fig. 2).

The climate of opinion depends on who talks and who keeps quiet

The hypothesis came to me out of the student unrest at the end of the sixties and the beginning of the seventies; I probably owe it to one particular student. I met her one day in the hall outside the lecture room and noticed that she was wearing a Christian Democratic button on her jacket.

"I didn't know you were a Christian Democratic supporter," I said to her. "I'm not," she said, "I just put the button on to see what it's like."

I met her again at noon. She was not wearing the button, and I asked about the change. "It was too awful," she said. "I took if off."

In the context of the commotion that characterized those first years of the new Ostpolitik, this was understandable. Followers of the Social Democrats and of the Christian Democrats might be equal in numbers, but they were far from equal in energy, enthusiasm, or in willingness to express and display their convictions. Only Social Democratic buttons and emblems appeared publicly, so it was no wonder that the relative strengths of the two parties were incorrectly assessed. A peculiar dynamic developed at this point. Those who were convinced the new Ostpolitik was right thought their beliefs eventually would be adopted by everyone. So these people expressed themselves openly, and self-confidently defended their views. Those who rejected the Ostpolitik felt themselves left out; they withdrew, and fell silent.

This very restraint made the view that was receiving vocal support appear to be stronger than it really was and the other view weaker. Observations made in one context spread to another and encouraged people either to proclaim their views or to swallow them and keep quiet until, in a spiraling process, the one view dominated the public scene and the other disappeared from public awareness as its adherents became mute. This is the process that can be called a "spiral of silence."

At first, all this was merely a hypothesis. It helped explain what had happened in 1965. During the summer of that election year, support for the government peaked as public attention focused on the combined activities of Chancellor Ludwig Erhard and the Queen of England. The popular Erhard was preparing for his first parliamentary campaign as chancellor, and the queen was traveling here and there throughout Germany in the beautiful summer weather of that year, meeting and being greeted by Erhard over and over again. Television news carried the images of their encounters everywhere. Although there was an almost even split between voter preference for the Christian Democrats and for the Social Democrats, it was pleasant to profess attachment to the Christian Democratic Union, the party in power, and this could be done easily and openly. The steep climb in the expectation of a Christian Democratic win in the parliamentary election reflected this climate of opinion (fig. 1).

Those who went along at the last minute

In neither 1965 nor 1972 were voting *intentions* swept along by this climate. Indeed, in both years just the opposite occurred. From top to bottom, intentions remained almost untouched by what was paving the way for a change just before election day—the climate of opinion. This may be taken as a good sign; voting intentions do not twirl like weather vanes in a storm but possess considerable stability. Paul F. Lazarsfeld, the Austrian-American social psychologist and student of elections, once spoke of a hierarchy of stability, placing voting intentions right at the top as especially firm and subject only to slow change in response to new experiences, observations, information, and opinions (Lazarsfeld et al. 1948, xxxvi–xxxvii). Still, in the end the climate of opinion made its effect felt. Twice we saw a last-minute swing in the direction of the climate's pressure, and it resulted in a substantial shift: 3–4 percent of the votes. Lazarsfeld (1968, 107–9) had already noted this "bandwagon effect" in the American presidential election of 1940. Everyone wants to be on the winning side, to belong with the winner— that was how the bandwagon effect was usually explained. Always be on the winning side? Most people are probably not so pretentious. Unlike the elite, most people don't expect office or power from a win. We are dealing with something more modest, a desire to avoid isolating ourselves, a desire that apparently all of us share. No one wants to be as isolated as the university student who wore a Christian Democratic badge for a whole morning, so isolated that neighbors look the other way when they pass you on the stairs to your apartment, or fellow workers move away, leaving an empty seat next to you. We are only beginning to observe the hundreds of signals that let a person know he or she is not surrounded by a warm glow of sympathy but by a ring of avoidance.

Repeated questioning of the same people before and after the 1972 election revealed to us that those who feel they are relatively isolated from others—we identify them in our studies by the comment, "I know very few people"—are the ones most likely to participate in a last-minute election swing. Those with weaker self-confidence and less interest in politics are also likely to make a last-minute switch. Because of their low self-esteem, few of these people ever think of being on the winning side or playing the trumpet on top of the bandwagon. "Running with the pack" better describes the situation of those who "go along." Yet this situation applies, more or less, to all mankind. When people think others are turning away from them, they suffer so much that they can be guided or manipulated as easily by their own sensitivity as by a bridle.

The fear of isolation seems to be the force that sets the spiral of silence in motion. To run with the pack is a relatively happy state of affairs; but if you can't, because you won't share publicly in what seems to be a universally acclaimed conviction, you can at least remain silent, as a second choice, so that others can put up with you. Thomas Hobbes (1969, see especially 69) wrote about the meaning of silence in his book, *The Elements of Law*, published in 1650. Silence, he said, can be interpreted as an indication of agreement, for it is easy to say no when one disagrees. Hobbes is certainly wrong in saying that it is easy to say no, but he is right in supposing that silence can be interpreted as agreement; that is what makes it so tempting.

Drawing the phenomenon into the light of day

There are two possible ways of checking the reality, the validity, of a process like that envisioned in the spiral-of-silence hypothesis. If something like this really exists, if this is truly the process by which ideologies and social movements prevail or are swept away, then many authors from earlier centuries must have noticed and commented on it. It is highly unlikely that phenomena such as these would have escaped the attention of sensitive and reflective men who, as philosophers, students of law, and historians, have written about human beings and their world. As I began my search through the writings of the great thinkers of the past, I was encouraged when I found a precise description of the dynamics of the spiral of silence in Alexis de Tocqueville's history of the French revolution, published in 1856. Tocqueville recounts the decline of the French church in the middle of the eighteenth century and the manner in which contempt for religion became a general and reigning passion among the French. A major factor, he tells us, was the silence of the French church: "Those who retained their belief in the doctrines of the Church became afraid of being alone in their allegiance and, dreading isolation more than error, professed to share the sentiments of the majority. So what was in reality the opinion of only a part . . . of the nation came to be regarded as the will of all and for this reason seemed irresistible, even to those who had given it this false appearance."[1]

Feeling my way back into the past, I found impressive observations and remarks scattered everywhere. They included comments from Jean-Jacques Rousseau and David Hume, John Locke, Martin Luther, Machiavelli, John Hus, and even from the writers of antiquity. The topic never constituted a major theme; it was more often in the form of a marginal comment. My search was like a paper chase, but the reality of the spiral of silence became more and more firmly established.

A second way of testing the legitimacy of a hypothesis is to investigate it empirically. If a phenomenon such as the spiral of

1. Tocqueville 1952, 207; English: 1955, 155. Author's translation in part.

silence exists, it must be measurable. At least that should be the case today; after more than fifty years of testing instruments for use in representative survey research, a social-psychological phenomenon of this kind should no longer be able to escape observation. The following chapter describes the kinds of instruments we developed in order to bring the spiral of silence into the cold light of day.

2   Testing with Survey Research Instruments

*T*he word "instrument" may suggest some visible apparatus, whether a tiny machine or a mammoth piece of engineering such as a radio telescope. Still, what appears in a questionnaire and is presented in an interview as a set of questions is an instrument for observation—even if it looks like a game. The reactions of a representative cross-section of people to such questions reveal the existence of motives and modes of behavior, the very things which must provide the groundwork for a process like the spiral of silence. Hypothesizing such a process entails the claim that people observe their social environment; that they are alert to the thinking of those about them and are aware of changing trends; that they register which opinions are gaining ground and which will become dominant. Can we prove this claim?

"How should I know?"

In January 1971, Allensbach surveys began to come to grips with the spiral of silence. The first series of questions contained three queries which ran:

> A question about the DDR (East Germany): If you had to make the decision, would you say that the Federal Republic should recognize the DDR as a second German state, or should the Federal Republic *not* recognize it?
>
> Now, regardless for the moment of your own opinion, what do you think: are most of the people in the Federal Republic for or against recognizing the DDR?

What do you think will happen in the future: what will people's views be like in a year's time? Will *more* people or *fewer* people favor the recognition of the DDR then than favor it now?

"Now, regardless for the moment of your own opinion, what do you think: are most of the people for or against . . ."—"What do you think will happen in the future: what will people's views be like in a year's time?" It might well have happened that most people would have responded to such questions with "How should I know 'what most people think,' 'what's going to happen in the future'? I'm no prophet!" But that was not the way people answered. As though it were the most natural thing in the world, 80–90 percent of the people in a representative cross-section of the population over sixteen years of age offered their assessment of the opinions held by the people around them (table 1).

People's views about the future are somewhat less certain, but even questions concerning the future of an opinion do not meet with blank looks. In January of 1971, a full three-fifths expressed their estimate as to how opinion concerning recognition of the DDR would develop, and the estimates were quite clear; 45 percent expected more support, and only 16 percent expected less support (table 2). The results are reminiscent of the observations of 1965. The question "What do you think: who will win the election?" was not answered "How in the world should I know?" by the vast majority of respondents—although in view of the poll figures, which month after month indicated that we had a real horse race, that might have been a very reasonable response. No, at that time expectations were voiced more and more clearly, and not without effect, as the shift of voters at the last moment showed. Carrying over the observations of 1965–71, we would be led to expect a spiral of silence operating in favor of the eventual recognition of the DDR.

A new human ability discovered: perceiving the climate of opinion

Let us stay for the moment with our initial exploratory probes and see the extent to which they confirm the hypothesis of a spiral of silence. After the first attempt in January 1971, numerous sets of questions followed. Just as in 1965, they consistently confirmed the people's apparent ability to perceive something about majority and minority opinions, to sense the frequency distribution of pro and

Table 1. Environmental observation of the climate of opinion

Most people are willing to express an opinion about which side of a disputed issue the majority of the population is on. From among about 50 tests conducted on the basis of representative samples with either 1,000 or 2,000 respondents between 1971 and 1979, table 1 gives twelve examples. The text of the question for the first of these ran: "Now, regardless of your own opinion, what do you think: Are most of the people in the Federal Republic for or against recognizing the DDR (East Germany)?" The other questions were formulated analogously.

Issues	Percentage of respondents providing an estimate
Recognize East Germany? (January 1971)	86
Do something to prevent the spread of hashish and LSD? (January 1971)	95
Stricter laws to maintain the quality of air and water? (March 1971)	75
Allow termination of pregnancy through abortion? (April 1972)	83
For or against the death penalty? (June 1972)	90
More political influence for Franz Josef Strauss? (October/November 1972)	80
For or against the forced feeding of prisoners who go on hunger strikes? (February 1975)	84
Allow a member of the German Communist Party to be appointed a judge? (April 1976)	82
Is the Christian Democratic Union well liked? (August 1976)	62
Is the Social Democratic Party well liked? (August 1976)	65
For or against the building of new nuclear energy plants? (September 1977)	85
Should smokers smoke in the presence of nonsmokers? (March 1979)	88
Average concrete estimate for 55 subject-matter areas	82

Source: Allensbach Archives, surveys 2068, 2069, 2081, 2083, 2087, 3011, 3028, 3032/II, 3032/I, 3047, 3065

Table 2. Expectations as an expression of the climate of opinion

People's readiness to express themselves about the future development of opinion was tested in January 1971. The issue used was recognition of East Germany. *Question*: "What do you think will happen in the future—what will people's views be like in a year's time? Will more people or fewer people favor the recognition of East Germany then than favor it now?"

	Respondents 16 years and older (%)
In a year more people will favor recognition of East Germany	45
More will be opposed	16
Don't know	39
	100
	N = 1979

Source: Allensbach Archives, survey 2068

con viewpoints, and this all quite independently of any published poll figures (table 3).

In the election year of 1976, we systematically compared results to two questions which had been used to measure the perception of the strength of opinions in 1965 and from 1971 on: "Who will win the election?" and "What do most people think . . ." Both approaches brought similar results, but the question, "Do you think most people like party 'X' . . . or don't you think so?" showed itself to be more sensitive and thus a better measuring instrument than "Which party will win . . . ?" Its swings in estimates of the strength of the parties, while running parallel to the other measures, were clearly stronger (fig. 3).

The astonishing fluctuations in how respondents estimated the climate of political opinion made us eager to know whether their observations were correct. In December 1974, systematic checks on this question began. Following Lazarsfeld's rule of the hierarchy of stability, voting intentions showed little change during the next fifteen months, although what slight change did occur was continuous. The difference between the largest and smallest percentages intending to vote for the Christian Democratic Union was never more than six percentage points, while that for the Social Democratic Party varied no more than 4 percent. However, severe disturbances occurred in the climate of opinion as perceived by our respondents over this same period. These swings, amounting to changes of 24 percent, were not arbitrary; on the contrary, we could see that they were set off by slight changes in the actual orientations of the voting public which occurred from time to time (figs. 4 and 5). The puzzling question is: how was the population as a whole able to perceive these slight ups and downs in voting intentions? We continued the observations. Events taking place in the federal states, for example in Lower Saxony or Rhineland-Palatinate, added to our atlas of trends (fig. 6). The Gallup Institute in Britain was willing to check the ability of the British population to perceive

Table 3. Expectations about tomorrow's climate of opinion

Which camp will become stronger, which weaker? Most people will risk a judgment about which camp in a controversy will become stronger. From among about 25 tests based on 1,000–2,000 interviews with representative samples of the population conducted between 1971 and 1979, six examples are drawn. The text of the questions ran: "What do you think, the way things are going now—how will opinions look a year from now? Will more people than today or fewer people be for . . .?"

Issues	Percentage of respondents making an estimate about how opinions will develop in the near future (one year)
Recognize East Germany? (January 1971)	61
For or against the "achieving society"? (August 1972)	68
Should young adults live together without being married? (February 1973)	79
More political influence for Franz Josef Strauss? (March/April 1977)	87
For or against the death penalty? (July/August 1977)	87
Should new nuclear energy plants be built? (March 1979)	81
Average percentage of concrete answers about how opinion will develop in the future based on 27 different issues	75

Source: Allensbach Archives, surveys 2068, 2084, 2090, 3013, 3046, 3065

their political climate. Voting intentions in Britain did not seem nearly as firmly established as those in the Federal Republic of Germany, but the British too seemed able to perceive the climate of opinion (fig. 7).

How many issues are encompassed in this ability to recognize

Figure 3

Who Will Win the Election?

This is a question which has been used for decades in voter research in order to measure the climate of opinion. Another indicator of the climate of opinion—"Do most people like the CDU/CSU . . .?"—measures the same thing but more precisely, that is, with stronger swings of opinion.

Indicator 1:
The coming parliamentary election will be won by the CDU/CSU ▰▰▰

Indicator 2:
The majority like the CDU/CSU ▭▭▭

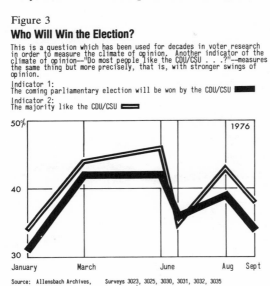

Source: Allensbach Archives,   Surveys 3023, 3025, 3030, 3031, 3032, 3035

Figure 4

Small Variations in the Number of Party Followers Are Perceived as Changes in the Climate of Opinion By a Much Larger Number of People

Voting intention: CDU/CSU ▰▰▰
Perception of the climate of opinion:
"I think that most people like the CDU/CSU" ▤▤▤

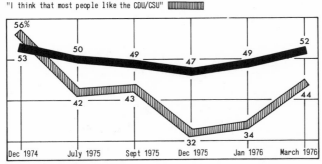

Source: Allensbach Archives,   Surveys 3010, 3019, 3022, 3023, 3025

the climate of opinion? We have to assume that hundreds of issues are constantly included in the observations people make. From March 1971 on, we have data comparing people's attitudes toward the issue of the death penalty to their perception of the climate of opinion on that subject. Because other empirical tasks were more pressing than testing the spiral of silence between 1972 and 1975, data are missing for that period. The six measures taken between 1971 and 1979, however, confirm that the actual changes in opinion

Figure 5

The Climate of Opinion Made Visible

Traditional questions about voting intention do not show how much disquiet the intention carries.
For example: SPD 1974 – 1976
Voting intention: SPD
Perception of the climate of opinion:
"I think that most people like the SPD."

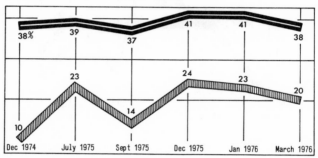

Source: Allensbach Archives,   Surveys 3010, 3017, 3019, 3022, 3023 and 3025

Figure 6

Sudden Stormy Weather in the State Elections in Rhineland-Palatinate

Voting intention: CDU
Perception of the climate: "I think most people in Rhineland-Palatinate like the CDU"

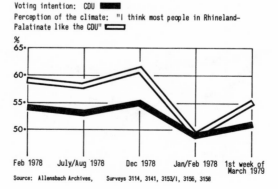

Source: Allensbach Archives,   Surveys 3114, 3141, 3153/I, 3156, 3158

were reflected reliably in the people's perceptions of the climate (figs. 8 and 9).

Sometimes this perception goes awry, and, because it generally functions so well, every instance of a distortion of it is exciting. Somehow, in these instances, the signals on which people base their

Figure 7

The Quasi-Statistical Ability to Perceive the Climate of Opinion is Found in England as Well

Questions: "If parliamentary elections were being held tomorrow, which party would you support?"
"Quite apart from how you feel about it, do you believe that most people in Great Britain find the Conservatives to be congenial and likeable, or don't you think so?"
Would support the Conservatives:
Most people find the Conservatives likeable:

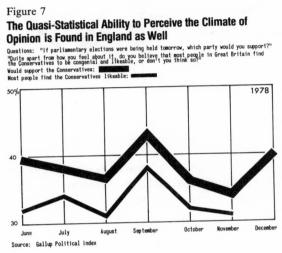

Source: Gallup Political Index

Figure 8

Opinions and the Climate of Opinion

How do people know collectively that an opinion has increased or decreased?
Opinion: "I favor the death penalty."
Climate of opinion: "Most people favor the death penalty."

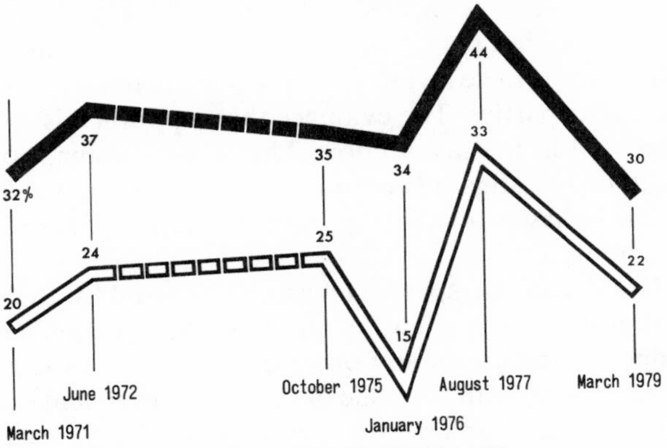

Source: Allensbach Archives, Surveys 2069, 2083, 3020, 3023, 3046 and 3065

Figure 9

The Control Test: Quasi-Statistical Perception of the Increase and Decrease in Opponents of the Death Penalty

Opinion: "I am against the death penalty."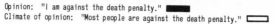
Climate of opinion: "Most people are against the death penalty."

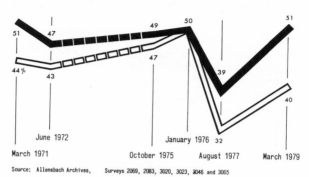

Source: Allensbach Archives,   Surveys 2069, 2083, 3020, 3023, 3046 and 3065

perception of the climate of opinion must get crossed. As long as we know so little about these signals, the distortions themselves are not easy to explain. Chapter 22 is devoted to this topic.

The train test

We do, however, venture an explanation for the distortion observed back in 1965, when the expectation of which party would win ran far ahead of the actual development of voting intentions. According to the spiral of silence hypothesis, this is explained by the differences in the willingness—indeed, the eagerness—of those in the two camps to express their opinions in public, to expose their views openly where the signals can be seen. The hypothesis can only be upheld if we find empirical evidence for two assumptions. The first is that people have an intuitive grasp of the relative strengths of the contending parties. The evidence that supports this assumption was presented in the last section. The second assumption, which remains to be investigated empirically, is whether people in fact do adapt their behavior to the apparent strength or weakness of the various camps.

In January 1972 a specific question appeared for the first time in an Allensbach interview, a question that had never, to our knowledge, appeared on any other questionnaire in Germany or elsewhere. It dealt with the issue of raising children and occurred in the context of an interview with housewives. The interviewer presented the respondent with a sketch showing two housewives in conversation, and said: "Two mothers are discussing about whether a child who has been very naughty should be spanked or not. Which of the two would you agree with, the top one or the bottom one?" (fig. 10).

One of the women presented in the sketch declares: "It is basically wrong to spank a child. You can raise any child without spanking." In January 1972, 40 percent of a representative sample of housewives agreed with this view.

The other woman says: "Spanking is part of bringing up children and never yet did a child harm." Forty-seven percent of the housewives agreed with this opinion; 13 percent were undecided.

The following question, however, was the crucial one: "Suppose you are faced with a five-hour train ride, and there is a woman

Figure 10

Test of Willingness to Speak Out or Tendency to Keep Silent in the Event of an Argument About Raising Children

sitting in your compartment who thinks . . ." Here the text of the quesion split; women who had said they believed spanking to be basically wrong were given ". . . that spanking is part of bringing up children," while women who approved of spanking were given ". . . that spanking is basically wrong." Thus, in both instances the housewives were confronted with a fellow traveler who represented a point of view diametrically opposed to their own. The question closed in uniform fashion with "Would you like to talk with this woman so as to get to know her point of view better, or wouldn't you think that worth your while?"

This "train test" was repeated from then on with changing subject matter. In one case it would be a conversation that presented people's views on the Christian Democrats and the Social Democrats. At other times it dealt with racial segregation in South Africa, young adults living together without being married, nuclear power plants, foreign workers, abortion, the danger of illegal drugs, or allowing radicals in civil service jobs.

The hypothesis to be checked was whether the various camps differed in their readiness to stand up for their views and convictions. The camp that shows more readiness to proclaim its stand will have greater impact and will thereby exert more influence on others, who may join its apparently stronger or increasing battalion of followers. In individual instances something like this might be observed, but how can such a process be measured in a way that fulfills the scientific requirements of an experiment? Measurements must be repeatable, endlessly retestable, and known to be independent of the subjective impressions of any observer. An attempt must be made to simulate reality, and this under conditions in which measurements can be made. Such conditions can be found, for example, in a survey interview, which runs its course uniformly; its questions are read aloud in a predetermined phrasing and a predetermined order; and its cross-sections of 500, 1,000 or 2,000 respondents are questioned by hundreds of interviewers, so that it is impossible for any one interviewer to have a decisive influence on the results. But what a weak situation is offered by an interview of this kind—how different it is from life, from experience, from the sensations of reality!

Simulating a public situation

Our first task consisted of simulating the public situation in the interview so as to investigate the latent readiness of the respondent to behave publicly in a particular way. Clearly, people draw their conclusions about the strength or weakness of a position not only from family discussions; so we had to simulate more than the family circle to obtain their general public behavior. Even lonely people, those with few acquaintances, manage to perceive the signals, as our analysis of the "last minute swing" showed. Further, when a swing in the climate occurs for or against a party, a person, or a particular idea, it seems to be sensed everywhere at almost exactly the same time, by all population groups, all age groups, all occupational groups (figs. 11–13). This is possible only if the signals are completely open and public. Behavior in the family, in the primary circle, may be the same as that in public places or it may differ; for the spiral of silence, this is a secondary matter. We quickly learned this when we attempted to paint a scene in the interview in which

Figure 11

Climate Swing Perceived By All Groups in the Population: An Expression of Being Public

Example: "The Federal Republic should grant the DDR recognition."

September 1968 to September 1970/January 1971

Before the climate swing: September 1968 ■

After the climate swing: September 1970/January 1971 ▫

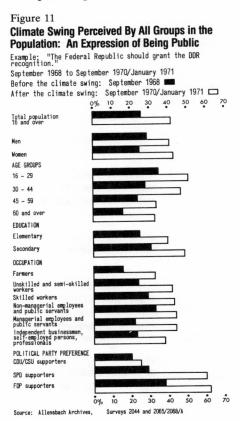

Source: Allensbach Archives, Surveys 2044 and 2065/2068/A

respondents were supposed to indicate their tendencies to talk or be silent. We told respondents they should imagine being invited somewhere with a fair number of other guests, some of whom they do not know. The conversation at this gathering turns to a certain controversial subject, and at this point the text of the question introduced some concrete issue. Would the respondent enjoy taking part in the ensuing conversation or would he or she not want to take part? The question did not work. The setting was not public enough, and considerations of courtesy to the host and to other guests with respect to the opinions they expressed strongly influenced the reactions of the respondents. We then tried the train test. It presented a public situation somewhat like a public thoroughfare: it allowed everyone entry, and people were there whose names and attitudes the respondent did not know. At the same time

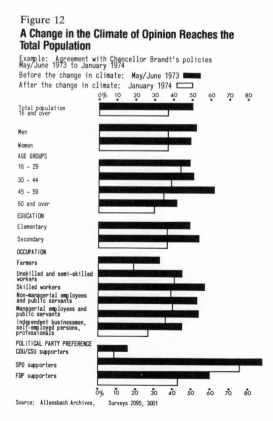

Figure 12

A Change in the Climate of Opinion Reaches the Total Population

Example: Agreement with Chancellor Brandt's policies May/June 1973 to January 1974

Before the change in climate: May/June 1973 ■■
After the change in climate: January 1974 ▭

Source: Allensbach Archives,   Surveys 2095, 3001

it involved so little exposure that even a shy person might participate, were he in the mood to do so. But would it provide an
indication of people's natural behavior in genuine public settings, as
on the street, in a grocery store, or as a spectator at a public event?
The interview occurs in privacy, perhaps in the presence of other
members of the family. Would people express their real responses
here, or would the impulse to do so be too weak in the face of a
merely imaginary situation?

**The second assumption is confirmed: those confident of victory
speak up, while losers tend toward silence**

As we evaluated one "train test" after another in the surveys
conducted in 1972, 1973, and 1974, it became evident that we could
measure the willingness of people in various camps to speak up or

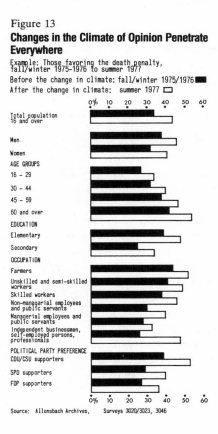

Figure 13
Changes in the Climate of Opinion Penetrate Everywhere

Example: Those favoring the death penalty,
fall/winter 1975-1976 to summer 1977

Before the change in climate: fall/winter 1975/1976 ■
After the change in climate: summer 1977 ▢

Source: Allensbach Archives, Surveys 3020/3023, 3046

keep quiet on particular subjects. The 1972 election year presented ideal conditions and issues for such tests. Enthusiasm for the Nobel Prize–winning chancellor, Willy Brandt, reached its height, yet opinions were sharply divided on the subject of Ostpolitik, which Brandt symbolized. One did not need particularly sensitive perceptual abilities to sense which camp was publicly the stronger, whether one supported or opposed Brandt. "What do you think: are most people in the Federal Republic for or against the treaties made with the East?" So ran the May 1972 question. "Most are in favor" was the answer of 51 percent; "Most are opposed," 8 percent; "About half and half," 27 percent; and 14 percent sidestepped the issue with the response, "Impossible to tell."

In October 1972, with the election campaign already underway, the train test was included in a survey: "Assume you are faced with a five-hour train ride and someone in your compartment begins to talk very favorably" (in every second interview the question read "very unfavorably") "about Chancellor Brandt. Would you like to enter conversation with this person so as to get to know his or her point of view more closely, or wouldn't you think it worth your while?" Fifty percent of Brandt's supporters (who numbered twice as many as the opponents) indicated that they would like to enter into conversation; only 35 percent of his opponents said they would. "Would not think it worth their while" was the response of 42 percent of Brandt's supporters and 56 percent of his opponents (table 4). Thus, Brandt's supporters were much stronger in actual numbers than his opponents, but beyond that their strength was multiplied by their greater willingness to convey their point of view.

A campaign button is a way of talking too

In connection with this hypothesis, we must understand what is meant by talking and by keeping quiet in the broadest terms. Wearing a campaign button, putting a bumper sticker on the car—these are ways of talking; not doing these things, even if one has firm convictions, is a way of keeping quiet. Openly carrying around a newspaper which has a well-known political slant is a way of talking; keeping it out of sight, in a briefcase or beneath a less partisan paper, is a way of keeping quiet (of course, one is not trying to hide the paper—it just happens to get wrapped up that way). Distributing handbills is a way of talking, as is putting up posters, defacing the opposition posters, tearing them down, or slashing tires of cars that carry the other party's stickers. In the sixties, men

Table 4. The train test

People's readiness to speak up and tendency to or preference for remaining silent in a "minimal public situation" was tested in October 1972, with Chancellor Brandt as the subject matter.

	Majority: Persons who agree with Brandt (%)	Minority: Persons who disagree with Brandt (%)
Would be glad to talk with a fellow train traveler about Brandt	50	35
Would not think it worthwhile	42	56
Undecided	8	9
	100	100
	N = 1011	N = 502

Source: Allensbach Archives, survey 2086/I + II

wearing shoulder-length hair were talking; just as today, wearing jeans in Eastern European countries is talking.

Even without the train test, the election year of 1972 gave us more than enough empirical evidence that one side in a controversy will be active and open in its "talk" while the other side, though not necessarily smaller in numbers, perhaps even larger, holds its peace. Former Vice President Agnew's complaint about the "silent majority" became justifiably famous because it touched on a reality that many people felt. It was a reality in which they themselves had participated, although they were not fully conscious of it since it had not been explicitly labeled.

One survey question after the federal election of 1972 graphically demonstrated how unequal the strengths of the two parties were perceived to be, even though the parties remained practically identical when it came to a count of their supporters. The question, asked in December, ran: "The different parties had posters, campaign buttons, and bumper stickers for cars. What is your impression: which party was supported by the most bumper stickers, posters, or campaign buttons?"

"More for the Social Democrats" was the answer given by 53 percent; "More for the Christian Democrats," by 9 percent. A second question checked out the same issue from a different angle: "The way a party fares in an election depends greatly upon its ability to get its followers to participate in the election campaign. What was your impression: which party's supporters showed more idealism and personal involvement in this past election campaign?" "Supporters of the Social Democrats" was the answer of 44 percent; "Supporters of the Christian Democrats," of 8 percent. One can read such results as indicating that at that time—the fall of 1972—a person favoring the Christian Democrats would look in vain among the campaign buttons and bumper stickers for a fellow sympathizer, for all such had fallen into silence, thereby contributing to a situation in which those who shared Christian Democratic convictions and sought for some kind of a sign must truly have felt isolated and alone. The spiral of silence could hardly have been wound more tightly than it was at that time.

At first these bits and pieces of evidence, assembled in an effort to make the climate of opinion visible, created a rather uncertain picture. Wear a campaign button—paste on a bumper sticker— aren't these things simply questions of taste? Some people are inclined to such actions and others are not; might it not well be that the more conservatively inclined voters are also more retiring, more disinclined to flaunt their convictions? Or, with respect to the "train test," there are some people who like to converse during a journey and others who do not. Can the train test really be regarded as an indication that an influence process like the spiral of silence is taking place?

The advantage of having talkative groups on your side

Our survey results support the proposition that, regardless of subject matter and conviction, some people *are* more prone to talk and others to remain silent. This is also true for whole groups in the population. In a public situation, men are more disposed to join in talk about controversial topics than are women, younger people than older ones, and those belonging to higher social strata than those from lower strata (table 5). This has definite consequences for the public visibility of various points of view. If a faction wins many young people or many well-educated people to its side, it automatically has a better chance of appearing to be the faction destined to gain general acceptance. But that is only half the story. There is a second factor that influences willingness to speak up: the agreement between your own convictions and your assessment of the trend of

Table 5. Willingness to discuss a controversial subject, by population subgroup

	Willing to discuss* (%)	Un-willing to discuss (%)	Un-decided (%)	N
Total population 16 and over	36	51	13	9966
Men	45	45	10	4631
Women	29	56	15	5335
Education				
Elementary (8 or 9 years of school)	32	54	14	7517
Secondary (10 or more years of school)	50	42	8	2435
Age groups				
16–29	42	47	11	2584
30–44	39	50	11	2830
45–59	35	52	13	2268
60 and over	27	56	17	2264
Occupation				
Farmers	19	63	18	621
Unskilled and semiskilled workers	28	54	18	2289
Skilled workers	37	51	12	2430
Nonmanagerial employees and public servants	41	49	10	2628
Managerial employees and public servants	47	44	9	1051
Independent businessmen, self-employed persons, professionals	40	49	11	927
Net monthly income				
Less than 800 DM**	26	56	18	1448
800–999 DM	32	53	15	1875
1000–1249 DM	35	52	13	2789
1250–1999 DM	42	48	10	2979
2000 DM or more	48	43	9	866
Residence				
Villages	32	52	16	1836
Small towns	37	52	11	3164
Medium-sized cities	36	51	13	1797
Large cities	38	49	13	3160

Table 5. *continued*

	Willing to discuss* (%)	Un- willing to discuss (%)	Un- decided (%)	N
Political party preference				
Christian Democratic Union	34	55	11	3041
Social Democratic Party	43	47	10	4162
Free Democratic Party				
(Liberals)	48	44	8	538

*Persons willing to hold a discussion in the train compartment about: the spread of socialism to West Germany; outlawing the German Communist Party; Federal Chancellor Brandt; and young adults living together without being married (Allensbach Archives, surveys 2084, 2085, 2086/I + II, 2089, 2090—1972/1973).
**Approximately 2.50 DM = $1.00 in 1983

the times, the spirit of the age, the mood of those who seem to be more modern, more reasonable, or simply the feeling that the "better" people are on your side (table 6).

Feeling in harmony with the spirit of the age loosens the tongue
In the fall of 1972, those who supported Willy Brandt were more prone than his opponents to participate in a conversation about Brandt in a public setting, *regardless* of whether they were old or young, male or female, or had lesser or greater amounts of education (table 7). The train test proved valuable. With this instrument it was possible to carry out a continuing series of investigations over the following years and so to reveal which side in a controversy spoke up and which preferred silence. On a journey, 54 percent of the Social Democratic supporters would have wanted to take part in a discussion about the Social Democratic Party, while only 44 percent of the Christian Democratic supporters would have wanted to talk about the Christian Democratic Union (1974). After the change in the office of federal chancellor, 47 percent of Helmut Schmidt's supporters but only 28 percent of his opponents wanted to talk about him (1974). When it came to force-feeding prisoners on hunger strikes, 46 percent of those in favor but only 33 percent of the opponents were willing to express themselves (1975).[2]

2. Allensbach Archives, surveys 3010, 3006, 3011.

Table 6. Willingness to converse as an indicator of the social climate and self-confidence of population subgroups

Comparisons over time between 1972 and 1978 showed a general increase in people's willingness to talk; it was particularly pronounced among Christian Democratic Union supporters

	Would be glad to talk about controversial subjects with fellow train travelers		
	1972/73 (%)	1975/76 (%)	1977/78 (%)
Total population 16 and over	36	37	44
Men	45	43	52
Women	29	32	37
Age groups			
16–29	42	41	51
30–44	39	41	49
45–59	35	35	42
60 and over	27	30	33
Education			
Elementary (8 or 9 years of school)	32	34	39
Secondary (10 or more years of school)	50	46	53
Occupation			
Farmers	19	30	29
Unskilled and semiskilled workers	28	29	35
Skilled workers	37	37	44
Nonmanagerial employees and public servants	41	41	48
Managerial employees and public servants	47	46	54
Independent businessmen, self-employed persons, professionals	40	40	47
Residence			
Villages	32	37	41
Small towns	37	36	46
Medium-sized cities	36	38	45
Large cities	38	37	44

Table 6. *continued*

	Would be glad to talk about controversial subjects with fellow train travelers		
	1972/73 (%)	1975/76 (%)	1977/78 (%)
Political party preference			
Christian Democratic Union	34	38	44
Social Democratic Party	43	40	47
Free Democratic Party			
(Liberals)	48	38	49

Sources:

1972/73: Allensbach Archives, surveys 2084, 2085, 2086/I + II, 2089, 2090 (between August 1972 and February 1973). The topics for discussion in the train compartment were: the spread of socialism to West Germany; outlawing the German Communist Party; Federal Chancellor Brandt; and young adults living together without being married. Total number of interviews was 9,966.

1975/76: Allensbach Archives, surveys 3011, 3012, 3013, 3020, 3031, 3033/I, 3035, 3037 (between February 1975 and December 1976). The topics for discussion in the train compartment were: forced feeding of prisoners; the death penalty; letting Franz Josef Strauss have more political influence; the way Spain was being governed; liking for the SPD; liking for the CDU/CSU; living together without being married; and smoking in the presence of nonsmokers. Total number of interviews was 14,504.

1977/78: Allensbach Archives, surveys 3046, 3047, 3048, 3049, 3060 (between August 1977 and October 1978). The topics for discussion in the train compartment were: the death penalty; building new nuclear energy plants; the death penalty for terrorists; sympathy for terrorists; and a United States of Europe without Russia and the East European countries. Total number of interviews was 10,133.

A shift in opinion helps research

We had come to what was then called in Germany a *Tendenzwende*, a turning point in the strength of political attitudes. Up to this point we could not tell why supporters of leftist positions and political leaders were more willing to join in discussions; it might have been their favorable political climate, but it could also have been that those who tended to favor leftist positions simply enjoyed arguing more.

Two observations were made during the following period that refuted the second possibility. First, Social Democratic supporters became less inclined to join in arguments about their party between

Table 7. In every population subgroup the supporters of the dominant opinion are more willing to voice their view than those in the minority

Example: Supporters and opponents of the policies of Federal Chancellor Brandt in 1972

	Would be glad to talk to fellow train travelers	
	Representatives of the dominant view: Brandt supporters (%)	Representatives of the minority view: Brandt opponents (%)
Total population	49	35
Men	57	44
Women	42	27
Age groups		
16–29	53	43
30–44	47	37
45–59	55	30
60 and over	42	34
Education		
Elementary (8 or 9 years of school)	45	29
Secondary (10 or more years of school)	61	51
Occupation		
Farmers	39	13
Unskilled and semiskilled workers	40	24
Skilled workers	45	30
Nonmanagerial employees and public servants	57	43
Managerial employees and public servants	62	47
Independent businessmen, self-employed persons, professionals	55	49
Residence		
Villages	46	28
Small towns	46	42
Medium-sized cities	48	40
Large cities	54	36

Table 7. *continued*

	Would be glad to talk to fellow train travelers	
	Representatives of the dominant view: Brandt supporters (%)	Representatives of the minority view: Brandt opponents (%)
Political party preference Christian Democratic		
Union	46	36
Social Democratic Party	52	35

Source: Allensbach Archives, surveys 2086/I + II, October 1972. The base for the percentages of Brandt supporters is 1011; the base for the percentages of Brandt opponents is 500.

1974 and 1976, that is, during a so-called political turning point. This was measured as a change from 54 percent willing to talk in 1974 to 48 percent in 1976. In this regard, however, the overall change was less striking than the sudden sensitivity supporters showed to the wording of the train question: whether it made their fellow traveler, who initiated the conversation, speak favorably or slightingly about the Social Democratic Party. In 1974, the supporters of the Social Democratic Party had seemed almost immune to influence from the nature of their fellow traveler's opinions; 56 percent joined in when the Social Democratic Party was praised and 52 percent when it was criticized. In 1976, 60 percent indicated an interest in joining a conversation with those who saw things as they did, but when the fellow traveler spoke out against the Social Democratic Party, their readiness to participate in the conversation sank to 32 percent! For Christian Democratic supporters, matters were exactly reversed. In 1974 they showed great sensitivity to the nature of the conversational environment by indicating completely different degrees of readiness to participate in the conversation, depending on whether their fellow train traveler was friendly or unfriendly toward the Christian Democratic Union; in 1976, the fellow traveler's view made no difference (Noelle-Neumann 1977a, esp. 152).

After the experiences of 1972 and 1973, we were ready to simplify the wording of the train test so that it would no longer shift between settings in which one confronted either opponents or supporters of a particular idea, direction, or person. The results up to that time showed that this aspect of the environment made little difference in how talkative or reticent a respondent was likely to be. Not until 1975/76 did we learn that dropping this variation in the test would have been premature. As already described, only when a spiral of silence has practically run its course and one faction possesses total public visibility while the other has completely withdrawn into its shell, only when the tendency to talk or to keep quiet has stabilized, are people liable to participate or to remain silent regardless of whether or not the others in the situation are expressly friend or foe. Aside from such settled situations, however, there remain the open controversies, arguments as yet undecided, or instances where latent conflict has yet to break the surface. In all these instances, as later investigations indicated, sensitivity to the tenor of the train conversation is considerable and can be very revealing.

Refuting the notion that those on the left are less attuned to the climate of opinion

The second discovery that refuted the presumption that left-leaning respondents have a greater tendency to participate in discussions arose out of a preoccupation with a phenomenon which, like the bandwagon effect, had attracted the attention of election researchers for decades. If, on the one hand, there was a recognizable preelection tendency for some of the voters to shift their votes in the direction of the expected winner, there was, on the other hand, a postelection tendency for more people to claim they had voted for the winning party than actual winning votes were cast. Just like the bandwagon effect, this could be interpreted as an effort to be on the winning side, this time through selectively "forgetting" that one in fact had voted differently.

To check out this state of affairs, we went back through the Allensbach archives to the first federal election in 1949 and worked forward. We could not find support in our data for the simple rule that after *every* election more people claimed to have voted for the winning party than the actual voting figures indicated. For the most part, the information people gave about the way they voted tallied quite well with the official election results (figs. 14 and 15). Once, in 1965, a suspiciously large number claimed to have voted for neither of the two major parties—the Social Democratic Party, which had lost the election, or the Christian Democratic Union, which had won. In 1969 and 1972 the numbers claiming to be Social Democratic voters substantially exceeded the actual proportion of votes the Social Democratic Party received. Two striking findings emerged, however, when we looked at the so-called panel method results, where the same people were questioned repeatedly over a period of time. The first was that if people corrected their previous voting decision in a later interview, indicating a party different than

Figure 14

A Way to Measure the Climate of Opinion

A "high" is registered for a party when more people claim to have voted for that party than the party's actual vote indicates.
A "low" occurs when the claims fall behind the actual voting results.
For example: the CDU/CSU shows a low after the end of the Adenauer era

The hatchmarked area's height shows the proportion of votes the CDU/CSU received in each of nine consecutive national elections

● Percentage of respondents who claim to have voted for the CDU/CSU in the previous national elections

Explanation: Theoretically the black circles should lie exactly at the top of the hatchmarked area. Circles that rise above it indicate exaggeration of the vote, while circles that fall below it indicate reticence to admit a CDU/CSU vote.

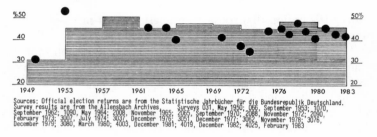

Sources: Official election returns are from the Statistische Jahrbücher für die Bundesrepublik Deutschland. Survey results are from the Allensbach Archives. Surveys 031, May 1950; 066, September 1953; 1070, September 1962; 1090, May 1964; 2008, November 1965; 2065, September 1970; 2088, November 1972; 2090, February 1973; 3007, July 1974; 3037, December 1976; 3051, December 1977; 3062, November 1978; 3076, December 1979; 3080, March 1980; 4003, December 1981; 4019, December 1982; 4025, February 1983

Figure 15

A Way to Measure the Climate of Opinion

The highs for the SPD in the sixties and seventies show an almost continual tendency for people to exaggerate their vote for the SPD in the last national election.

The hatchmarked area's height shows the proportion of votes the SPD received in each of nine consecutive national elections

○ Percentage of respondents who claim to have voted for the SPD in the previous national election

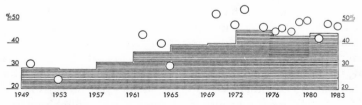

Sources: Official election returns are from the Statistische Jahrbücher für die Bundesrepublik Deutschland. Survey results are from the Allensbach Archives. Surveys 031, May 1950; 066, September 1953; 1070, September 1962; 1090, May 1964; 2008, November 1965; 2065, September 1970; 2088, November 1972; 2090, February 1973; 3007, July 1974; 3037, December 1976; 3051, December 1977; 3062, November 1978; 3076, December 1979; 3080, March 1980; 4003, December 1981; 4019, December 1982; 4025, February 1983

the one they had indicated immediately after the election, the change was not always in the direction of the winning party (the Social Democratic Party) but occurred *in the direction of the majority view of the group to which those people belonged.* For example, with younger voters the move favored the Social Democratic Party, but with older it favored the Christian Democratic Union; with workers it favored the Social Democratic Party, but with the self-employed the Christian Democratic Union. This suggested less a tendency toward wanting to be on the winning side than an attempt to avoid isolating oneself from one's own social milieu. Since most groups in 1972 had decided by and large in favor of the Social Democratic Party, the overall balance of the results in the postelection survey ran distinctly toward an inflated vote for the Social Democratic Party.

A new procedure for measuring the pressure of opinion
The second remarkable finding was that the tendency to overstate the vote for the Social Democratic Party did not remain constant during the period following the federal election, and neither did the tendency to understate the vote for the Christian Democratic Union. Both appeared to move in subtle response to changes in the climate of opinion. At first, in 1972/73, too many people claimed to have voted for the Social Democratic Party in the previous election, and too few for the Christian Democratic Union. Then, as if in slow motion, people began to recollect having voted for the Social Democratic Party or the Christian Democratic Union, and their statements moved closer to the actual electoral proportions. An excerpt from this series of observations is shown in figure 16. Even as the recollection came closer to the actual results again in 1976, the changes were by no means over. As election day drew near, the old lack of willingness of Christian Democratic Union voters to confess their prior vote began to show itself again (fig. 17).

Today the Allensbach institute routinely measures the strength of these trends, calculating the degree of polarization and the sharpness of the current political discussions by the observed month to month over- or underestimate of the votes claimed for the two major parties in the previous national election. We will later return to the meaning of such distortion. For the moment we want to take some frames out of the slow-motion picture from 1974 to 1976, the turning point in political tendencies, and to show thereby that

Figure 16

Overestimation or Underestimation of the Vote for a Party as an Indication of the Climate of Opinion

The Figure illustrates the degree to which the claimed vote for the SPD exceeded the official election return during the period 1973 to 1976. The SPD's actual vote of 49 percent is shown throughout by the open line. ===
The Figure also shows the degree to which the vote admitted for the CDU/CSU fell below the actual, official voting return during the same period. The CDU/CSU's actual vote of 45 percent is shown throughout by the filled-in line.——The trend suggests the supporters of the CDU/CSU were gathering courage during the period.

Eligible voters who stated in an interview that they had voted for the CDU/CSU ●●●
Eligible voters who stated in an interview that they had voted for the SPD○○○

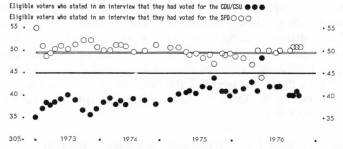

Source: Allensbach Archives, Surveys 2089-3004, 3006, 3008-3010, 3012-3023, 3025 - 3035

Figure 17

Increase in Opinion Pressure During the Struggle for Voters

Distortions in information respondents gave in election year 1976 about the last party they had voted for

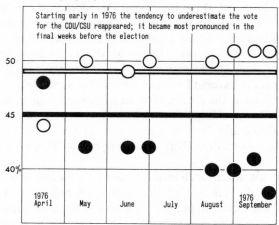

Explanation: The Figure shows the extent to which too many or too few people claimed to have voted for each of the two major parties, the SPD and the CDU/CSU, as compared to the official election returns from the 1972 national election. The 1972 returns for the SPD are marked with the open line ===== at 49 percent. The returns for the CDU/CSU at that time are marked with the filled-in line at 45 percent. ▬▬▬ Eligible voters who stated in an interview that they voted for the CDU/CSU ●●● ; for the SPD ○○○ .
Source: Allensbach Archives,   Surveys 3028 - 3035

eagerness to join in discussions and an inclination toward silence are not necessarily connected to left- or rightwing political orientation.

Since 1972 we have been able to interpret the exaggerating of votes for one side and the minimizing of votes for the other as forms of "talking" and "remaining silent." Without any effort of our own, a procedure for measuring the changes in the pressure of opinion that cause people to speak or to remain silent had become available to us.

Ready to take a public stand? A battery of pertinent questions

During these years, new test questions and new instruments continued to be developed. In 1975 we first inserted into a survey a battery of questions that were intended to indicate how ready the individual was to support a political party publicly. The text of the lead-in question ran: "Now a question about the political party that comes closest to your own point of view. If someone were to ask you whether you would be willing to do something to help this party, for example, some of the things listed on the cards in this stack, would you agree to do any one or more of these things for the party you prefer?" Eleven possible ways to provide support for a party were presented in the set of cards the interviewer gave the respondent. Not all of them required *public* activity, since people who were unwilling to engage in public actions but who still desired to express their party loyalties needed to be able to find something in the set they could do, such as making a financial contribution. The other suggested alternatives were:

I'd wear a campaign button or stick-on badge.

I'd attach a bumper sticker to my car.

I'd go door to door to talk with strangers about the party platform.

I'd hang up a party poster or sign on my house or in my window.

I'd go out and put up signs for this party in public places.

I'd take part in street discussions and stick up for this party.

I'd attend a rally for this party.

If it seemed important, I'd stand up in a meeting of this party and say something in the discussion.

I'd defend this party's point of view in other parties' meetings.

I'd help distribute campaign literature.

For analytic purposes, a simple but valuable measure that emerged from this question was the answer: "I would not do any of these things for the party of my choice." An instrument like this proves its usefulness in its ability to detect and measure subtle or slight changes, just like a postal scale that distinguishes between 18 and 21 grams when the ordinary household scale will not even distinguish between 10 grams or 30.

The battery of questions aimed at measuring how prepared people are to provide public support for their party proved to be a delicate and responsive instrument. A falling-off in a party's following registered itself immediately, as for example during the state elections in the Rhineland Palatinate, where quarrels among party leaders almost managed to help them pull defeat from the jaws of victory. Before the conflict among the leaders broke out (December 1978), 39 percent of the supporters of the Christian Democratic Union said they would do "none of these" when questioned about helping their preferred party. Shortly before the election, 48 percent of the remaining Christian Democratic supporters answered they would do "none of these." Meanwhile, the opposition, the Social Democratic Party, maintained a stable 30 percent of inactive supporters who wished to provide support in "none of these" ways between December 1978 and February/March 1979 (Noelle-Neumann 1979, 10). The relative psychological strengths had shifted, even though the voting intentions had changed so slightly that, following the principles of sampling statistics, the shift was not detectable as significant. Nevertheless, the shift eventually led the Christian Democrats to the brink of an electoral defeat.

This concrete instance serves to illustrate how social research attempts to make the invisible visible. Of course, people could be asked directly whether or not they wear a campaign button or have a bumper sticker on their car. From the point of view of measurement technique, this direct approach would have the advantage of observing or determining real circumstances, instead of relying on perhaps dubious expressions of a respondent's intentions. The disadvantage lies in the fact that the group that actually wears campaign buttons or puts bumper stickers on its cars consists largely of hard-core activists, whose reactions to the changing fortunes of a party are liable to be much less sensitive than those of more marginal supporters. Using only the hard core's less sensitive behavior can easily lead to results that lie below the threshold of statistical detection, and so allow the disturbances in the climate of opinion to escape observation.

In checking to see whether persons with leftist political views are more inclined to discuss and show their convictions, we have uncovered another question. Granted, people seem to have an extraordinary gift for sensing the climate of opinion. There also seem to be factions that understand how to capture the public spotlight and other factions that let themselves be pressured into silence. But how can we tell what motives underlie this behavior? Does a fear of social isolation explain this process, as the spiral of silence hypothesis claims? We investigate this question in the next chapter.

3   Fear of Isolation as a Motive

In the early fifties, Solomon Asch (1951, 1952), a social psychologist, reported an experiment he had conducted more than fifty times in the United States. The task of the subjects in this experiment was to judge which of three lines best matched a fourth test line in length (fig. 18). One of the three was always exactly the same length as the test line. At first glance, the task appeared easy; the correct match was quite evident and all subjects spotted it easily. From eight to ten persons took part in each experimental session, all guided by the following format. The test line and the three lines that were candidates for the match were hung up where all could see them. Then each of the subjects in the room, starting from the left, stated his or her judgment as to which line was the best match for the test line. Each session repeated this procedure twelve times.

However, after two rounds in which all participants agreed unequivocally on the correct match to the test line, the situation suddenly changed. The experimenter's assistants, seven to nine persons who were in on the purpose of the experiment, all named as the correct line one that was visibly too short. The one naive subject, the only unsuspecting person in the group, sat at the end of the row. At this point his behavior was scrutinized to see what

Figure 18
The Asch Length-of-Line Experiment:
Testing Conformity Due to Fear of Isolation

Subjects in the experiment were asked the following
question: Which of the three lines on the right is
equal to the standard line on the left?

Standard line   Comparison lines

Source: Solomon E. Asch, "Group Forces in the Modification and Distortion
of Judgments." Social Psychology, New York, Prentice-Hall, 1952, p. 452.

would happen to it under the pressure of a unanimous judgment at variance with the evidence of his senses. Would he waver? Would he join the majority view, regardless of how much it contradicted his own judgment? Or would he stand fast?

Solomon Asch's classical laboratory experiment shows how scarce self-reliant individuals are

Two out of every ten naive subjects stuck resolutely to their own impressions. Two of the remaining eight agreed with the group only once or twice during the ten critical passes through the procedure. But the remaining six more frequently announced as their own opinion the obviously false judgment made by the majority. This means that even in a harmless task which does not touch their real interests and whose outcome should be largely a matter of indifference, most people will join the majority point of view even when they can have no doubt that it is false. This was what Tocqueville described when he wrote: "Dreading isolation more than error, they professed to share the sentiments of the majority."[3]

When we compare Asch's research method to the survey method involving questions like the train test, we realize immediately that Asch's method possesses a completely different attraction and a completely different kind of persuasive power. Asch is working in the tradition of what is called "the laboratory experiment." He can arrange to control conditions during the experiment down to the last pertinent detail—how the chairs are placed, how his assistants behave during the sessions, how visually

3. Tocqueville 1952, 207; English: 1955, 155. Author's translation in part.

obvious the differences in the lines to be matched are, etc. The testing setup, the "laboratory," allows him to create an unequivocal situation and to hold it constant for all subjects. The survey interview is a much "dirtier" research tool because it is subject to a variety of disturbances and contaminations. We cannot be certain about how many respondents really do not understand the thrust of a question, how many interviewers do a poor job of reading the questions in the proper order and sticking to the prescribed wording, or how many make independent "improvements" and free improvisations, or provide explanations that get out of hand when the respondent seems uncertain as to the sense of the question. How much of a burden is placed on the imagination of a typical person when he is asked, "Suppose you are faced with a five-hour train ride, and in your compartment someone begins to . . . ?" In the usual interview, the stimulation to imagine such a situation must be relatively weak. Besides, everything depends on how the question is read, how the answer is transcribed, and how humanly responsive and talkative the particular subject happens to be. All of these unknowns introduce uncertainties in the results. In a laboratory like Asch's, by contrast, a "real situation" can be called into existence. Here, influences that are close to actual experience are allowed to work uniformly on all subjects in the experiment—for example, feeling like an idiot when everyone else seems to see things differently.

Two motives for imitation: learning and fear of isolation

"They dreaded isolation more than error" was Tocqueville's explanation. At the end of the century, his fellow countryman, the sociologist Gabriel Tarde, dedicated a large part of his work to studying the human ability and tendency to imitate, speaking of a human need to be in public agreement with others (Tarde 1969, 318). Since then, imitation has remained a topic of social science research; for example, an extensive article is devoted to it in the 1968 *Encyclopedia of the Social Sciences* (Bandura 1968). In this entry, however, imitation is explained not as a result of the fear of being singled out for disapproval but as a form of learning. People observe others' behavior, learn that this or that behavioral possibility exists, and, given an appropriate opportunity, try out the behavior for themselves. Our interest in determining the role played by the fear of isolation becomes more complicated. If we call it imitation when someone repeats what has been said or done by others, then this kind of imitation can occur for very different reasons. It might be because of a fear of isolation; but it might also reflect the desire of adding to one's stock of knowledge, particularly in a democratic civilization that equates numerical majority with better judgment. The beauty of Asch's laboratory experiment lies precisely in its ability to eliminate all such ambiguity. The subjects in the experiment see with their own eyes that the line selected by the majority as the best match is not the best match. When these subjects join the judgment of the majority, it must be unequivocally because of a fear of isolating themselves, not out of hopes of adding something to their repertory of behaviors or store of knowledge.

As may already be supposed from the unpleasant ring of labels like "conformist" or "hanger-on," the tendency to imitate goes against ideals of individal autonomy. It is not an image with which most people like to be identified, although many would agree that it might describe "the other guy."

The question has been raised whether the Asch length-of-line experiment might not have revealed an *American* tendency to conform. Stanley Milgram (1961) repeated the investigation in a somewhat changed form in two European countries whose populations were widely regarded as being, in the one case, strikingly individualistic (the French) and as having, in the other, a strong sense of solidarity, a high level of cohesiveness (the Norwegians).[4] Although the subjects in the Milgram version of the study heard rather than saw the deviating majority, this sufficed to produce the impression that they stood all alone in their perceptual experience. Most Europeans—80 percent of the Norwegians and 60 percent of the French—frequently or almost always joined the majority view. There were later variations in the experiment. For example, checks were run to see how the number of people who sat ahead of the naive subject and made correct judgments about the matching line affected the subject's ability to depart from the majority view and say what was there before his or her eyes.

We do not need to follow these refinements; the Asch experiment in its original version has served an important purpose for our research question. We assume that the normal individual's fear of isolation sets the spiral of silence in motion, and the Asch experiment shows for a fact that this fear can be substantial.

4. See in this connection a later study, Eckstein 1966.

And it would have to be substantial to explain the results brought to light by the survey research method. Only by assuming that people greatly fear becoming isolated can we explain the enormous feat they collectively accomplish in being able to say with accuracy and reliability which opinions are on the increase and which on the decrease, and do this without assistance from any instruments of survey research. Humans invest their attention with great economy. The effort spent in observing the environment is apparently a smaller price to pay than the risk of losing the goodwill of one's fellow human beings—of becoming rejected, despised, alone.

Are we denying the social nature of human beings?

The problem is to make the attention individuals pay to group judgments both empirically visible and theoretically intelligible. Previous work on the phenomenon of imitation seems to regard learning as practically its only motive. Such work reveals a pervasive tendency to deny, or at least fails to recognize, the *social nature* of human beings, unfairly defaming it with the label of "conformity." Our social nature causes us to fear separation and isolation from our fellows and to want to be respected and liked by them. In all likelihood, this tendency contributes considerably to successful social life. But the conflict is not to be avoided. We consciously praise rational, independent thought and unshakable firmness in the judgment that we assume each person should reach by himself.

The psychoanalyst Erich Fromm systematically sought out as many different domains as he could find where contradictions between the conscious and the unconscious impulses of people in our time were as large as the contradictions Freud found in his time between conscious and unconscious sexuality. Among such modern contradictions, Fromm (1980, 26) pinpoints:

> consciousness of freedom—unconscious unfreedom
> conscious honesty—unconscious fraudulence
> consciousness of individualism—unconscious suggestibility
> consciousness of power—unconscious sense of powerlessness
> consciousness of faith—unconscious cynicism and complete lack of faith

Freedom, sincerity, individualism—all these are adopted consciously as expressions of the values we feel in our own beings, but they simply do not fit the ways we must assume people behave, given our description of the spiral of silence. It is therefore un-reasonable to expect that people will consciously admit to a fear of isolation if asked directly about their motives in a survey interview. However, just as we are able to simulate a public situation in an interview in order to test for tendencies to speak out or keep quiet, we can also simulate the threat of isolation in the interview setting and observe whether respondents react to it as the hypothesis of a spiral of silence would lead us to expect.

A field experiment to simulate the threat of isolation

The procedure about to be described is called a "field experiment" in technical language. "Field" here stands in distinction to "laboratory." The subjects remain in the field, in their natural setting. They are not hauled into an alien laboratory. An interviewer comes into their homes to ask some questions, something that falls a little outside the everyday, ordinary course of events yet approximates the familiar experience of a conversation between two persons.

Why in fact do researchers stick with such a flawed and transitory investigative tool as the survey interview, an approach that provides relatively weak kinds of stimuli and is difficult to control? Because one gains thereby the advantage hinted at in the catchword "field"—the naturalness of all the conditions—and because the method includes the possibility of observing a representative sample of the population, not just those well-known groups which can be obtained for laboratory purposes and on which so much of experimental social research rests—students, the military, and patients in institutions. The very things that constitute the strength of the laboratory approach—its possibilities of painstaking control and of planned variations in the conditions that might influence results—are the things that also constitute its weakness. Those portions of real life that may play a decisive role in the behavior one wants to investigate may well unintentionally be cut out by the laboratory setting.

Smoking in the presence of nonsmokers: the threat test

Our first attempt to simulate the dangers of social isolation in a field experiment occurred in 1976 and dealt with the topic "Smoking in the presence of nonsmokers" (Noelle-Neumann 1977a, esp. 154–55). This theme seemed suitable since public opinion on the topic was still developing and the strength of the two main camps seemed to be fairly well balanced. In a hypothetical dialogue, which was read aloud during the interview, 44 percent selected the following point of view: "In the presence of nonsmokers one should refrain from smoking. To smoke would be inconsiderate; for those who do not smoke, it is very unpleasant to have to breathe smoke-filled air." Exactly the same percentage, 44, took the opposite stance: "One can't expect people to refrain from smoking just because nonsmokers are present; it's really not that much of an annoyance to them anyway." In a test of willingness to speak out on the subject or the tendency to keep quiet, 45 percent of the critics of smoking in the presence of nonsmokers and 43 percent of those who defended the rights of smokers declared themselves ready and willing to participate in a discussion on this topic while riding on a train.[5]

We move now to simulating the danger of social isolation: The core of the series of questions that we asked our representative cross-section of 2,000 persons was framed in the format of the train test:

1. Use the two statements already presented to obtain the personal opinion of the respondent about the issue of smoking in the presence of nonsmokers.
2. Obtain an estimate of what they suppose "most people" think about the topic by asking: "Now, regardless of your own opinion, what do you think most people think about this? Are most people here in the Federal Republic of the opinion that smokers should refrain from smoking in the presence of nonsmokers, or that smokers should continue to smoke if they wish?" (Results for the total population: 31 percent, "Most think smokers should refrain from smoking in the presence of nonsmokers"; 28 percent, "Most think smokers can continue their smoking"; 31 percent, "Opinion is equally divided"; 10 percent, "Impossible to say.")
3. Test for speaking up or keeping quiet: "Suppose you are faced with a five-hour train ride, and someone in your compartment strikes up conversation and says: 'In the presence of nonsmokers, people ought to refrain from smoking.' Would you want to join in this conversation, or would you not think it worth your while?" (In every other interview the fellow train traveler was given the point of view that "One cannot require someone to

5. Allensbach Archives, survey 3037.

refrain from smoking just because there are nonsmokers present.")

4. Determine whether the respondent is a smoker or a nonsmoker.

In order to simulate the threat of social isolation, the 2,000 respondents were divided into two representative groups of 1,000. The experimental group, i.e. the group that was to be subjected to the experimental factor of a threat of social isolation, was shown a sketch of two persons engaged in a conversation. One of them exclaims: "It seems to me that smokers are terribly inconsiderate. They force others to inhale their health-endangering smoke." The other person begins to answer: "Well, I . . ." The model for this question comes from the sentence-completion approach used in diagnostic psychology (fig. 19). The text of the lead-in question runs: "Here are two men in conversation. The upper one has just said something. Would you read it please. The lower one was interrupted in mid-sentence, but what do you think the lower one would have answered? How might he have finished the sentence he started?" With this invitation should come a strong increase in the otherwise weak stimuli that may occur when one simply listens passively to someone scolding those who smoke in the presence of nonsmokers. That such a sentence-completion test does not demand too much of people in a representative sample or overtax the possibilities of a survey interview can be seen by the fact that fully 88 percent of the respondents completed the sentence from the sketch.

The second sample of 1,000 persons constituted the control group. It was treated exactly like the experimental group in every respect, with the sole difference that the sentence-completion test and its threat of social isolation were missing. Following the logic of the controlled experiment, any overall differences in results that are found when the experimental group is compared to the control group can be traced back to the threat test, since all conditions otherwise were the same.

The results confirmed the expectation. After being threatened verbally, smokers who had defended their right to smoke in the presence of nonsmokers showed noticeably less interest in taking part in a discussion on this topic in a train compartment (table 8).

Smokers are particularly intimidated when a double threat of isolation is simulated. First they are given the sentence-completion test with a radical opponent of smoking in the presence of nonsmok-

Figure 19

The Threat Test

Picture used with a sentence-completion test in an interview with smokers to simulate the reality of being intimidated by a strong contrary opinion. The necessity of completing the sentence which has been started leads to experiencing the situation more intensely. Afterwards, one measures to see whether the verbal threat has influenced the tendency to speak out or remain silent.

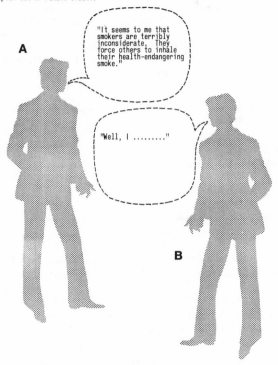

ers, and then they are faced with a fellow traveler in the train compartment who opens the conversation with the demand that "in the presence of nonsmokers people ought to refrain from smoking." Under these conditions, only 23 percent of the smokers are inclined to participate in the conversation.

Empirical tests can also make the other side of the spiral of silence visible. Nonsmokers tend to be less self-assured and consequently less inclined to try to make their point of view stick. When the sentence-completion test shows them, however, that they are by no means alone in their views, they become noticeably more inclined to join in the conversation (table 9). Shyer nonsmokers reach a high point in their readiness to speak up when, besides having an

Table 8. Train test of the silence hypothesis: danger of isolation will lead people to be silent

An aggressive climate of opinion can be simulated in an interview. After the threat test, smokers are less prone to speak out in their own defense.

| | Smokers who claim the right to smoke even in the presence of nonsmokers | |
	where the danger of social isolation has *not* been made clear (%)	where the danger of social isolation has been made clear (%)
Willing to participate in a conversation on the topic of smoking in the presence of nonsmokers?		
Yes	49	40
No	41	45
Undecided	10	15
	100	100
	N = 225	253

Source: Allensbach Archives, survey 3037, December 1976

aggressive champion in the threat test, their fellow traveler in the train compartment forcefully declares that people should refrain from smoking in the presence of nonsmokers. Under these circumstances, only 23 percent of the smokers are inclined to join in, as against 56 percent of the nonsmokers. One can see how, as the spiral of silence runs its course, the standpoint that it is unconscionable to smoke in the presence of nonsmokers can become dominant to the point where it is impossible for a smoker publicly to take the opposite position—that smokers ought to be allowed to smoke even in the presence of non-smokers. What is being expressed here is quite evidently a cumulative effect; step by step, through hostile responses of the environment, one becomes unnerved. The more self-assured smokers do not react to the threat test by itself. When, immediately following the threat test, they are placed in a train compartment with someone who represents their own point of view—that smoking in the presence of nonsmokers is all right—they forget the previous threat. With it, 54 percent, and without it, 55 percent, are inclined to join in the conversation.

Table 9. Train test of the silence hypothesis: with social support, nonsmokers become more inclined to talk

	Nonsmokers who ask that smokers refrain from smoking in the presence of nonsmokers	
	without the social support of an aggressive person of similar views (%)	with the social support of an aggressive person of similar views (%)
Willing to participate in a conversation on the topic of smoking in the presence of nonsmokers?		
Yes	37	48
No	51	37
Undecided	12	15
	100	100
	N = 330	297

Source: Allensbach Archives, survey 3037, December 1976

If, however, following the threat test, another unsettling experience occurs—the fellow train traveler also thunders against smoking in the presence of nonsmokers—then smokers prefer to take refuge in silence (table 10). For people who are less self-confident, a lesser threat of isolation will suffice. Women, for example, and members of the lower classes generally react to the threat test alone and are not immediately reassured merely by having a fellow traveler take their point of view (table 11).

Reacting to interview situations as though they were reality
The results of the threat test not only allow us to unveil the process of the spiral of silence; they lead us further in another respect. They encourage the assumption that many people have the imagination to experience situations described in an interview so vividly that they react to them as if they were reality. So we do not have to do our research in a secret laboratory, complete with railroad train and scientists, disguised as fellow travelers, conducting their experiments on outspokenness versus silence with unsus-

Table 10. Train test of the spiral of silence among self-assured smokers

In the presence of someone sympathetic to their views in a train compartment, smokers are willing to speak up even when they have been threatened previously.

	Smokers who claim the right to smoke even in the presence of nonsmokers	
	where the danger of social isolation has *not* been made clear (%)	where the danger of social isolation has been made clear (%)
Willing to participate in a conversation on the topic of smoking in the presence of nonsmokers when a fellow traveler has shown sympathy for smokers by saying "You can't expect people not to smoke just because nonsmokers are present"?		
Yes	55	54
No	33	30
Undecided	12	16
	100	100
	N = 119	135

In a hostile conversational environment, smokers too are intimidated, especially if they have previously been threatened.

Willing to participate in a conversation on the topic of smoking in the presence of nonsmokers when a fellow traveler has attacked smokers by saying: "In the presence of nonsmokers you should refrain from smoking"?		
Yes	41	23
No	51	63
Undecided	8	14
	100	100
	N = 106	118

Source: Allensbach Archives, survey 3037, December 1976

Table 11. Train test of the spiral of silence among less self-confident smokers: women

After a double-barreled verbal threat, most women smokers are reduced to silence

	Women smokers who claim the right to smoke even in the presence of nonsmokers	
	where the danger of social isolation has *not* been made clear (%)	where the danger of social isolation has been made clear (%)
Willing to participate in a conversation on the topic of smoking in the presence of nonsmokers when a fellow traveler has attacked smokers by saying: "In the presence of nonsmokers, you should refrain from smoking"?		
Yes	42	10
No	54	74
Undecided	4	16
	100	100
N =	48	49

Source: Allensbach Archives, survey 3037, December 1976

pecting subjects. Nevertheless, in developing the instruments for use in our interviews, we encountered repeated disappointments.

We wanted to go one step further and see if we could make it empirically evident that certain points of view were so stigmatized, so despised, that to adopt them was to isolate oneself. For this purpose we included a test in a number of Allensbach surveys in 1976 which used a drawing that was supposed to be a visual presentation of social isolation. At one end of a table a number of people are shown, congenially close to each other, while at the other end one person sits alone. Cartoonists' balloons plant the suggestion that an argument is taking place involving the members of the group and the loner. The test consisted of asking the respondents to assign particular points of view to the loner. For example, what does the isolated person stand up for? Is he in favor of allowing members of the German Communist Party to become judges, or is he against it?

The text of the question ran: "Coming back, now, to the earlier question whether someone who is a member of the German Communist Party should be appointed as a judge—here you see several people talking about that issue. There are two opinions: one favors appointing such men as judges and one opposes such appointments. What do you think the individual sitting alone here might have said? That he is in favor of, or that he is against, appointing a communist as a judge?" (figs. 20, 21).

A test that did not work

The picture of people around the table turned out to be something like the unresponsive household scales already mentioned—it showed no results. There was a substantially high proportion of "don't know" answers, 33 percent, which in itself pointed toward the possibility that people's imaginations were being overtaxed. Furthermore, the point of view that was put into the mouth of the evidently isolated person at the table seemed to have nothing to do with minority or majority opinion. Although response to the direct question, "Should members of the Communist Party be allowed to become judges?" resulted in a resounding majority "no" at the time it was asked (60 percent no, 18 percent yes, in April 1976), and although the population knew perfectly well which point of view

Figure 20

The Isolation Test

Question: "Which opinion does the lone person at the end of the table represent?"
Proposed test for determining whether certain points
of view tend to isolate a person.

Figure 21
The Isolation Test

Second version: Instead of sitting at a table, the group is standing.
The test was sometimes misunderstood; the isolated person
was thought to be a superior.

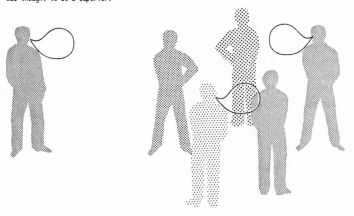

was in the majority and which might tend to isolate a person (80 percent said most people do not want members of the Communist Party as judges while only 2 percent said most people have nothing against it), the guesses about which opinion the loner in the picture expressed were distributed almost equally between supposing that he was in favor of allowing communists to become judges (33 percent) and supposing that he was opposed (34 percent). Judging from the actual, and quite correctly estimated, popular opinion at this time, most of the people should have taken him to be an advocate of the notion that "a member of the Communist Party should be able to be appointed as one of our judges"—that is, *if* people were actually aware that unpopular opinions might lead to isolation, and *if* they saw the man at the end of the table as isolated. Was the effect of the scene at the table too intimate? Was it insufficiently public? Does someone sitting at the end of a table still belong to the group and therefore not seem isolated to our respondents?

In any event, the second test picture, in which people stood rather than sat, turned out to be somewhat more useful. This time only 21 percent were undecided, and most others (46 percent) guessed that the isolated person represented the minority position, that is, that members of the Communist Party should be given access to judgeships. Even so, 33 percent came down on the opposite side. Those who themselves took the position that one should allow communists the chance to become judges turned out to have a sharper sensitivity to the isolating possibilities of their position; they identified the isolated person with this opinion to the tune of 65 percent (table 12). This test, however, also proved unsatisfactory; even in the instance of an overwhelming majority opinion on a particular side, the results were too unclear. For example, during another test run with the same pictures but using a less polarized issue, a completely unexpected misunderstanding showed up. The question was: "Who would you like to have as the next Federal Chancellor?" Forty-four percent said Helmut Schmidt and 35 percent said Helmut Kohl (April 1976). Each of these two groups, however, tended to assign their own point of view to the person standing off by himself.

For the time being the test was given up; later (see the end of chapter 22) we will encounter it again, albeit with a different diagnostic assignment. We did not, however, give up the goal we had pursued with these picture tests: finding an empirical check for whether people knew which points of view would tend to isolate a person. For the spiral of silence to work, of course, it would be sufficient if such knowledge existed only unconsciously. The tendency indicated by Fromm's work for each person to feel conscious of himself or herself as an individual, an emancipated citizen, and the concomitant neglect of efforts to make us conscious of our social nature (surely a more appropriate term than Fromm's deprecatory "mass man"), are hardly conducive to conscious observations and admissions of the type we seek. Nevertheless, despite its weaknesses the survey interview can provide clear evidence that people know which opinions at a particular time are liable to result in social isolation. To achieve this result, the test question had to be sharpened, and it had to involve such an extreme situation that even a thick-skinned person would clearly recognize the inherent dangers of isolation.

Who gets their tires slashed?

Shortly before the federal elections in September 1976, two questions of the following type appeared in Allensbach interviews. One ran: "Here is a picture of a car that has had its tire slashed. On the right rear window is a sticker for a political party, but you can't read which party the sticker was for. What is your guess: with which party's stickers do people run the greatest risk of having a tire

Table 12. Member of the German Communist Party as a judge? A test of social isolation

Does the population realize that certain points of view expose their adherents to the risk of social isolation? *Question:* "Coming back to our earlier question, whether someone who is in the German Communist Party should be appointed as a judge. . . . here you see several people who are talking about that issue. There are two opinions: one in favor of appointing such men as judges and one opposing such appointments. What do you think this individual standing here alone might have said? (In every other interview it read: "sitting alone at the table.") That he is in favor, or that he opposes appointing a communist as a judge?"

	Presentation of a picture with	
Total population	persons sitting (%)	persons standing (%)
The person off by himself is—		
in favor of appointing Communist Party members as judges	33	46
opposed	34	33
Undecided	33	21
	100	100
	N = 466	516

Those who hold the minority opinion—Communist Party members should be allowed to be judges—know better than the general population that one isolates oneself from other people by adopting this position.

Holders of the minority opinion—Communist Party members should be able to be judges		
The person off by himself is—		
in favor of appointing Communist Party members as judges	45	65
opposed	29	21
Undecided	26	14
	100	100
	N = 83	79

Source: Allensbach Archives, survey 3028, April 1976

slashed?" (table 13). Almost half the sample, 45 percent, left the question unanswered. Nevertheless, the result was clear. Those who did answer differentiated sharply among the three parties represented in parliament: 21 percent named the Christian Democratic Union, 9 percent the Social Democratic Party, and 1 percent the Free Democrats (or Liberals). Table 13 shows the complete

Table 13. The development of further tests to measure the climate of opinion

Which opinions can isolate a person? *Question:* "Here is a picture of a car that has had its tire slashed. On the right rear window there is a sticker for a political party, but you can't read which party the sticker was for. What is your guess: With which party's stickers do people run the greatest risk of having a tire slashed?"

	September 1976			
	Total population (%)	Christian Democratic supporters (%)	Social Democratic supporters (%)	Free Democratic supporters (%)
Christian Democratic Union	21	28	12	21
Social Democratic Party	9	7	11	13
Free Democratic Party (Liberals)	1	2	x	4
National Democratic Party of Germany	11	10	12	10
Communist parties	16	14	22	15
No definite response	45	42	46	43
	103	103	103	106
	N = 556	263	238	45

Source: Allensbach Archives, survey 2189; x = less than 0.5%

results. Christian Democratic supporters felt themselves most endangered; Free Democratic supporters were aware of their own
lesser danger and of the relatively greater danger run by Christian
Democratic supporters. Social Democratic supporters did not feel
themselves particularly endangered; if they had, they would have
estimated their own danger as substantially higher than the estimates they gave the other parties, and this was not the case.

The second test question from this series was superior to the
first; it led to fewer refusals and it dealt with behavior that was more
permissible than damaging other people's property. Consequently,
the second question provided a more realistic indication of what
people regarded as popular or unpopular; it provided a better
simulation of the signals that indicate public rejection. In any event,
it clearly made supporters of the Social Democratic Party and the
Free Democratic Party less inhibited in indicating their feelings
about being accepted.

The question ran: "I want to tell you now about another case
and ask you what you think. Someone drives into a strange city and
can't find a parking space. He finally gets out of the car and asks a
pedestrian, 'Can you tell me, please, where I can find a place to
park?' The pedestrian replies, 'Ask somebody else, buddy!' and
walks away. I should mention that the driver is wearing a political
badge on his jacket. What do you think: which party did this badge
support? What is your guess?" (table 14).

Fully 25 percent of the Social Democratic supporters, and 28
percent of the Liberals guessed that it was a Christian Democratic
badge, more than double the number who named the Social Democrats. The Christian Democratic supporters apparently hesitated to
admit their own unpopularity (table 14). In that month, September
1976, as we have already noticed, the tendency to deny having
voted for the Christian Democratic Union during the previous
election—a tendency that had evened out for a while—reached its
highest point.

Nevertheless, the psychological situation for Christian Democratic supporters was much less threatening at that point than it had
been four years earlier during the federal election of 1972. We see
this from the answers to a question which symbolically threatened
public isolation. The question was asked in both 1972 and 1976 in
postelection studies and ran: "In the election campaign, posters
again were ripped up and defaced. According to what you saw,
which party's posters were most often damaged?" In 1972, the

Table 14. Test question for the climate of opinion: What points of view may cause social isolation?

Question: "I want to tell you, now, about another case and ask you what you think. Someone drives into a strange city and can't find a parking space. He finally gets out of the car and asks a pedestrian: 'Can you tell me, please, where I can find a place to park?' The pedestrian replies, 'Ask somebody else, buddy!' and walks away. I should mention that the driver is wearing a political badge on his jacket. What do you think: Which party did this badge support? What is your guess?"

Answers	September 1976			
	Total population (%)	Christian Democratic supporters (%)	Social Democratic supporters (%)	Free Democratic supporters (%)
Christian Democratic Union	23	21	25	28
Social Democratic Party	14	19	12	8
Free Democratic Party (Liberals)	2	4	1	x
National Democratic Party of Germany	8	7	10	7
Communist parties	21	21	21	21
No definite response	35	34	35	40
	103	106	104	104
	N = 546	223	264	50

Source: Allensbach Archives, survey 2189

Christian Democratic Union was named by a wide margin; that is, 31 percent regarded Christian Democratic posters as subject to the most damage, while the Social Democrats came in second with 7 percent. In 1976, the Christian Democratic posters were again most often seen as the most damaged, although now by only 23 percent instead of 31 percent (table 15).

Slashed tires, defaced or torn posters, help refused to a lost stranger—questions of this kind demonstrate that people can be on uncomfortable or even dangerous ground when the climate of opinion runs counter to their views. When people attempt to avoid isolation, they are not responding hypersensitively to trivialities;

Table 15. Destroying and defacing posters: a symbolic threat of isolation

Question: "In the election campaign, posters again were ripped up and defaced. According to what you saw, which party's posters were most often damaged?"*

	Postelection studies	
	1972 (%)	1976 (%)
Posters from the —		
Christian Democratic Union	31	23
Social Democratic Party	7	12
Free Democratic Party (Liberals)	1	2
All the same	27	22
Don't know	35	41
	101	100
	N = 912	990

*The wording of the question in 1972 was slightly different: ". . . which party, more than the rest, had damage done to its posters?"
Source: Allensbach Archives, surveys 2129, 2191

these are existential issues that can involve real hazards. Society demands quick conformity over issues that are undergoing change. It must require this to maintain a sufficient degree of unity to remain integrated. As a German jurist, Rudolph von Ihering (1883, 242; cf. 325) noted in his essay *Der Zweck im Recht* (Intention in Law), the disapproval that punishes someone who strays from the majority view does not have the rational character of the disapproval that arises from "an incorrect logical conclusion, a mistake in solving an arithmetic problem, or an unsuccessful work of art; rather it is expressed as the conscious or unconscious *practical reaction of the community* to *injury* of its interests, a defense for the purposes of common security."

4 Public Opinion: What Is It?

"**W**ell, I still don't know what public opinion is," said a participant in the morning session of a conference about public opinion as he left the auditorium for the noon break. That was in 1961 in Baden-Baden at a symposium of media practitioners and researchers. He was not alone in his annoyance. Generations of philosophers, jurists, historians, political theorists, and journalism scholars have torn their hair in the attempt to provide a clear definition of public opinion.

Fifty definitions

Moreover, no progress has been made since that time. On the contrary, the concept unraveled and dissolved more and more until it was for all practical purposes useless. In the mid-1960s a Princeton professor, Harwood Childs (1965, 14–26), undertook the tedious task of collecting definitions and was able to assemble around fifty from the literature. In the fifties and sixties, the demand to abandon the concept increased. Public opinion was said to be a fiction that belonged in a museum of the history of ideas; it could only be of historical interest. Remarkably enough, this was of no avail. "The concept simply refuses to die," complained a German professor of journalism, Emil Dovifat (1962, 108). Also in 1962, in his inaugural dissertation, "Structural Change in the Concept of the Public: An Investigation of a Category in Bourgeois Society," Jürgen Habermas commented that "not only colloquial usage . . . clings to it, but so do scientists and scholars, especially those in jurisprudence, political studies, and sociology, who are apparently incapable of replacing traditional categories such as 'public opinion' with more precise terms" (1962, 13).

W. Phillips Davison, professor of journalism at Columbia University, began his article "Public Opinion," written for the 1968 edition of the *International Encyclopedia of the Social Sciences*, with the sentence: "There is no generally accepted definition of 'public opinion.' Nevertheless," he continued, "the term has been employed with increasing frequency. . . . Efforts to define the term have led to such expressions of frustration as 'public opinion is not the name of some thing, but a classification of a number of somethings'" (Davison 1968, esp. 188). Here he cites Childs's collection of some fifty definitions.

This perplexity is found also in the writings of the German historian Hermann Oncken, who, in an article published in 1904, put it thus: "Whoever desires to grasp and define [the concept of public opinion] will recognize quickly that he is dealing with a Proteus, a being that appears simultaneously in a thousand guises, both visible and as a phantom, impotent and surprisingly efficacious, which presents itself in innumerable transformations and is forever slipping through our fingers just as we believe we have a firm grip on it. . . . That which floats and flows cannot be understood by being locked up in a formula. . . . After all, when asked, everyone knows exactly what public opinion means" (Oncken 1914, esp. 224–25, 236).

It is remarkable that a scholar of Oncken's sagacity and conceptual power retreats to the evasion "after all . . . everyone knows" and reduces the search for definitions, which are the prerequisites for applying the scientific method, to "locking up in a formula."

The spiral of silence as a process that creates and spreads public opinion

In the early 1970s, I was developing the hypothesis of the spiral of silence in an effort to clarify the puzzling findings of 1965—voting intentions that did not change, yet an increasing expectation that one side would win. At that point I began to ask myself whether we perhaps had a handle on a part of that monster, "public opinion." "In innumerable transformations and . . . forever slipping through our fingers," as Oncken described it (1914, 225). The spiral of silence might be one of the forms in which public opinion appeared; it might be a process through which a new, youthful public opinion develops or whereby the transformed meaning of an old opinion spreads. If this were so, it would still be necessary to attempt a definition of public opinion, in order to avoid having to state that "the spiral of silence is that process by which something indefinable is spread."

The scholarly controversy swirled around both parts of the concept, around both "public" and "opinion."

Meinung and "opinion" are understood differently

For the meaning of what in German is termed *Meinung* (opinion), our research led back to Plato's *Republic*. On the occasion of a festival in the port city of Piraeus, in a discussion on the state with Glaucon and other friends, Socrates works out an idea of opinion which is roughly the same as the traditional German one:

> Think you then, said I, that opinion is more obscure than knowledge, but clearer than ignorance?
> Far, said he.
> Does it lie then between them both?
> Yes.
> Opinion then is between the two?
> Entirely so. (Plato 1900, 165–66)

Opinion takes a middle position. As Plato saw it, it was not completely worthless. However, many other voices differentiated it only negatively from knowledge, belief, and conviction. Kant (1893, 498) characterized opinion as "insufficient judgment, subjectively as well as objectively." The Anglo-Saxons and the French, in contrast, saw "opinion" as more complex. They left it open how valuable or worthless opinion might be, but considered it the unified agreement of a population or a particular segment of the population. "Common opinion" is what the English social philosopher David Hume called it in a work published in 1739 (Hume 1896, 411). Agreement and a sense of the common is what lay behind the English and French "opinion."

Agreement that demands recognition

In the context of what we have learned about the spiral of silence, the French and English approach makes much more sense than the German preoccupation with the value or lack of value of opinion. Individuals would observe the consensus in their environment and contrast it with their own behavior. It was not thereby necessarily the consensus of *opinion* that would be at issue; it might deal with concurrent *behavior*—wearing or not wearing a badge, offering one's seat to an old person or remaining seated in a public vehicle. For the spiral of silence process, it was immaterial whether a person isolated himself through an opinion or through behavior. These considerations forced us to see that, in the definition we sought, opinion was to be understood as a synonym for the expression of something regarded as acceptable, thereby hinting at the element of consensus or agreement found in the English and French usage.

Three meanings of "public"

The interpretation of "public" proved to be at least as critical as that of "opinion." Many scholars have argued over the concept "public." As Habermas contended, "the use of 'public' and of 'the public' betrays a multiplicity of competing meanings" (1962, 13). To begin with, there is the legal sense of "public," which emphasizes the etymological aspect of its openness: it is open to everyone—a public place, a public path, a public trial—as distinguished from the private sphere (from the Latin *privare*), something distinguished or set aside as one's own. A second meaning can be found in the concepts of public rights and public force. Here "public" expresses some involvement of the state. According to this second usage, "public" has to do with public interests, as expressed, for example, in the phrase "the public responsibility of journalists." This means we are dealing with issues or problems that concern us all, that concern the general welfare. States base the legalized use of force on this principle: the single individual has surrendered the possibility of using force to the organs of the state. The state has the monopoly to use force. Finally, in the phrase "public opinion," "public" must have a related but different meaning. Legal scholars such as Ihering and von Holtzendorff have marveled at the amazing power public opinion has in making regulations, norms, and moral rules prevail over the individual without ever troubling legislators, governments, or courts for assistance. "It is cheap" was the praise public opinion received in 1898 from the American sociologist Edward Ross (1969, 95). The equation of "public opinion" with "ruling opinion" runs like a common thread through its many definitions. This speaks to the fact that something or other clinging to public opinion sets up conditions that move individuals to act, even against their own wills.

The social skin

The third meaning of "public" could be characterized as social-psychological. The individual does not live only in that inner space where he thinks and feels. His life is also turned outside, not just to other persons, but also the collectivity as a whole. Under certain conditions (I am thinking of the famous distinction of Ferdinand Tönnies, *Gemeinschaft* and *Gesellschaft*), the exposed individual is

sheltered by the intimacy and trust engendered through, for example, a shared religion. In great civilizations, however, the individual
stands exposed even more openly to the demands of society (Tönnies 1922, 69, 80). What is it that "exposes" the individual and
continually requires that he attend to the social dimension around
him? It is fear of isolation, fear of disrespect, or unpopularity; it is a
need for consensus. This makes a person want to focus his attention
on the environment, thus leading to an awareness of the "public
eye." Ordinary individuals always know whether they are exposed
to or hidden from the public view, and they conduct themselves
accordingly. To be sure, people seem to differ greatly in the way
they are affected by this awareness. The individual directs his
anxious attention toward this anonymous court, which deals out
popularity and unpopularity, respect and scorn.

Fascinated by the ideal of the self-reliant, independent individual, scholars have hardly noticed the existence of the isolated
individual fearful of the opinion of his peers. Instead, they have
explored many other possible meanings and dimensions of the
concept, often as barren academic exercises. They have considered
the *content* of public opinion: this is assumed to consist of relevant,
"public affairs" issues. Next they have considered whose opinion
constitutes public opinion: those persons in a community who are
ready and in the position to express themselves responsibly about
questions of public relevance and thereby exercise an office of
criticism and control over the government in the name of the
governed. They have also considered the forms of public opinion:
those which are openly expressed and are therefore generally ac-
cessible—opinions made public, and particularly those made public
in the mass media. Only the social-pyschological aspect of "public"
seems practically to have been neglected in the twentieth century's
wealth of definitions. Yet this is the meaning felt by people in their
sensitive social skin, their social nature.

Opinions that one can express in public without isolating oneself
In the preceding chapters I have tried to identify elements that
seem to be linked with the process of public opinion and are
amenable to empirical investigation: (1) the human ability to realize
when public opinions grow in strength or weaken; (2) the reactions
to this realization, leading either to more confident speech or to
silence; and (3) the fear of isolation that makes most people willing
to heed the opinion of others. It is on these three elements that an
operational definition of public opinion may be built: opinions on

controversial issues that one *can* express in public without isolating oneself. This definition, then, will serve as our tentative guideline for further investigations.

Of course, this interpretation of public opinion needs to be supplemented, because it applies only to situations in which opinions vie with one another, whenever newly arising ideas are being approved or existing conceptions overthrown. Ferdinand Tönnies, in his 1922 publication *Kritik der Öffentlichen Meinung* (Critique of Public Opinion), was of the view that public opinion existed in various degrees or states of aggregation: solid, fluid, and gaseous (1922, 137–38). If one uses Tönnies's analogy, the spiral of silence appears only during the fluid state. For instance, when one camp speaks of *Radikalenerlass*, not allowing radicals into public service jobs, and the other camp speaks of *Berufsverbot*, prevention of a person's right to pursue his or her profession, then each camp has its own language, and we can follow the movement of the spiral of silence by noting the frequency with which each term is used by the majority. Where opinions and forms of behavior have gained a firm hold, where they have become custom or tradition, we can no longer recognize an element of controversy in them. The controversial element, a prerequisite for the potential of isolation, enters only after a violation, when firmly established public opinion, tradition, and morals have been injured. In the late nineteenth century, Franz von Holtzendorff (1879–80, 74) spoke of the "censor's office" of public opinion, and von Ihering (1883, 340) called it the "task-mistress of all things moral," removing from it all trace of the intellectual. This is what he meant when he spoke of the conscious or unconscious "reaction of an interest against its own injury, a defense in the service of the common security" (Ihering 1883, 242). The definition of public opinion remains to be completed; for in the field of consolidated traditions, morals, and, above all, norms, the opinions and behaviors of public opinion are opinions and behaviors that one *must* express or adopt if one is not going to isolate oneself. The existing order is preserved on the one hand by the individual's fear of isolation and his need to be accepted; and on the other by the public's demand, carrying the weight of a court sentence, that we conform to established opinions and behaviors.

Public opinion as approval and disapproval

Can a proper definition ignore what has been presented as public opinion in hundreds of books, that is, opinion only about matters of political significance? By our definition, public opinion—

whether it refers to change or to defending established and consolidated positions—is not restricted in subject matter. What we are speaking of is the approval and disapproval of publicly observable positions and behavior. We are speaking of the approval or disapproval that makes itself noticeable to the individual. The spiral of silence is a reaction to openly visible approval and disapproval among shifting constellations of values. The question of whose opinion should count is equally unrestricted. In this view, public opinion is not just a matter for those who feel a calling, or for talented critics—the "politically functioning public" of Habermas (1962, 117). Everyone is involved.

A venture into the past: Machiavelli, Shakespeare, Montaigne

To find out whether the concept of public opinion as it has developed out of the spiral of silence is well founded, we may go back two hundred years and to the land in which the term "public opinion" first appeared—eighteenth-century France. In a famous novel first published in 1782, *Les Liaisons Dangereuses*, Choderlos de Laclos casually uses the term *l'opinion publique* as everyday language. Laclos's passage concerns an exchange of letters between a sophisticated woman and a young lady. The older woman advises her friend against keeping company with a man of bad repute: "You believe him capable of change for the better, yes, and let us further assume that this miracle actually occurs. Would not public opinion persist in remaining against him, and would not this suffice to make you adjust your relationship with him accordingly?" (Choderlos de Laclos 1926, 1:89).

We find public opinion active here as a court of judgment in spheres far removed from politics and far removed from persons especially distinguished by their political judgment. The author of the letter assumes that the vaguely described and anonymous group characterized as the public will, through its opinion, so influence the recipient of the letter as to lead to appropriate adjustments in her behavior. But we can go back even further into the past, to a time before the expression "public opinion" had been coined. Here we encounter the same anonymous court passing judgments, and, although under a different name, it bears witness to an almost identical conflict. Shakespeare describes an exchange between King Henry IV and his son, the future Henry V. The king reprimands his son for being seen too often in bad company. He should have more regard for opinion. Opinion is of the greatest importance: the king says that he himself was raised by opinion to the throne: "Opinion that did help me to the crown" (*Henry IV, Part I*, act 3). If Shakespeare could use "opinion" so decidedly on the stage at the end of the sixteenth century, then it is not surprising that the longer expression "public opinion" was first coined not in England but in France. The English word "opinion" apparently contained enough of the element of "publicness"—the court-of-judgment quality by which reputations were created and destroyed—that it did not require the additional element of "public" at all.

The idea that a ruler or a future king must pay attention to the opinion of his environment, to his general public, was certainly nothing odd or new to Shakespeare. His century was acquainted with Machiavelli's 1514 *The Prince*, which contained important sections advising rulers on how best to deal with the public. There are never, says Machiavelli, more than a few who "feel" a government or, one can translate, who feel themselves directly affected by it. But everyone *sees* it, and everything depends on its seeming, in the eyes of its viewers, to be powerful and virtuous. "The vulgar are always taken by appearances." "It is not, therefore, necessary for a prince to have all the desirable qualities [mercy, faithfulness, humanity, sincerity, religiousness, etc.], but it is very necessary to seem to have them." The prince, Machiavelli said, must avoid everything that could lead to his becoming hated or that might make him appear contemptible. He must trouble himself to make sure that the people are satisfied with him (Machiavelli 1950, 64–66, 56, 67; Rusciano n.d., 35, 40, 33, 25, 37).

The theory that lay at the foundation of Henry IV's admonition to his son ran like this in Machiavelli's Discourses on the First Decade of Livius' Roman History: "There is no better indication of a man's character than the company he keeps; and therefore very properly a man who keeps respectable company acquires a good name, for it is impossible that there should not be some similitude of character and habits between him and his associates" (Machiavelli 1971/1950, 509–11; Rusciano n.d., 64).

Here we are in the first half of the sixteenth century, and yet we hardly feel that we have strayed into a time when people were less sensitive than they are today about what a good reputation means, or less sensitive to the critical court of public opinion.

We have, however, obtained a new insight from Machiavelli and Shakespeare, namely, that the court of judgment called public opinion does not merely make little people tremble for their reputation. Princes, lords, and rulers are likewise subject to its dicta. Machiavelli warns the prince he is trying to instruct that, in order to rule, he must know the nature of his subjects thoroughly (Machiavelli 1971, 257). The power of the people lies in their capacity to reject the government of the prince and to overthrow him if he is insensitive to their desires (Rusciano n.d., 49).

Discoverer of the public dimension: Montaigne

At the University of Mainz, we began some systematic studies of literature by putting together a questionnaire with twenty questions to be asked of texts rather than of persons. Does the text contain the concept of public opinion or related concepts? Does it describe the fear of isolation? Does it describe conflicts between the individual and the collective, between the prevailing opinion and deviant opinion? We combed texts as one might comb the countryside—the Bible, myths, fairytales; works by philosophers, essayists, poets.

In a paper by Wilhelm Bauer (1920), who wrote several works on public opinion, Kurt Braatz (a doctoral student) found a comment to the effect that Machiavelli had used the concept in Italian. There was no citation, however, and we could not locate the passage. Although English translations of Machiavelli have used the expression "public opinion," the *Discorsi* use such terms as *opinione universale* (I, 58), *commune opinione* (II, 10), or *pubblica voce* (III, 34).

To determine the meaning of public opinion, we believed, we needed to see how the concept was first used, in what context, based on what observations—just as one can gain knowledge of a plant by studying its habitat. Our expectation was confirmed. Michael Raffel (1984) summarized the findings of his master's thesis in an article titled "Creator of the Concept of Public Opinion: Michel de Montaigne." In the 1588 edition of his essays, about seventy years after the appearance of Machiavelli's *Discorsi*, Montaigne twice used the collective singular *l'opinion publique*. Explaining why he sprinkled his writings with so many quotations from writers of antiquity, he said, "It is really for the sake of public opinion that I appear with this borrowed finery" (Montaigne 1962, 1033). The second time he used the expression "public opinion" was in addressing the question of how customs and moral notions can be changed. Plato, he said, considered pederasty a dangerous passion. To combat it, Plato (in his *Laws*) recommended that it be condemned by public opinion. He demanded that poets portray this vice as execrable, thus creating public opinion on the subject. Although the new, negative view might still go against majority opinion, it would, if presented as the prevailing view, later become valid for slaves and free men alike, women and children, and the entire citizenry (ibid., 115).

It is no accident that Montaigne was so attentive to the social nature of man and to the effect of publicity, public approval, and public condemnation. To my knowledge, every scholar or writer to have made an important contribution to the topic of public opinion has had firsthand experience of it. Machiavelli wrote of it after a change of government in Florence, after he had been accused of involvement in a conspiracy and had been incarcerated, tortured, and then set free, retiring to his estate at San Casciano. Montaigne's experience was threefold. First, he had the experience of his immediate family. The corporate system that had been entrenched throughout the Middle Ages had begun to change; a newly formed group of wealthy but nonaristocratic citizens was striving to be recognized as having equal rights with the aristocracy. A battle was raging over dress codes and status symbols—what furs, what jewels, what kinds of material could be worn appropriate to one's rank—a battle over the public, visible conditions of life. Montaigne had witnessed this in his own family. His father's family had acquired its wealth in the wine and dye trades and had bought the Château Montaigne in 1477; his father had added "de Montaigne" to the family name. Montaigne's sensitivity to symbols and new modes of behavior had been learned at home.

Even more important was the experience of changing beliefs, the religious struggle between Catholics and Protestants initiated by Luther's posting of the ninety-five theses in 1517, a struggle which, in France, took the form of the wars of religion (1562–89). Montaigne complained that there was no escape from the wars anywhere in France, and that his home town of Bordeaux, of whose *parlement* he was a member, was particularly restless, an arena for continual clashes. One had to observe the social environment and the strength of the respective camps carefully, and to adjust one's behavior accordingly. After all, three to four thousand Huguenots were murdered in Paris in the notorious massacre of Saint Bartholomew's Eve (23 August 1572), and twelve thousand others had perished elsewhere in France.

These, surely, were the conditions that prompted Montaigne to withdraw from public life on his thirty-eighth birthday (28 February 1571). He had an inscription placed over the entrance to his library in the tower of the Château Montaigne, stating that he wished to spend his remaining days there in peace and solitude. This is where he wrote his famous Essays. He did eventually return to public life, becoming mayor of Bordeaux in 1582 and traveling on a variety of diplomatic missions across Europe. Hence he was much aware of the contrast between public and private life and of the way different convictions were held in different countries and, in each case, regarded as binding. "What kind of truth is it," he asks, "that is delimited by mountains and becomes a lie on the other side of those mountains?" (Montaigne 1962, 563). "If mountains can set limits to 'truth,' then opinion must have a social aspect and strict boundaries to its realm" (203). "So Montaigne sees prevailing opinions as tied to a particular place and time—something observable as a social reality with only temporary validity. It is legitimated only by the fact that it presents itself as an opinion without alternative, one that is binding: . . . 'so that we really have no standards of truth and reason other than the examples and ideas of opinions and habits that we see around us every day" (Raffel 1984).

By alternating essentially public and essentially private phases in his life, Montaigne in his writing becomes the discoverer of the public dimension. He consciously divides up his life: "A wise man ought inwardly to retire his minde from the common presse, and hold the same liberty and power to judge freely of all things, but for outward matters, he ought absolutely to follow the fashions and forme customarily received" (Montaigne 1962/1908, 129). For Montaigne, the public sphere has its own inherent laws. It is a sphere dominated by a consensus inimical to individuality. "Of our habitual actions, not one in a thousand concerns us as individuals" (Raffel 1984). Montaigne invents a variety of new concepts for this new element. He coins the term *le publique*, and, in addition to the new concept *l'opinion publique*, he speaks of *l'opinion commune* (Montaigne 1962, 174), *l'approbation publique* (ibid., 1013), and *référence publique* (ibid., 9).

Why did the concept of *opinion publique* not become established then rather than a century and a half later? "Perhaps a letter from a friend of Montaigne's, Estienne de Pasquier, to an acquaintance is of some help here," suggests Michael Raffel. Pasquier complains that Montaigne frequently takes the liberty of using uncommon words "which, if I am not mistaken, he will have a hard time making fashionable" (Raffel 1984; Frame 1965).

John Locke, David Hume, and Jean-Jacques Rousseau read Montaigne. But it was not until the second half of the eighteenth century, in the decade preceding the French Revolution, that he became a fashionable writer.

After our description in previous chapters of empirical investigations, our search through the past has taken us to the first appearance of the concept of public opinion in the sixteenth century. Everything described as public opinion, general opinion, public approbation, public propriety in the works we have looked at is so remarkably familiar to us from empirical work that it is as if we were now seeing two views, which are really of a piece, coming together again. This encourages us to continue looking for historical evidence in the hope that it will help us toward a better understanding of public opinion.

5 The Law of Opinion: John Locke

*I*n his *Essay Concerning Human Understanding*, published in 1671, John Locke (1894, 1:9) reports that five or six of his friends used to meet regularly for conversation in his London apartment. The meetings led to a fascinating discussion in which, however, they made no progress at all. It occurred to them that they may have taken the wrong approach and that they would be better served by another. Locke's friends found this very convincing and urged him to make a few notes about the course of the conversation before they met again. To comply with their request, Locke took more and more notes, and, from these notes, his book eventually emerged.

London around 1670 must have been a wonderful city. Discussions were held everywhere—in Parliament, in the editorial offices of newspapers, in coffeehouses, and in private circles. What Locke, then in his late thirties, jotted down on paper—written incoherently, he says, and not meant for great and learned men—has the freshness of an early summer morning. After the book's publication, however, Locke lamented: "The imputation of novelty is a terrible charge amongst those who judge of men's heads, as they do of their perukes, by the fashion, and can allow none to be right but the received doctrines. Truth scarce ever yet carried it by vote anywhere at its first appearance: new opinions are always suspected, and usually opposed, without any other reason but because they are not already common. But truth, like gold, is not the less so for being newly brought out of the mine" (1894, 1:4).

We must distinguish between three kinds of laws, says Locke. First the divine law, second the civil law, and third the law of virtue and vice, the law of opinion or of reputation, or—Locke uses the terms interchangeably—the law of fashion.

Locke expounds on the third law as follows: "To comprehend it aright, we must consider that men's uniting into political societies, though they have resigned up to the public the disposal of all their force, so that they cannot employ it against any fellow-citizen, any further than the law of their county directs—yet they retain still the power of *thinking* well or ill, approving or disapproving the actions of those they live amongst and converse with" (1894, 1:476).[6]

Reputation and fashion: the standards of a certain place at a given time

> The measure of what is everywhere called and esteemed "virtue" and "vice" is this approbation or dislike, praise or blame, which, by a secret and tacit consent, establishes itself in the several societies . . . in the world; whereby several actions come to find credit or disgrace amongst them, according to the judgment, maxims, or fashions of that place. . . . But no man escapes the punishment of their censure and dislike, who offends against the fashion and opinion of the company he keeps. . . . Nor is there one of ten thousand, who is stiff and insensible enough, to bear up under the constant dislike and condemnation of his own club. He must be of a strange and unusual constitution, who can content himself to live in constant disgrace and disrepute with his own particular society. Solitude many men have sought, and been reconciled to: but nobody that has the least thought or sense of a man about him can live in society under the constant dislike and ill opinion of his familiars and those he converses with. This is a burden too heavy for human sufferance. (Locke 1894, 1:476, 479)

6. Cited as in first edition, cf. footnote (emphasis added).

The description stands complete: men, through fear of isolation, are forced into conformity by the court of public opinion. But John Locke's work brought him no happiness. Persecuted by his enemies, he altered the passage in the third edition of his book, substituting stilted phrases (1:476–77, n. I).

He was accused of making good and evil relative, and this in a destructive way. That which arose out of divine law he was said to have transformed into a matter of consensus among private individuals; he was accused of degrading moral issues into matters of fashion. He did not even seem to realize what constituted a law, for, as everyone knows, it is authority—something private individuals surely lack. Authority is what pertains to law, namely, the authority and power to enforce its observance. Locke writes:

> I think I may say, that he who imagines commendation and disgrace not to be strong motives to men to accommodate themselves to the opinions and rules of those with whom they converse seems little skilled in the nature or history of mankind: the greatest part whereof we shall find to govern themselves chiefly, if not solely, by this *law of fashion*; and so they do that which keeps them in reputation with their company, little regard the laws of God, or the magistrate.
>
> The penalties that attend the breach of God's laws some, nay, perhaps most men, seldom seriously reflect on: and amongst those that do, many, whilst they break the law, entertain thoughts of future reconciliation, and making their peace for such breaches.
>
> And as to the punishments due from the laws of the commonwealth, they frequently flatter themselves with the hopes of impunity. But *no man* escapes the punishment of their censure and dislike who offends against the *fashion* and opinion of the company he keeps, and would recommend himself to. (1:476–77; emphasis added)

Locke sketches a terminology on three levels: with reference to the divine law, one speaks of duties and of sins; with reference to the civil law, of the legal or criminal; with reference to the law of opinion and reputation, of virtue and vice. Using the example of a duel, he shows that these different standards do not necessarily produce the same results: "Thus the challenging and fighting with a man . . . is called *duelling*: which, when considered in relation to the law of God, will deserve the name of sin; to the law of fashion, in some countries, valour and virtue; and to the municipal laws of some governments, a capital crime (1: 481–82).

Our twentieth-century methods of social research have allowed us to see how people perceive the environment of opinion in ways that are very close to what Locke had seen. With a variety of expressions, Locke describes the social nature of human beings. "Men commonly regulate their assent, and . . . pin their faith more than anything else . . . [upon] *the opinion of others* . . . men have reason to be Heathens in Japan, Mahometans in Turkey, Papists in Spain . . ." Put another way, that which we call our opinion does not belong to us but is a simple reflection of the opinions of others (2:367–68).

John Locke places no limits on content when he deals with his "law of opinion." But he stresses that what matters is the element of evaluation; praise or blame is always expressed. The consensus these opinions cling to he characterizes as a "secret and tacit consent" (1:476). That there is something mysterious about it can be confirmed by twentieth-century research.

Something else about Locke's description arrests our attention: one is dealing, he says, with the opinion, with the standard of "that place" (1:477). The body of opinion which the individual respects, this agreement, exists in a particular place at a particular time. Consequently, individuals can alter their intercourse with opinion by removing themselves to a sufficiently distant place, and they can hope that, in time, things will change. Opinions are transient. Although the phrase "public opinion" does not occur in John Locke's work, it is present indirectly in two ways: first, in his idea of agreement, which can only be interpreted as a matter of social unity and thus public; second, in his stress on "place," with its connotation of the most public setting possible. Compared to the concept of *l'opinion publique* as developed in France, Locke's "law of opinion or reputation" (1:475–76) is harsher and less merciful, but he wanted to express it that strongly.

When Locke uses the expression "law," he does not do so frivolously, casually, incidentally; nor does he use it in the sense of the natural scientist, speaking of the laws of nature. He means law in a legal sense and he makes it quite plain: when an action involves a law, a reward or punishment that is not intrinsic to the act itself must follow from it (1:476). Even the label he gives his law is instructive. When Locke speaks of "the law of opinion or reputation," one sees how close his idea of opinion comes to being completely enveloped in reputation; the two are almost identical in meaning.[7]

John Locke speaks constantly of "fashion" as he considers his topic (1894, 1:476, 478ff.). This peculiarity of the text, which at first has a ludicrous effect, in fact marks especially clearly the pioneering nature of his thought. People judge opinions as they do perukes—men's wigs. Locke pinpoints how superficial and transitory opinion is, how bound up with place and time, but also how coercive while it reigns, by emphatically characterizing it as "fashion." He uses the word distinctly as a key in order that he not be misunderstood. This opinion of which he speaks in his "law of opinion or reputation" cannot be regarded as a source of political wisdom. Its intellectual value is wide open to question, and criteria for evaluating it will have to be sought in other ways.

Locke also insists on concepts such as "reputation," hence on social-psychological concepts that show human beings in their complete dependence on the social environment, on the many, on others. Because people tend to mistrust new opinions and to disregard them just because they are new and not yet in fashion, Locke seeks out classical authorities to provide himself with ammunition. He cites a passage of Cicero: There is nothing in the world better than integrity, praise, dignity, and honor. Then he adds, Cicero knew very well that these are all different names for the same thing (1:478).

For the same thing? And what is that?

According to our understanding, these are all marks of approval given to the individual by the public.

---

7. That John Locke dealt with the negative aspects of public judgment as well as with the positive aspects is shown by his essay "Some Thoughts Concerning Education" in Locke 1824, 8:1–210.

6 *Government Rests on Opinion: David Hume, James Madison*

*I*n 1711, seven years after John Locke's death, David Hume was born. In his *Treatise of Human Nature*, first published 1739 and 1740, he takes up Locke's thoughts and turns them to a theory of the state. Although people may have relinquished the use of force since the founding of the state, they have not surrendered their capacity to approve and disapprove; and because people have a natural tendency to heed opinions and to conform to the environing opinions, opinion is vital to state affairs. The concentrated power of similar opinions held by private persons brings forth a consensus, and this constitutes the actual basis of any government. Hume guides himself by the principle: "It is . . . on opinion only that government is founded" (Hume 1963, 29).[8]

> Nothing appears more surprising to those who consider human affairs with a philosophical eye, than the easiness with which the *many* are governed by the *few*; and the implicit submission, with which men resign their own sentiments and passions to those of their rulers. When we inquire by what means this wonder is effected, we shall find, that . . . the governors have nothing to support them but opinion. It is, therefore, on opinion only that government is founded; and this maxim extends to the most despotic and most military governments, as well as to the most free and most popular. (Ibid., emphasis added)

With Hume, the perspective we use to deal with opinion shifts from the pressure it exercises on individuals to the pressure it exercises on government—exactly the point of view that Machiavelli presented to the prince. Locke was attentive to normal people, those who were subject to the law of opinion or reputation in their everyday existence and whose fear of disapproval was such that not one in ten thousand would have been unmoved had his neighbors regarded him with disdain. In his *Essay Concerning Human Understanding*, Locke investigated human nature in general. Hume directed his interest to the government. His sphere was the court,

---

8. My thanks to Professor Ernst Vollrath of the University of Cologne for a stimulating exchange of letters on this topic.

diplomacy, and politics. He too was fearful of the punishments, with which the law of opinion or reputation threatened anyone who provoked disapproval, and, as a precaution, published his first work, *A Treatise of Human Nature*, anonymously. However, in keeping with his love of an elevated life, he was less sensitive to the punishments than to the rewards which, according to the law of opinion, await those who find approval and recognition.

The love of fame: the sunny side of public opinion

Hume titles the chapter in which he discusses public opinion "Of the Love of Fame" (1896, 316–24). After describing how virtue, beauty, wealth and power—that is, how objectively advantageous conditions—allow men to feel pride, and how poverty and servitude oppress them, he continues: "But beside these original causes of pride and humility, there is a secondary one in the opinions of others, which has an equal influence on the affections. Our reputation, our character, our name are considerations of vast weight and importance; the other causes of pride; virtue, beauty and riches have little influence, when not seconded by the opinions and sentiments of others. . . . [Even] men of the greatest judgment and understanding . . . find it very difficult to follow their own reason or inclination, in opposition to that of their friends and daily companions" (316).

Hume, who was caught up in the pursuit of a good life (he describes with great fondness the advantages of wealth and power), expresses himself in this passage as if matters depended above all on the good opinion of the reference group—to use a concept from modern sociology. His formulation depends less on publicness, or approval and disapproval of "that place." Nevertheless, he sees the breadth of effects that arise when men do not wish to place themselves in contradiction to their environment. "To this principle," he says, "we ought to ascribe the great uniformity we may observe in the humours and turn of thinking of those of the same nation" (ibid.). He expressly approves this human sensitivity to the environment and regards it in no way as a weakness (see his *An Enquiry Concerning the Principles of Morals*): "A desire of fame, reputation, or a character with others, is so far from being blameable, that it seems inseparable from virtue, genius, capacity, and a generous or noble disposition. An attention even to trivial matters, in order to please, is also expected and demanded by society; and no one is surprised, if he find a man in company to observe a greater elegance of dress and more pleasant flow of conversation, than when he passes his time at home, and with his own family" (Hume 1962, 265–66).

It is sufficiently obvious that Hume does not pause long over society's rejects, those who suffer the punishments of a disapproving public. Instead, he concerns himself with those on the sunny side, and it troubles him somewhat to draw a boundary beyond which the love of fame might go too far. "Wherein, then, consists Vanity, which is so justly regarded as a fault or imperfection? It seems to consist chiefly in such an intemperate display of our advantages, honours, and accomplishments; in such an importunate and open demand of praise and admiration, as is offensive to others" (266). Hume clearly realizes that his reflections apply primarily to the upper social circles. He notes: "A proper regard to . . . station in the world, may be ranked among the qualities which are immediately agreeable to others" (ibid.).

Hume certainly moves within Locke's general outline of the relationship between the individual and the public, grounded in a given "place," but he sees this relationship in a completely different light. His idea of the public is much closer to the one Habermas thought was taken for granted by the Greeks (Habermas 1962, 15). "In the public light, that which is, shines forth; and it will be seen by all. As citizens converse with one another, things are brought into the discussion and acquire form; as the same people argue with one another, the best distinguish themselves and win being, the immortality of fame. . . . In this way the city-state offers an open field for honorable achievement: the citizens' intercourse with each other as equal with equal . . . but each strives to stand out . . . The virtues catalogued by Aristotle prove themselves true, one by one, in public, and they find their recognition there (Habermas 1962, 15–16).

Hume's elevated stance, however, in which the public is the arena in which achievements are recognized, is not shared by other eighteenth-century authors writing about public opinion at the same time or after he did. David Hume's basic principle, "It is . . . on opinion only that government is founded," became the doctrine of the founding fathers of the United States. We now recognize the weight of opinion in the political sphere, but, at the same time, we now again see the role of the individual through the eyes of John Locke.

Man is timid and cautious

In *The Federalist*, James Madison warily investigated the implications of the principle that "all governments rest on opinion." The dogma in these essays has great power and constitutes the foundation of American democracy. How weak and vulnerable in contrast is the human nature that is supposed to provide this foundation. "If it be true," wrote Madison in 1788, "that all governments rest on opinion, it is no less true that the strength of opinion in each individual, and its practical influence on his conduct, depend much on the number which he supposes to have entertained the same opinion. The reason of man, like man himself is timid and cautious, when left *alone*; and acquires firmness and *confidence*, in proportion to the number with which it is associated." (Madison 1961, 340; Draper 1982).

We find here that realistic evaluation of human nature and its application to political theory to which we, in the second half of the twentieth century, must return; the methods of public opinion research now force us to seek explanations for what stubbornly arose to confront us in our series of observations.

Threat, not fame, sets the spiral of silence in motion

If we compare, on the one hand, how David Hume regards the topic of the individual and the public and, on the other, how John Locke or James Madison treats it, we see a distinction that is similar to the one we found in our earlier interpretation of the bandwagon effect. "Wanting to be on the side of the victors" is one interpretation; "Not wanting to isolate oneself" is the other. The public as a stage on which one distinguishes oneself is what fascinates the one; the public as a threat, an arena in which one may lose face impresses the others. Why, then, should we be concerned with the spiral of silence and its relation to public opinion less as a domain in which to win laurels than as a threat, a menacing public tribunal? Because only the menace, the individual's fear of finding himself alone, as Madison so empathically described it, can also explain the symptomatic silence we found in the train test and in other investigations, the silence that is so influential in the building of public opinion.

Revolutionary times sharpen the capacity to sense public exposure as a threat

Could it be that Locke's and Madison's intuitive gift for sensing the threats of the public may have been sharpened by the revolution

that each of them experienced? Attention to how one should behave in order not to become isolated is first made necessary in times
of drastic change. In a stable order of things, most people will not
run afoul of public opinion as long as they do not violate the
ordinary rules of decorum; they will not be drawn into even an eddy
of the spiral of silence. What one is to do or say or leave unsaid and
undone is so obvious that the pressures of conformity become like
the pressures of the atmosphere that we live under: we remain quite
unaware of them. In prerevolutionary and revolutionary times,
however, new impressions arise. The support of opinion slips away
from governments until they finally collapse, and individuals torn
out of a secure confidence about what is to be praised or blamed
seek to relate to new standards. In such exciting times and under
these impressions, it is easier to understand how public opinion
works and to find adequate words to describe it.

1661: Glanvill shapes the concept "climate of opinion"

In a quiet age, one would not expect to find someone setting up
the law of opinion or reputation, complete with punishments and
rewards. It appears unthinkable, then, that the English philosopher
Joseph Glanvill, in peaceful times, would have happened upon the
powerful term he included in his treatise about the vanity of dogmatizing. He made up the phrase "climate(s) of opinions" and set it off
in italics in the text. He wrote: "So they [the dogmatists] that never
peep't beyond the belief in which their easie understandings were at
first indoctrinated, are indubitately assur'd of the Truth, and comparative excellency of their receptions, while the larger Souls, that
have travail'd the divers *Climates of Opinions*, are more cautious in
their resolves, and more sparing to determine" (Glanvill 1661,
226–27).

"Climate of opinion"—without a doubt, one would have
thought this a modern expression, born in our own time. That
assumption can be attributed to our sensitivity which, like Joseph
Glanvill's, is tuned to precarious conditions and to convictions that
have become uncertain. Without such vacillating conditions, the
concept "climate" would be uninteresting to us, but, out of the
experiences of our times, we can appreciate its appropriateness.
Climate totally surrounds the individual from the outside; he cannot escape from it. Yet it is simultaneously there within us, exercis-
ing the strongest influence on our sense of well-being. The spiral of
silence is a reaction to changes in the climate of opinion. The idea of

a frequency distribution, of the relative strength of various contradictory tendencies is suggested more clearly by the expression "climate of opinion" than by "public opinion." "Climate" also brings to mind the image of time and space—something like Kurt Lewin's concept of "field"; and "climate" also includes the most complete sense of "public." In revolutionary times, including our own, it pays to search for observations that will reveal the nature of public opinion.

Descartes intuitively understood the spiral of silence

Descartes, whom Glanvill admired and recommended, lived under completely different circumstances in France than Glanvill did in England. The England of Glanvill was torn by dissension, while France in Descartes's time was going through a period of unchallenged values and social hierarchies. Descartes's thought illustrates the accuracy of our speculation that in revolutionary periods the public is experienced more as a threat, while in periods of order it is experienced more as a sphere in which one can distinguish oneself. Descartes appears to understand the spiral of silence intuitively as a process that nourishes newly developing public opinion. He knew how to advance his own fame. In 1640 he transmitted *Meditations on First Philosophy* to "The most wise and illustrious: The dean and doctors of the sacred faculty of theology in Paris." In a cover letter he requested that they, considering the great public respect they enjoyed, provide "public testimony" in support of his thoughts. This request, said he, arose in hopes that it would "easily cause all men of mind and learning to subscribe to your judgment; and your authority will cause the atheists, who are usually more arrogant than learned or judicious, to rid themselves of their spirit of contradiction or lead them possibly themselves to defend the reasonings which they find being received as demonstrations by all persons of consideration, lest they appear not to understand them" (Descartes 1964/1931, 1:136).

7 Launching the Term "Public Opinion": Jean-Jacques Rousseau

What kind of a situation first prompted Jean-Jacques Rousseau to use the term *l'opinion publique*?

Venice, 1744: Rousseau, now in his early thirties, is secretary to the French ambassador. It is a year full of excitement. Involved in the Austrian Wars of Succession, France has declared war on Maria Theresa. On 2 May 1744, Rousseau writes a letter apologizing to Amelot, the French minister of foreign affairs, for having too plainly warned the Venetian nobleman Chevalier Erizzo that "public opinion" already regarded him as sympathetic to Austria (Rousseau 1964a, 1184). He assures Amelot that his comment apparently has had no adverse consequences and that, in the future, he will not be guilty of such blunders. Rousseau here uses the phrase "public opinion" in the same way that a woman of sophistication will later use it concerning "liaisons dangereuses," in the warning to a young lady who has paid too little attention to her reputation: public opinion here is regarded as a tribunal from whose disapproval one must protect oneself.

Those who interpret public opinion as a politically critical judgment that involves the government, as became the practice from the nineteenth century on, will find little support in Rousseau's use. Searching his works for ideas relating to the topic of public opinion has had little attraction for historians and political scientists.

One would expect that the man who launched the term *l'opinion publique* must have had a deep feeling for the phenomenon, and the expectation is not disappointed. From 1750 on, concern with the strength of public opinion permeates Rousseau's writings. However, because he had no organizing principle to guide his treatment of this topic, a special technique is required to create a consistent picture. The first systematic investigation was presented by Christine Gerber (1975), a master's student in journalism at Mainz. She threw a net, as it were, over Rousseau's six major works and investigated every passage in which the words "opinion," "public," "publicity" or "public opinion" occurred. Using content analysis, she worked through Rousseau's works of social criticism (1750–55),

Julie or the New Heloise, The Social Contract, Emile, The Confessions, and finally the *Letter to d'Alembert* (1758). She found 16 uses of "public opinion," around 100 uses of "opinion" connected with some adjective or substantive other than "public," and 106 instances of "public" or "publicity"—which, aside from the context of public opinion, was used most frequently in connection with public respect. The first French investigation of the topic was a doctoral thesis by Colette Ganouchaud (1977–78).

Public is what everyone can see

The upshot of this research was the realization that Rousseau was highly sensitive to the threatening aspect of publicity. As an outsider in society, he had unusual opportunities to gather experience in this regard. "I saw nothing but the horror of being recognized, publicly proclaimed, in my presence as a thief, liar, slanderer" (Rousseau 1968, 1:122). "All this did not hinder the excited crowd, incited by whom I know not, from getting stirred up against me little by little to the point of rage, insulting me publicly in broad daylight and not only outdoors and on country paths, but even in the middle of the street" (2:398).

"In broad daylight," "not only on country paths": being in full view, unprotected from the public, aggravated the evil. Rousseau's repeated combination of the words "public respect" indicates how clearly he relates "public opinion" to "reputation," in the tradition of Machiavelli, Locke, and Hume, but he discusses the concept at incomparably greater length in his writing. He is torn by ambivalent evaluations. Seen in terms of society, public opinion seems to be a blessing: it fosters social cohesiveness; insofar as it makes individuals adjust to morals and traditions, it is a conservative force; and it protects morals from decay. Its value lies in moral rather than intellectual functions.

Public opinion as the guardian of morality and traditions

Rousseau believed that social life was better regulated in the far distant past, when savages lived together in a natural state. Therefore he held the more stable forms of public opinion—namely, customs and tradition—to be the most important resources a society had to protect; in them the essential qualities of a people were collected. According to Rousseau, there are three kinds of laws upon which the state is built—public law, criminal law, and civil law. He then explained: "In addition to these three types of law there is a fourth, the most important of all, which is graven not in marble or bronze, but in the hearts of the citizens; which forms the real constitution of the state; which day by day acquires new strength; which revives or replaces the other laws when they grow old or are extinguished, which preserves the people in the spirit of its original institutions, and imperceptibly substitutes the force of habit for that of authority. I am speaking of manners, morals, customs and above all, of public opinion, a factor unknown to our political theorists, but on which the success of all the rest depends." (Rousseau 1953, 58).

In the middle of the century of English revolution, John Locke emphasized relativity: what the law of opinion or reputation demands, what finds approval or disapproval will depend upon the current attitudes "of that place." For Rousseau, overwhelmed by his impressions of the power and splendor of the French court in the middle of the eighteenth century, constancy seems to prevail. The fourth law is written in the hearts of all the citizens and must only be protected from corruption and decay. In *The Social Contract*, Rousseau invents a special tribunal, the "censor," an office which had never existed. He creates it for the sole purpose of strengthening public opinion as the guardian of public morality. The only definition of public opinion that Christine Gerber could find in Rousseau occurs in this connection: "Public opinion is a species of the law which the censor administers, and which he, like the prince, merely applies in specific cases" (Rousseau 1953, 140). Rousseau also explains to what effect the censor is an instrument. "The censorship preserves manners and morals by preventing opinions from growing corrupt, by preserving their rectitude through wise applications, sometimes even by making them definite when they are still uncertain" (141).

An unspoken agreement upon a moral standard establishes, for Rousseau, the basis from which a society may arise, and that collectively stable moral consensus is the "public" of Rousseau's: "This public personality is usually called the *body politic*, which is called by its members the State" (Rousseau 1964d/1957, 424). It follows logically that party divisions can bring no good: there is a single, collective foundation for a society, and it can be threatened only by the egotism of particular individuals. This conviction exposes the roots of Rousseau's hostility toward the private as opposed to the public—a negative sensibility that finds its strongest twentieth-century expression in neo-Marxism.

Rousseau is quite cautious in his claim of how the censors affect opinions, "sometimes even . . . making them definite when they are still uncertain" (1953, 141). He explains the office of the censor with these "special cases" in mind. The censor strengthens what is best in the collective convictions of a people; he expresses, or announces, or brings those convictions into "consciousness," as we would say today. As soon as the censor makes himself independent, as it were, and proclaims that something has been agreed upon when in fact there is no popular consensus, then his words make no impression; they find no response and will be ignored (140). This is the sense in which the censor is an instrument; he is only a mouthpiece. How much more cautiously Rousseau structures this operation of public opinion than do his followers in the twentieth century. According to Rousseau, no coercion may be used. All that may be done is to emphasize basic moral principles through a censor. The censor shares this limitation with the prince, as Rousseau conceives of him. The prince, too, possesses no means of power and cannot issue laws. "We have seen," Rousseau says, "that the legislative belongs, and can only belong, to the people" (60). The initiative for issuing laws, however, comes from the prince. To discharge this office he needs a good vantage point from which to survey the climate of opinion, a matter "with which the great legislator is secretly concerned" (58). In this observational task he is helped by the activities of the censor. The prince must decide which convictions of the people are active enough to support legislation; law may be based only on prior agreement, on the sense of community which constitutes the actual foundation of the state. "Just as an architect, before erecting a great edifice, observes and sounds out the ground to see if it can support the weight, the wise legislator does not begin by drawing up laws which are good in themselves, but first investigates whether the people for whom they are intended is capable of bearing them" (46).

Rousseau does not specify the precise relationship between the *volonté générale* (which sets itself apart from the private and egotistical *volonté de tous*) and public opinion. "Just as the law is the means whereby the general will declares itself, the censorship is the means of declaring the judgment of the people (140). The *volonté générale* could perhaps be imagined as a consolidation of public opinion; in turn, it becomes consolidated in the laws that follow from it. "Laws are nothing but authentic acts of the general will" (98). David Hume affirmed the legitimizing power of public opinion in his principles as: "It is . . . on opinion only that government is founded" (Hume 1963, 29). Rousseau affirms it, too: "Opinion, queen of the world, is not subject to the power of kings; they are themselves her first slaves" (Rousseau 1967/1960, 73–74).

In his letter to d'Alembert, Rousseau is more specific about who could fill the office of the censor in France. To the surprise of those who see Rousseau as a radical democrat—"the legislative belongs, and can only belong, to the people"—he proposes that the role of censor would be best filled by the honorary court tribunal of the marshals of France (Rousseau 1962b, 176). Rousseau thereby equips that office with the highest prestige. To him, the weight of "public respect" is a clear factor of influence on the people, and no dissonance may be allowed to arise in regard to it—on pain of having that public respect rapidly destroyed. He requires that the government as well become subject to the censor, or the honorary court tribunal of the marshals of France, whenever it proclaims something pertaining to public opinion, or, that is, whenever it expresses public approval or disapproval. Here Rousseau sets public opinion up as a moral authority. Perhaps it was such a thought, and also such a role, that the German Nobel Prize–winning novelist Heinrich Böll had in mind when he spoke of the present pitiful condition of public opinion in the Federal Republic of Germany: the office of censor was not in the right hands.

Moved by the idea of a collective conception of what is good and bad among the people, Rousseau shaped a concept which would first come into its own in the twentieth century: "civil religion" (Rousseau 1953, 142). Not until the number of believers in metaphysical religions declined could the thought of a "civil religion" first begin to spread. As we might expect, the term "civil religion" refers to a collection of principles that one cannot publicly contradict without becoming isolated, to wit, a product of public opinion.

Public opinion as the protector of society and the enemy of individuality

As Rousseau saw it, however full of blessing public opinion might appear to be in its role as the guardian of public morality, it remained nonetheless a disaster in its influence on the individual. To the degree that the individual respected such opinion as a guardian of morals—both out of a fear of isolation and in order not to be exposed to painful disapproval, "not only outdoors and on country paths, but even in the middle of the street"—Rousseau could see nothing really against it, despite the memories of his own suffering. "Whoever judges manners and morals judges honour; and he who judges honour takes opinion [of the people] as his law" (1953, 140).

Its disastrous effect grows out of the need people feel to distinguish themselves; out of a "Love of Fame," to cite the title of the eleventh chapter of David Hume's treatise; or, somewhat more modestly and simply, out of the human need to receive recognition, to count for something socially, to have prestige, to be contrasted positively with others. The corruption of human society began with this need, as Rousseau explained in the essay that made him famous in 1775, *Concerning the Origins of Inequality among Men*: "Finally, consuming ambition, the zeal to increase one's wealth—less out of a genuine need than in order to set oneself above others—create in all men the dark inclination to injure one another" (Rousseau 1964b, 175). "I would make clear how greatly this almighty craving for reputation, honor and distinction that devours us all governs our talents and powers and allows itself to be measured; how greatly it excites the passions and multiplies them; how greatly it turns all men into rivals or, worse, into enemies" (ibid., 189).

The "savage" is free of this devouring drive; "the savage lives in himself" (ibid., 193), although from the beginning he had differentiated himself from animals through free will, a capacity to empathize, and the ability to preserve himself. Then the process giving rise to society began. Rousseau tells us, as "public respect started to be valued" (Gerber 1975, 88), the nature of man's being changed. Now, he claims, we must accept this fact of our nature as irrefutable: "Man, as a social being, is always oriented outward; he first achieves the basic feeling of life through the perception of what others think of him" (Rousseau 1964b, 193).

According to Rousseau, man is split into two beings, one of which contains his real nature, his "genuine needs," inclinations, and interests, and the other of which shapes itself under the yoke of opinion. He clarifies the difference by using the example of the scholar. "We should always differentiate the inclinations which arise out of nature from those which come out of opinion. There is a passion to know which is based only on the desire to be respected as a learned person; there is another which is born out of man's natural craving for knowledge about everything, be it near or far, that can be of interest to him" (1964d, 429).

Rousseau sees the compulsion to consume as a byproduct of public opinion: "As soon as they desire a cloth because it is costly, their hearts already have been delivered captive to luxury and all the whims of opinion, for this taste certainly did not arise spontaneously out of themselves" (1964d, 372).

Legality, honor, respect—there is nothing better. So John Locke cited Cicero, and then reasoned these qualities back to their single root, enjoying the favorable judgment of one's society. Rousseau, concerned as he was with the contrast between the true nature of man and that arising through opinion, attempted to erect a concept of honor which sprang from self-esteem rather than from the esteem of others. "In what is called honor I differentiate that which is the result of public opinion and that which is to be regarded as the consequence of self-esteem. The first consists of empty prejudices, which are as changeable as the tossing waves" (1964c, 2:84).

At this point one cannot overlook Rousseau's ambivalence any longer: he speaks of public opinion as empty prejudice, but on other occasions he finds it to have the purpose of protecting that which is most lasting and of most value: customs, tradition, and morality. It is easy to catch Rousseau in such contradictions. One reads at times: "It is a matter of public concern to distinguish between vile and upright people" (1964b, 222–23). Rousseau admired the artistry with which the Spartans managed the distinction: "When a man of bad moral character made a good proposal in the Spartan assembly, the ephors, without paying any attention to him, had a virtuous citizen make the same proposal. What an honour for the one, what a rebuke to the other, even though neither of them had been blamed or praised!" (1953, 141–42). Here there can be no doubt about Rousseau's high evaluation of public respect. Then one reads in *Emile*: "And if the whole earth should reproach us, what then? We do not strive for public recognition; thy happiness suffices us" (1964d, 758).

Compromise as a necessary part of one's dealings with public opinion

In what appears as a contradiction, Rousseau, more clearly than anyone before him, captures the essential aspect of public opinion, allowing us finally to recognize all its manifestations: it presents a compromise between social consensus and individual convictions. The individual is forced to seek a middle-of-the-road solution, forced by the "yoke of opinion" and by his vulnerable nature, which makes him dependent on the judgment of others and averse to being singled out or to living in isolation. In *Emile*, Rousseau puts it this way: "Since she depends both on her own conscience and on public opinion, she must learn to know and reconcile these two laws, and to put her own conscience first only when the two are opposed to each other" (1964d/1957, 731/346). In other words, only when it is absolutely impossible to avoid doing so.

"I must learn to bear with censure and ridicule"

Compromise can lead to very different results. Exactly where David Hume claimed one should adjust to public opinion, in the clothing one chooses to wear in public—precisely there Rousseau decided to manifest his individuality. As a guest of Louis XV, in the great proscenium box of the royal theater in Fontainebleau at the premiere performance of an operetta he had written, he appeared "ungroomed," in a badly combed and unpowdered wig, in robes inappropriate to the festivities, and without a brocade vest. "I have dressed as I always dress, neither better nor worse. My outside is simple and neglected, but not dirty or unclean, my beard is also neither of these in itself, because nature gives it to us and because, according to the time and the fashion, it is occasionally even an ornament. Perhaps some find me ridiculous or impudent, but should that affect me? I must learn to bear with ridicule and censure when they are not merited" (cited in Harig 1978). This attitude gives rise to the danger of being too unwilling to compromise, as Rousseau also understood. In *Julie, or the New Heloise*, he writes, "I am worried that that undaunted love of virtue which gives him the strength to despise public opinion may drive him to the other extreme and lead him to speak disparagingly of the holy laws of decorum and propriety" (Rousseau 1964c, 623).

"To find a form of association which defends and protects the person and property of each member with the whole force of the community, and where each, while joining with all the rest, still obeys no one but himself, and remains as free as before. This is the fundamental problem" (Rousseau 1953, 14–15).

8 Public Opinion as Tyranny: Alexis de Tocqueville

*I*f the purpose of our historical investigation is to find out what those who shaped the concept of "public opinion" meant by it, then we can now conclude: there are indeed good historical reasons to adopt a concept of public opinion which is based on fear of isolation and its result, the spiral of silence.

It is possible that societies differ in the degree to which its members fear isolation, but all societies contain pressures to conform, and the fear of isolation makes those pressures effective. Stanley Milgram (1961) found in his experiments that Norwegian subjects showed slightly more conformity than Americans did, and French ones slightly less. Milgram transferred his experiments to Europe because the suspicion had arisen that conforming behavior such as Solomon Asch had established was perhaps an American peculiarity.

In fact, what Thorstein Veblen described as American status-seeking behavior at the beginning of the twentieth century in *The Theory of the Leisure Class* (1970; first published 1899) was the same kind of practice Rousseau decried in his opposition to what Veblen later termed conspicuous consumption. The compromise between public opinion and individual nature, to use Rousseau's pair of opposites, in the United States favored public opinion and expected submission from the individual. So Rousseau's countryman, Tocqueville, explained and described the phenomenon in the records of his trip, *Democracy in America* (1948; first published 1835–40).

So far as I can see, Tocqueville was the first discerning observer of the spiral of silence at work. He took as an example the decline of the French church before the revolution, and alluded at every opportunity to the significance of talk and silence in connection with public opinion (1948, 1:263). Furthermore, his approach to public opinion most closely approximates what can be seen today with our empirical methods of observation. He saw, just as we do now, a fear of isolation and a tendency toward silence at its center. Tocqueville wrote no book about public opinion, nor did he entitle a chapter after it. Yet his book is full of accounts, assessments, explanations, and analyses of the consequences of public opinion. This is not to say that he regarded it as a purely American phenomenon. He saw the universal characteristics of public opinion and how they affected Europe as well. He believed, however, that they had progressed further in America and had taken on a role there that they might later play in Europe. For Tocqueville, public opinion in America was a heavy pressure, a burden, a coercion to conform or, to use Rousseau's terms, a yoke under which the individual member of society had to stoop:

> In aristocracies men often have much greatness and strength of their own; when they find themselves at variance with the greater number of their fellow countrymen, they withdraw to their own circle, where they support and console themselves. Such is not the case in a democratic country; there public favor seems as necessary as the air we breathe, and to live at variance with the multitude is, as it were, not to live. The multitude require no laws to coerce those who do not think like themselves: public disapprobation is enough; a sense of their loneliness and impotence overtakes them and drives them to despair. (1948, 2:261)
>
> I know of no country in which there is so little independence of mind and real freedom of discussion as in America. (1:263)
>
> In any constitutional state in Europe every sort of religious and political theory may be freely preached . . . for there is no country in Europe so subdued by any single authority as not to protect the man who raises his voice in the cause of truth from the consequences of his hardihood. If he is unfortunate enough to live under an absolute government, the people are often on his side; if he inhabits a free country, he can, if necessary, find a shelter behind the throne. The aristocratic part of society supports him in some countries, and the democracy in others. But in a nation where democratic institutions exist, organized like those of the United States, there is but one authority, one element of strength and success, with nothing beyond it. (1:263)

This one power, according to Tocqueville, is public opinion. How did it become so powerful?

Equality explains the power of public opinion

In the introduction to his book on America, Tocqueville wrote: "Among the novel objects that attracted my attention during my stay in the United States, nothing struck me more forcibly than the general equality of condition among the people. I readily discovered the prodigious influence that this primary fact exercises on the whole course of society; it gives a peculiar direction to public opinion and a peculiar tenor to the laws" (1948, 1:3).

While trying to discover the causes for that insatiable striving toward equality, he became alert to a worldwide development (Tischer 1979, 18).

> If, beginning with the eleventh century, we examine what has happened in France from one half-century to another, we shall not fail to perceive that at the end of each of these periods a two-fold revolution has taken place in the state of society. The noble had gone down the social ladder, and the commoner has gone up; the one descends as the other rises. Every half-century brings them nearer to each other, and they will soon meet. Nor is this peculiar to France. Wherever we look, we perceive the same revolution going on throughout the Christian world. . . . The gradual development of the principle of equality is, therefore, a providential fact. It has all the chief characteristics of such a fact: it is universal, it is lasting, it constantly eludes all human interference, and all events as well as all men contribute to its progress. . . . The whole book that is here offered to the public has been written under the influence of a kind of religious awe produced in the author's mind by the view of that irresistible revolution which has advanced for centuries in spite of every obstacle and which is still advancing in the midst of the ruins it has caused.
>
> It is not necessary that God himself should speak in order that we may discover the unquestionable signs of his will. (Tocqueville 1948, 1:6–7)

Tocqueville explains why equality in social conditions leads to the predominance of public opinion:

> When the ranks of society are unequal, and men unlike one another in condition, there are some individuals wielding the power of superior intelligence, learning, and enlightenment, while the multitude are sunk in ignorance and prejudice. Men living at these aristocratic periods are therefore naturally induced to shape their opinions by the standard of a superior person, or a superior class of persons, while they are averse to recognizing the infallibility of the mass of the people. The contrary takes place in ages of equality. The nearer the citizens are drawn to the common level of an equal and similar condition, the less prone does each man become to place implicit

faith in a certain man or a certain class of men. But his readiness to believe the multitude increases, and opinion is more than ever mistress of the world. . . . At periods of equality, men have no faith in one another, by reason of their common resemblance; but this very resemblance gives them almost unbounded confidence in the judgment of the public; for it would seem probable that, as they are all endowed with equal means of judging, the greater truth should go with the greater number. (Tocqueville 1948, 2:9–10)

As we see, Tocqueville interprets public opinion as the opinion of the numerical majority.

Tocqueville claims he is dealing with the will of God, which no one can withstand. He is overcome, however, with a sympathy for the fate of the individual in such a society: he lapses into deep pessimism about its spiritual consequences, and he rebels. Concerning the fate of the individual, he writes:

When the inhabitant of a democratic country compares himself individually with all those about him, he feels with pride that he is the equal of any one of them; but when he comes to survey the totality of his fellows and to place himself in contrast with so huge a body, he is instantly overwhelmed by the sense of his own insignificance and weakness. The same equality that renders him independent of each of his fellow citizens, taken severally, exposes him alone and unprotected to the influence of the greater number. (1948, 2:10)

Whenever social conditions are equal, public opinion presses with enormous weight upon the minds of each individual; it surrounds, directs, and oppresses him; and this arises from the very constitution of society much more than from its political laws. As men grow more alike, each man feels himself weaker in regard to all the rest; as he discerns nothing by which he is considerably raised above them or distinguished from them, he mistrusts himself as soon as they assail him. Not only does he mistrust his strength, but he even doubts of his right; and he is very near acknowledging that he is in the wrong, when the greater number of his countrymen assert that he is so. (1948, 2:261)

Tocqueville describes how the pressure of public opinion affects not only individuals, but the government as well. As an example he selects the behavior of the American president during an election campaign. During this time, the president no longer rules in the interest of the state but in the interest of his reelection (Tischer 1979, 56). "He adopts its [public opinion's] likings and its animosities, he anticipates its wishes, he forestalls its complaints, he yields to its idlest cravings" (Tocqueville 1948, 1:138).

Tocqueville grants that equality in a society can also have a beneficial effect. Because authority has been dethroned, equality can open the minds of men to new thoughts. On the other hand, the individual might stop to think entirely: "It [the public] does not persuade others to its beliefs, but it imposes them and makes them permeate the thinking of everyone by a sort of enormous pressure of the mind of all upon the individual intelligence. In the United States the majority undertakes to supply a multitude of ready-made opinions for the use of individuals, who are thus relieved from the necessity of forming opinions of their own" (1948, 2:10).

Tocqueville reflects sadly on how democratic people once were able to overcome the powers which "checked or retarded . . . the energy of individual minds". But now, if "under the dominion of certain laws [Tocqueville means the authority of the numerical majority] democracy would extinguish that liberty of the mind . . . the evil would only have changed character. Men would not have found the means of independent life; they would simply have invented . . . a new physiognomy of servitude" (1948, 2:11).

"There is, and I cannot repeat it too often," writes Tocqueville, "there is here matter for profound reflection to those who look on freedom of thought as a holy thing, and who hate not only the despot, but despotism. For myself, when I feel the hand of power lie heavy on my brow, I care but little to know who oppresses me; and I am not the more disposed to pass beneath the yoke, because it is held out to me by the arms of a million men" (1948, 2:58).

Tocqueville opens up an issue on which, about fifty years later, James Bryce, one of the classic American writers on public opinion, focused in the fourth part of his book *The American Commonwealth* (1888–89), namely, the tyranny of the majority (2:337–44). This fourth part now finally bears the explicit title "Public Opinion." But somehow public opinion is never treated successfully when the subject is taken up explicitly and with total academic rationality. It must be something very irrational indeed if all those books that deal with it directly seem to fail. This applies also to the standard German works of the first decade of the twentieth century: Wilhelm Bauer, *Die öffentliche Meinung und ihre geschichtlichen*

Grundlagen (Public Opinion and Its Historical Basis) (1914), and Ferdinand Tönnies, *Kritik der öffentlichen Meinung* (Critique of Public Opinion) (1922).

"No one can accuse Bryce of having a systematic approach to the study of public opinion," wrote Francis G. Wilson fifty years later (1939, 426), referring to the famous book. Indeed, in the hundred-odd pages that Bryce devotes to the subject, comments are swept together from the most disparate authors and then decorated with his own observations, some of considerable interest. Consider, for example, his remarks on the "fatalism of the multitude" (Bryce 1888–89, 2:237–364, esp. 327–36), where he is the first to describe what will later be called "the silent majority."

---

9   The Concept of "Social Control" is Formed and the Concept of "Public Opinion" is Shattered

We enter the twentieth century with a 1950 definition of public opinion: "Let us understand by public opinion, for the purposes of this historical review, opinions on matters of concern to the nation freely and publicly expressed by men outside the government who claim a right that their opinions should influence or determine the actions, personnel, or structure of their government" (Spier 1950, 376).

A concept of public opinion tailor-made for scholars and journalists

How could "public opinion" come to mean something so different from what it had denoted for centuries? Publicly expressed opinions, influence on goverment—this part of Spier's definition we recognize; but the other part is something new: only opinions about questions of national significance, only the opinions of men whose judgments command respect, will count. This constitutes a radical narrowing of the concept and at the same time a qualitative change. We are dealing no longer with the middle term between knowledge and ignorance, as Socrates conceived of it. Instead, we have here a self-conscious power of opinion established close to the government, laying claim to an equal if not a superior judgment.

Such a transformation needs to be explained. When did public opinion lose its meaning as reputation? On first asking myself this question, I felt as if I had lost my wallet and had to go back and look for it. That was at the beginning of the sixties, almost at the same time that I noticed, and could find no explanation for, the remarkable discrepancy between the two curves of voting intentions and of expectations about who would win the election. It was not for seven years, however, that I noticed that the two questions were connected.

David Hume's thesis "Government is founded on opinion," the prominent place Rousseau granted public opinion in the state, the overwhelming strength of public opinion in the United States—all this must have tempted power seekers to pose as public opinion representatives. The throne of public opinion seemed to be left vacant, as it were, in various works written up to the middle of the nineteenth century. At this point, however, a number of hefty tomes began to treat the subject systematically and debate which kind of public opinion would most benefit the state. The influence of philosophers, scholars, writers, and journalists sought their proper place in claiming to represent public opinion. In Jeremy Bentham's treatment ([1838–43] 1962, 41–46) or in James Bryce's (1888–89, 2:237–364, "Public Opinion") we find many pointed social-psychological observations; but these are mixed with normative demands as to the character and role that public opinion *should* play and also who should be considered its representative. Even this confusion was still a long way from the public opinion conceptualized by Speier (1950), Wilhelm Hennis (1957a) or Jürgen Habermas (1962), which amounted to nothing more than a critical political judgment.

Shoveling snow off the sidewalk as public opinion

The turning point seems to have occurred in the very last years of the nineteenth century. Between 1896 and 1898, Edward A. Ross published a series of articles (reprinted as a book in 1901) in the *American Journal of Sociology*. It seems that from this time on, public opinion shed its centuries-old connotation of pressure to conform and continued to exist only with the abbreviated meaning of a tribunal that criticized and controlled the government (Ross 1969; Noelle 1966). Something of the earlier meaning remained, however. By way of example, when the social psychologist Floyd H. Allport (1937, 13) wrote "Toward a Science of Public Opinion" as the opening essay in the first issue of the later famous *Public Opinion Quarterly*, he used the act of shoveling snow off the sidewalk to illustrate the effectiveness of public opinion. He characterized its substance with the words: "The phenomena to be studied under the term public opinion are essentially instances of behavior. . . . [These instances of behavior] are frequently performed with an awareness that others are reacting to the same situation in a similar manner." But contemporary scholars, especially in Europe, were more irritated than intrigued by such ideas.

Until the dead member drops from the social body

What was it about Edward A. Ross's articles at the turn of the century that had such a profound effect as to change the concept of public opinion? To begin with, Ross spoke like a second John Locke, and it is indeed amazing that he never referred to Locke.

> The coarse, vital man may ignore the social stigma. The cultivated man may take refuge from the scorn of his neighbors in the opinion of other times and circles; but for the mass of men, the blame and the praise of their community are the very lords of life. . . . It is not so much the dread of what an angry public may *do* that disarms the modern American, as it is sheer inability to stand unmoved in the rush of totally hostile comment, to endure a life perpetually at variance with the conscience and feeling of those about him. . . . Only the criminal or the moral hero cares not how others may think of him. (Ross 1969, 90, 105, 104)

These words appear in Ross's work in the chapter entitled "Public Opinion." He sees public opinion, however, subordinated to a phenomenon he designates with a new term, which provided the title of his book: *Social Control*. Social control is exercised in human societies in many ways, says Ross. It may be completely visible and institutionalized—for example, in law, in religion, in national holidays, or in child-rearing practices. However, social control is also effective in the form of public opinion, which, though not institutionalized, possesses certain sanctions. Writing on social control more than half a century later, Richard T. LaPiere (1954, 218–48) divided these sanctions into three categories: physical sanctions, economic sanctions, and, most important, psychological sanctions—which begin, perhaps, when people stop greeting someone and end when the "dead member drops from the social body," as Ross put it (1969, 92).

Ross calls special attention to the advantages of social control through public opinion. In comparison with the law, it is "flexible" and "cheap" (1969, 95). His lively presentation was a great success, and "social control" became an established concept. The expression has all the attractions of the new, and it is filled with all that John Locke once called the law of opinion or reputation. Many sociologists have taken up the subject of social control, but no one now equates social controls with public opinion. The double-faced integrating power that coerces both government and individual to respect the social consensus thus disappears. Effects on the individual are now called social control; effects on government are called public opinion, which, as an intellectual construct, at once takes on characteristics of the norm. The relationship between the two types of effects is destroyed.

---

10   The Howling Chorus of Wolves

Why are the paths so overgrown? Why do we have to fight our way through the bushes in search of the real meaning of public opinion? What is the function of this phenomenon with an old-fashioned name? A "classic concept" from our "traditional store of concepts"; "You can neither just drop it nor take it seriously in its original meaning"—so begins the sociologist Niklas Luhmann's essay "Public Opinion," which first appeared in 1970 (1971, 9). Like Walter Lippmann, whose book *Public Opinion* was published in 1922, Luhmann discovered characteristics of public opinion that had never been described before (cf. chapter 18 below). Both authors, however, have helped to blur the historical traces of the subject. Luhmann writes: "A glance at intellectual history shows that belief in reason could not be maintained, nor could belief in the potential of public opinion to exercise critical control, to change government" (1971, 11). But who gave rise to this belief? Neither Locke nor Hume, neither Rosseau nor Tocqueville.

None of the modern literature on public opinion would have taken me back to these sources had I not had a strange experience on a Sunday morning in Berlin, early in the summer of 1964. At the time, I was spending the weekends in Berlin to prepare for my Monday lectures on survey research methods at the Free University. There was already a note of farewell in all of this, for in the fall I was going to the University of Mainz as professor of communication research. On this particular Sunday morning—I hadn't even had breakfast—something that looked like a book title suddenly came into my mind; but it had no connection with survey research methods, no connection with the work I had planned to do that day, absolutely no recognizable connection with anything. I ran to the table and wrote on a scrap of paper: "Public opinion and social control." I knew right away what sort of title it was; a year and a half later it was the title of my official inaugural lecture in Mainz (Noelle 1966).

It was this short title on a scrap of paper that prompted me to return to the topic of public opinion and to search for its historical traces. Why had it become so completely unfashionable to treat this subject as it had been understood for centuries, as involving the sensitive social nature of man, human dependence on the approval and disapproval of his environment? Doesn't such an interpretation fit the self-image of modern man? Does it run counter to the wonderful self-awareness won through emancipation, through coming of age? If it does, it is easy to imagine that uneasiness will arise from the following comparisons of human and animal societies.

The fear of isolation is a research topic that is noticeably avoided with respect to human beings but is treated in detail and uninhibitedly in research on animal behavior. Ethologists are so anxious to forestall accusations of anthropomorphism that they must often encounter reservations about comparing animal with human behavior. Erik Zimen, in *The Wolf* (1981, 43), writes that "we must certainly be very cautious in comparing human and animal behavior. Behavior patterns that appear similar may have entirely different functions, while others of entirely different appearance and phylogenetic origin may perform the same function. . . . Nevertheless, comparative observation of human beings and animals can stimulate new ideas, which must then be tested by exact observation or experiment, particularly when species socially organized in such a similar manner as wolf and man are being investigated."

In any event, language is quite without self-consciousness, and we have no difficulty in understanding the expression "to howl with the pack" (of wolves). One could as well speak of "howling with the dogs." "Howling in chorus" is just as common among dogs as among wolves, and chimpanzees too will sometimes howl in chorus (Alverdes 1925, 108; Lawick-Goodall 1971; Neumann 1981).

Getting in the mood for joint action

Wolves, according to Erik Zimen, howl primarily in the evening before setting out to hunt, and early in the morning as a preliminary to the morning's activities. "To a wolf the howling of another wolf is a powerful stimulus to follow suit. . . . But this does not invariably happen. The initial howl of an animal of low rank, for instance, is a less effective trigger than that of a superior animal" (Zimen 1981,71). Not included in the howling are all the oppressed wolves, the outcasts, and the excluded. The similarity between the situation of the oppressed and the outcasts and that of the low-ranking wolves indicates how important it must be not to isolate oneself and to be allowed to take part in what the American wolf researcher Adolph Murie (1944) called "the friendly get-together," in other words, howling in chorus. To be an outcast wolf also has concrete disadvantages: its food is taken away (Zimen 1981, 243).

What is the function of this howling? Erik Zimen: "This restriction to 'insiders' suggests that the ceremony reinforces the cohesion of the pack. The wolves confirm their friendly, cooperative feeling for one another, so to speak. The timing also suggests that it serves the purpose of synchronizing and coordinating the phase of activity that follows. The wolves that have just awoken from sleep are quickly put into a mood that facilitates a joint enterprise" (ibid., 75).

Flock behavior

According to a report by Thure von Uexküll, Konrad Lorenz also perceived synchronization, or being able to take common action, when he observed the acoustic signals jackdaws use to regulate their flock behavior.

> The flock of jackdaws, which flies out to the fields by day to hunt for food and to the woods in the evening to sleep, uses the calls of individual birds to agree on a common course. If the courses of the individual birds diverge in the morning or evening hours, the flock can be observed flying back and forth for a while. If the 'djak' calls predominate over the 'djok' calls, the flock flies in the direction of the woods or vice versa. This goes

on until all the birds are producing only one of the calls and the flock as a whole either flies into the woods or out to the fields. The flock is then prepared to take action by common agreement, whether it be looking for food or settling down to sleep. There is a common mood or something like a common emotion. Thus the flock of jackdaws is a voting republic. (Uexküll 1963–64, 174)

In *On Aggression*, Konrad Lorenz entitles his chapter on the group behavior of fish "Anonymity of the flock" (Lorenz 1966, 139–49).

> The most primitive form of a "society" in the broadest sense of the term is the anonymous flock, of which the shoal of ocean fishes is the most typical example. Inside the shoal, there is no structure of any kind, there is no leader and there are no led, but just a huge collection of like elements. Of course these influence each other mutually, and there are certain very simple forms of "communication" between individuals of the shoal. When one of them senses danger and flees, it infects with its mood all the others which have perceived its fear. . . . The purely quantitative and, in a sense, democratic action of this process called "social induction" by sociologists means that a school of fish is the less resolute the more individuals it contains and the stronger its herd instinct is. A fish which begins, for any reason, to swim in a certain direction cannot avoid leaving the school and thus finding itself in an isolated position. Here it falls under the influence of all those stimuli calculated to draw it back into the school. (ibid., 144–45)

Isolation, losing contact with the school, could mean sudden danger to the individual's life. For that reason, group behavior seems to be perfectly functional, and as advantageous for the survival of the individual as for the group.

What happens if an individual has no fear of isolation? Konrad Lorenz reports on an experiment conducted by Erich von Holst with a minnow, a fish that belongs to the genus of the carp.

> Erich von Holst removed from a common minnow, the forebrain, which, in this species, is the site of all shoaling reactions. The pithed minnow sees, eats, and swims like a normal fish, its only aberrant behavior property being that it does not mind if it leaves the shoal unaccompanied by other fishes. It lacks the hesitancy of the normal fish, which, even when it very much wants to swim in a certain direction, turns around after its first movements to look at its shoalmates and lets itself be influenced according to whether any others follow it or not . . . if

it saw food or had any other reason for doing so, it swam resolutely in a certain direction and—the whole shoal followed it.

Lorenz comments: "By virtue of its deficiency, the brainless animal had become the dictator!" (Lorenz 1966, 146).

Modern brain researchers say that in the human brain as well there are certain zones that supervise the relationship between the self and the world outside (Pribram 1979), which is to say, zones that are open to attack by the anonymous group. "We are more vulnerable . . . than we think," the analyst of human relations, Horst E. Richter (1976, 34), once said; and he meant that we are vulnerable to the way the environment judges and treats us. Must human beings really hide their social nature as if they were embarrassed by it?

"The reason of man, like man himself is timid and cautious, when left alone; and acquires firmness and confidence, in proportion to the number with which it is associated"; so James Madison described the phenomenon (Madison 1961, 340). In his book, *Les sociétés animales*, published in 1877, the French sociologist Alfred Espinas expressed similar ideas, basing them on a research report by a biologist, A. Forel: "The courage of an ant waxes in exact proportion to the number of its companions and friends of the same genus and wanes to the extent that it is separated from them. Any inhabitant of a strongly populated ant hill is much more courageous than the same ant belonging to a very small colony. The same worker that will let itself be killed ten times over if it is surrounded by its companions will be extraordinarily fearful and avoid the merest hint of danger if it is alone just twenty meters from its nest. The same is true of wasps" (cited in Reiwald 1948, 59).

Must we create a fiction of public opinion based on critical judgment because to acknowledge the real forces that keep human society together would not be compatible with our ego ideal?

11 Public Opinion among African and Pacific Tribes

*I*n his book *The Forest People*, Colin M. Turnbull (1961), an anthropologist, describes the life of pygmies in the Congo forests. We are introduced to a happy camp life: the men assemble in the evenings for group singing; in the mornings the young people awaken the sleepers with their cries and calls. Before a hunt, the people often dance. Men and women form a circle around the whole camp, singing a hunting song, clapping their hands together, peering to the left and to the right, and jumping great leaps, thereby imitating the animals they hope to kill.

In the background of this pastoral scene, dramatic conflicts occur. Cephu, a leader of five families who was once highly respected but has fallen on hard times through bad luck as a hunter, is often found on the fringes of collective enterprises. He transgresses the rules of solidarity by secretly spreading his net in the forest ahead of the nets of the others participating in a hunting drive. The women and children, who are the drivers, send the game to his nets first. On the evening of the day we are observing, no one talks to him and he is not even offered a place among the men at their evening gathering. He demands that a young lout move over and make a space for him, but the youth just sits there, and another person starts to sing a mocking song about Cephu to the effect that he is not a man at all but an animal. Unnerved, Cephu offers to give up the meat from the spoils of his hunt. His offer is immediately accepted, and everyone goes to the huts of Cephu's people, which are away from the body of the camp, and ransacks the huts, looking in every corner and take everything edible, including meat already stewing in a pot over the fire. Later that evening, one of Cephu's distant relatives carries a pot filled to the brim with meat and mushroom sauce back to Cephu and his people. Even later that night, Cephu is seen again among the circle of men around the dying fire, joining their song. Once again, he belongs among them (Turnbull 1961, 94–108).

One cannot survive alone

Another occurrence concerns a young man who has been caught in incest with a cousin. No one is willing to provide him protection in a hut, and his peers drive him with knives and spears out of the village and into the forest. Turnbull quotes an account given by one of the young man's tribe: "He has been driven to the forest and he will have to live there alone. Nobody will accept him into their group after what he has done. And he will die, because one cannot survive alone in the forest. The forest will kill him." Then, Turnbull says the informant—in a manner characteristic of pygmy men—suddenly broke into a smothered laugh, clapped his hands, and observed: "He has been doing it for months; he must have been very stupid to let himself get caught" (Turnbull 1961, 112). It was clear that this stupidity counted for more than the incest itself.

That same night, the hut of the young man's family took fire and a fight broke out between the families. During the fight, the original cause, the incest, was hardly mentioned in the general uproar and argument. But the next morning, the mother of the young girl who had been shamed was seen eagerly helping to fix the hut of the ones who had injured her, and three days later the young man crept back into camp in the evening and sat among the bachelors again. At first no one would talk to him, but then a woman sent a little girl to him with a bowl of something to eat, and the matter was laid to rest (ibid., 113–14).

Weapons of the outside world: spite and ridicule

In the cases described by Turnbull the conflicts were settled, but not before they had been discussed by the whole camp. There was, he said, no judge, no court, no jury. There was no formal procedure at all, no council that reached decisions, and no chief. Every case was treated so as not to endanger the cohesiveness of the group. A society living by hunting with nets had to retain above all else its capacity for cooperation. Its individual members were kept under control by two means: they feared, above all, being despised and being ridiculous. One is reminded of Edward Ross's description of public opinion as social control: "It is more effective than court judgments, it penetrates to every corner and is cheap" (Ross 1969, 95).

Margaret Mead's three kinds of public opinion

In the thirties, under the title "Public Opinion Mechanisms among Primitive Peoples," Margaret Mead (1937) described three types of public opinion processes encountered among primitive peoples. She found public opinion to be effective when anyone emerged as a violator of laws; when there was uncertainty about how the laws were to be interpreted; and when a conflict erupted or a decision had to be reached about future behavior or procedural issues. In such instances, the steps or the measures for reaching a consensus had to be established, and Mead thought that the mechanisms of public opinion were required to maintain the community's capacity for action.

The first type she describes is analogous to the pygmies' method (Mead 1937, 8–9). It only works, she says, in relatively small communities, around two hundred or, at the most, four hundred people. She illustrates it with the Arapesh tribe in New Guinea. In this tribe, dependence on fixed rules is minimal and many precepts are short-lived; they appear and are forgotten again. The community exists almost without any system of rules. There are scarcely any firm positions of authority and no political institutions, no judges, no courts, no priests, no medicine men, and no hereditary leadership castes.

A communal pork dinner

As a case of conflict resolution, Mead describes what happens when an Arapesh discovers a trespassing pig rooting in his garden. He does not act in a way we would call spontaneous; on the contrary, he is extremely careful. It is clear, at all events, that he will kill the pig because that is the generally accepted custom. While the pig is still rooting in the garden, however, or immediately after it has been killed and when it is still bleeding from the wound made by the spear, the owner of the garden calls a few friends in for consultation—his peers, brothers, brothers-in-law. Should he send the slain pig back to its owner, who at least will then have the meat to use to pay damages; or should he keep the meat and eat it as compensation for the irritation and the harm done to his garden? If these friends of his age and situation counsel him to go the conciliatory route, giving the animal back to the owner, then that will happen. If they plead the more risky approach, another round of counselors will be sought among the older generation—the father, the uncles. If they too favor keeping the meat, then, finally, a particularly respected man will be asked. If he also approves, the pig will be eaten jointly by all those who were in favor of the action as a sign that they will stick together and defend the decision should difficulties arise because of it, and to show that they are ready to share in any unpleasant consequences, such as black magic or the hatred of the pig's owner and his clique.

Unclear or changing rules require great attention

Exploring which behavior to adopt under such conditions in order not to be isolated must be a careful and circumstantial process because there are no clear rules. New situations continually arise in which the individual must decide for or against something. When he has reached a decision, he and his fellows must uphold it vigorously. On the other hand, alliances are short-lived. Discord is quickly laid aside, and, by the time the next conflict occurs, there will be new parties.

That we are dealing here with public opinion processes cannot be doubted, for all the ingredients are present: the controversy, the two camps, the attempt to act in such a way as not to isolate oneself, the excitement that comes of knowing oneself to be in the right—all these play their part. It may be doubted whether we are dealing with "public" opinion, whether the element of "publicness" is really present. It is certainly not present in the same sense that we understand the term in modern mass society. Today, "public" implies anonymity, equal opportunity of access, the individual finding himself among a formless mass of others whose names, faces, and dispositions he does not know. The Arapesh know the members of their little settlement community. What they experience too, however, is public exposure in the sense of that all-embracing social membership from which no one wants to be separated, excluded, or isolated.

The dual system or party mentality

To describe the second way in which public opinion processes are carried out, Mead uses an example from the Iatmul, a tribe of New Guinea headhunters (Mead 1937, 10–12). Like the Arapesh, they have no chiefs, no central authority and are nonetheless capable of making decisions and of acting effectively. Unlike the Arapesh, they do not resolve conflicts by having individuals carefully seek out the majority opinion. The Iatmul have developed a "dual" system: the tribe is split into two camps or parties, according to formal criteria, between which at any given time disputes are decided. Mead believes that this procedure is required for larger social units to achieve a consensus (among the Iatmul, tribes reach 1,000 persons). Individuals do not decide in favor of a particular point of view on the basis of the issue or because they have reflected on it, but because their group represents that viewpoint. How these groups are constructed and which side the individual ends up on appear to be arbitrary. People born in winter may belong to one party, people born in summer to the other. The parties may consist of those living north of the graveyard versus those living south of it. Or they may consist of those whose maternal line may not eat hawk versus those whose maternal line may not eat parrots, those who trace their paternal descent from clan A versus clan B, or those who belong to one or another of two neighboring age groups. The system functions only because these groups cut across one another in a variety of ways; people who may be opponents in one matter today will be allies on another issue tomorrow. In this way, the community is never split, although it always remains thoroughly dual; that is, it applies a pattern for easily achieved splits, corresponding to the "in favor" or "opposed" camps that characterize every public opinion process.

Decisions are not reached by majority consent. The people whose interests are affected the most seek a resolution, and members of each formal group adopt their catchwords, which are repeated informally. Mead thinks that in modern societies many questions are decided by similar dual arrangements: members of political parties, interest groups, or regional coalitions passionately fight on this side or that, not because of the substantive issues but because their camp has adopted a given position. Solutions are finally reached according to the strength shown by the members of the two camps. Modern political jargon betrays the direct relations this mechanism of public opinion bears to our present systems. The term "polarization" points to the dual form that arises when we must decide between opposing alternatives; the modern expression "party mentality" designates the attitude for which Margaret Mead used the Iatmul as an example.

The individual is powerless: formalism on Bali

Margaret Mead uses the south sea island people of Bali to illustrate the third way of holding a society together (1937, 12–14).

A rigid ceremonial order is at once apparent. Legal skill determines questions in dispute. All healthy adult men belong to the council, and, with the passing years, each moves to increasingly higher positions in office, and it becomes his duty to engage in the most painstaking interpretation of the inherited rules. Let us imagine that a case is presented to them. A couple have married, but doubts have arisen as to whether the marriage should be regarded as legitimate or as incestuous. They are first cousins even though two generations removed. Genealogically, the woman is the "grandmother" of the young man. Marriages between first cousins are prohibited. What is the determining point in this case: the first-cousin relationship or separation by two generations? A threatening tension builds for a full day. The council meets, and the leaders consider a series of arguments but come to no decision. No one takes sides and there are no lawyers for the families involved. No effort is made to determine the ruling opinion. Finally the council's expert for matters pertaining to the calendar decides: first order means first order; the marriage is to be regarded as a violation of the rules. The punishment for those who have violated the rules—isolation—now must follow. The houses of both spouses are picked up and carried outside the southern boundaries of the village, where they are deposited in the punishment zone. The whole population helps. The couple is expelled; it may no longer participate in any meetings or events in the village, other than services pertaining to burial rites.

Are we really still dealing with a public opinion mechanism when we consider how the Balinese resolve conflicts? The transition to other forms of social control is, to be sure, a smooth one. Edward Ross by no means restricted social control to public opinion but expressly added to it the system of justice. Events among the Balinese do remind one of a judicial system, albeit without written laws or speeches for the defense. Divine commandments, formal statutes, and the law of opinion—to stick to the trichotomy proposed by John Locke—converge and, in some circumstances, leave the individual no leeway to escape the fate of isolation, no matter how careful he is or how many supporters he might gather.

Margaret Mead bases the utility of investigating public opinion among primitive people on the possibility of studying there, in pure cultural form, that which in modern societies has become confused. We can differentiate the procedures of the Arapesh, the Iatmul and the Balinese by the degree to which the individual can or must take a part in reaching and maintaining a consensus. Among the Arapesh, the individual is required to exercise the greatest attentiveness, for the rules are in flux and what is correct today may be wrong tomorrow; one may quickly find oneself ousted. In the Iatmul system, the individual is still important as a follower of one of the two parties. Among the Balinese, for whom most of the rules have become rigidified, individuals may find themselves completely without influence. The great sensitivity that the Arapesh develop contrasts with the thorough fatalism of the Balinese. Under these latter circumstances, the quasistatistical organ for evaluating the environment must atrophy.

Control by neighbors

The composite model of public opinion that Margaret Mead describes among the Zuni is fluid (1937, 15–16). Everyone is constantly observed and judged by his or her neighbors; public opinion is continually present as a negative sanction. This puts the brakes on all occupations and prevents many actions from ever occurring. If we look for modern analogies, we can certainly see that neighborhood control not only limits but also elicits action, as for example, when in Europe a family airs bedclothes out of the window in the morning in a demonstratively visible fashion to signal that here the norms of cleanliness are being maintained. How precisely mechanisms of public opinion like the Zuni's have been developed in other cultures can be seen in particular customs: not drawing drapes in the evening so that all those outside can see into the well-lit rooms; disapproving of hedges between yards as symbolic unfriendliness against neighbors; or disapproving if someone closes the inside doors of an office or home.

---

12 Storming the Bastille: Public Opinion and Mass Psychology

*T*hese accounts from New Guinea or Bali could easily be misunderstood as exotic travelogs. Margaret Mead, therefore, sought modern Western parallels in order to show what is common to the processes of public opinion. As a parallel to the procedures of the Arapesh, she selected an example that would reach her American readers, the lynch mob (1937, 7). She believed that, in both cases, individuals acted spontaneously in response to the situation; they acted the way they felt was right and obtained, thereby, a political result, although they made no effort to come to a collective agreement.

It is strange that Margaret Mead does not notice the huge difference between the situation of the careful Arapesh in whose garden another man's pig is rooting, and that of the individual participant in the middle of a lynch mob. The Arapesh never allows himself to be drawn into a spontaneous action "in terms of his own feeling on the subject" (ibid.). He manages the affair with extreme circumspection, as Mead herself describes it, for he is subject to social control and attempts to secure for himself by his caution the support of influential individuals, accomplishing this, among other ways, by letting them take part in the pork dinner, or even insisting that they do so.

Being in a crowd reduces the necessity of monitoring the environment

For those who participate in a lynching, quite the opposite is true. They abandon all caution; they cease to be single individuals under scrutiny from others who approve or reject their behavior, and become completely absorbed instead by the anonymous mass. Thus they become freed from social controls which otherwise would dog every step they take within reach of public sight or sound.

Mead's modern illustrative example is a phenomenon which can be characterized better as a spontaneous crowd. L. von Wiese (1955, 424) calls it a *konkrete Masse*, i.e. a mass of people in physical contact or at least in sight of each other who, for a short time, emerge as a group and act together as a group as though they were a single being. That is surely not an analog to the Arapesh. In solving the problem of the trespassing pig, a consensus was sought from what was regarded as a sufficiently respected set of people, but each participant remained a wholly separate and distinct person, with a particular role.

The kind of behavior typified by the lynch mob, or collective behavior in general, has fascinated scientists and educated audiences since the French revolution and the storming of the Bastille. In the nineteenth and twentieth centuries, a flood of essays and books on crowd psychology have focused on this puzzling manifestation of human nature. Unfortunately they have probably impeded the understanding of public opinion processes more than they have advanced it. In the twentieth century, mass eruptions and public opinion were perceived to be at least diffusely connected one to another, when they were not outright identified, as by Margaret Mead. Such a conception, however, obliterated the characteristic elements of the social-psychological phenomenon of public opinion that had previously been so clearly delineated by seventeenth- and eighteenth-century writers.

What is the relationship between mass psychological explosions and public opinion? To start this investigation, it seems useful to bring to mind the storming of the Bastille as the French historian Taine described it.

> Each district serves as a center, and the Royal Palace is the largest one of all. From one to another, there circulate a stream of proposals, complaints, debates, and simultaneously a stream of humanity, which pushes its way in or tumbles forward, with no guidance other than its own momentum and the accidents of its course. A crowd assembles itself here, then there; its strategy amounts to shoving and be shoved. The crowds manage to get in only to those places where they are let in. When they get into the Invalides, it is only with the assistance of the soldiers. They shoot at the walls of the Bastille from ten in the morning until five in the afternoon—walls that are 40 feet high and 30 feet wide—and only accidently does a shot hit one of the Invalides on the towers. . . . The masses are spared as one spares children, taking pains to assure that they damage as little as possible. At the first demands, the governor withdraws the cannon from the firing ports and invites the first deputation to breakfast with him. He makes the men of the garrison swear not to shoot if they are not attacked. When he finally allows them to fire, it is only in the last extremity, to defend the second bridge, and only after he has announced to the attackers that he is going to allow the troops to fire. In short, his forbearance, patience, and longsuffering are extraordinary and fully reflect this era's conception of the humane. The unfamiliar sensations of attack and resistance, the smell of powder, the violence of the attack drives the people wild. They seem to know nothing more than that they must throw themselves against this massive pile of stone. Their remedies are at the same level as their tactics: some believe they have captured the governor's daughter and want to burn her to force her father to yield. Others set fire to a projecting portion of the building that is filled with straw, and thereby obstruct their own

path. "The Bastille was not taken by force," said the courageous Elie, one of the fighters. "It surrendered before it ever could be attacked."

Capitulation occurs on the condition that no one will be harmed. The garrison does not have the heart to shoot at so many living beings while their own protective cover is so good, and the soldiers are, furthermore, confused by the sight of the enormous mass assembled about them. Only eight or nine hundred people are attacking, but the area in front of the Bastille and the surrounding streets are full of the curious who have come to see the spectacle. As one eyewitness relates, there are among them "a number of elegant, good-looking women who have left their carriages some distance away." From the height of the fortress's breastworks, it must appear to the 120 men of the garrison as if all Paris has poured itself out against them. So it is they who let down the drawbridge and allow the enemy to enter. Everyone has lost their head, the besieged as well as the besiegers—though the latter to a greater extent as they are drunk with triumph. They have scarcely entered before they begin to break everything; those who come late shoot at those who came earlier, completely according to chance. Sudden omnipotence and the freedom to kill are too strong a wine for the nature of men; giddiness overtakes them, they see red, and all ends in a wild delirium.

. . . The French guards, who know the laws of war, attempt to keep their word, but the masses behind them do not know whom they encounter and strike out with random violence. They spare the Swiss who shot at them because, from their blue uniforms, they take them to be prisoners. In their stead, they fall upon the Invalides who opened the Bastille to them. The one who prevented the governor from blowing up the fortress has his hand cut off at the wrist with a sabre stroke, is stabbed through twice, and his hand, which rescued a quarter of Paris, is carried in triumph through the streets. (Taine 1916, 66–69)

Such a scene of mass hysteria is very different from what we have defined here as public opinion by empirical and historical analysis. Public opinion inheres in those attitudes and models of behavior at a specific time and place which are adhered to with vigor; which, in any environment of established viewpoints, one must exhibit to avoid social isolation; and which, in an environment of changing viewpoints or in a newly emerging area of tension, one *can* express without isolating oneself.

Do such outbreaks of the crowd have anything at all to do with public opinion? There is a simple criterion with which to answer this question. All instances of public opinion entail a threat of isolation. Whenever individuals are not free to speak or act according to their own inclinations but must consider the views of their social environment in order to prevent becoming isolated, we are dealing with some manifestation of public opinion.

In this regard, there can be no doubt about the concrete mass, or excited crowd. The people who went along with the storming of the Bastille, like those who only thronged the streets as sensation-hungry onlookers, knew perfectly well how they had to behave in order to avoid being isolated: they had to show approval. By the same token, they knew what sort of behavior would expose them to a life-endangering isolation, namely, rejection and criticism of the crowd's course of action. The unequivocal character, the sharpness of the threat of isolation against every deviant from a crowd in this acute stage teaches us that, at root, crowd hysteria is a manifestation of public opinion. In place of the storming of the Bastille, we could easily substitute scenes of mass activity from the present—the outcry at a football stadium against a referee's decision or against a team that has disappointed its fans. Or at the scene of an accident: a large Cadillac with out-of-state license plates has hit a child; it makes no difference whether the child ran into the car's path or whether the driver is to blame—everyone in the crowd will know that they dare not take the part of the driver. Or a demonstration concerning the death of a victim of police brutality; it is impossible to defend the policeman.

Whereas in other settings one must, with more or less difficulty, orient oneself to the kinds of behavior that are approved, in a scene of mass excitement these are as clear as daylight. The understanding that unites the participants and binds them to the crowd may, of course, have a variety of origins. According to these, mass scenes can be characterized.

An active mob can draw its strength from elements that are either timeless, or springing from the *Zeitgeist*. The timeless condition is related to what Tönnies called the "firm" conditions of aggregation, and the time-bound is related to the "fluid" state. Mobs based on timeless elements are typically aroused by instinctive reactions: hunger riots; protecting a small child who has been run over; closing ranks against a stranger or a foreigner; taking sides with one's own team or nation. It is on this basis that the Nazi minister of propaganda Goebbels was able to mobilize a full stadium with his rallying call, "Do you want to have total war?"

Timeless, or at least not dependent on topical conditions: so we would describe communal anger over the transgression of shared moral traditions. By contrast we might say that mass demonstrations that evolve out of fluid conditions, changing values, or new conceptions of value are determined by particular historical conditions.

The concrete mass can be used as a strategic device to speed up the spread of new ideas. In the normal course of events, it takes a very long time for the separated individuals of a dispersed mass to come around to a new idea. If you succeed in organizing the individuals into a concrete mass that favors the new idea, the process of value change will be considerably speeded up because the mass demonstrates that the idea can be supported openly without risk of isolation. The time-bound mass is a typical phenomenon of revolutionary periods. So the concrete mass may serve as an enormously intensified kind of public opinion.

The situation of the individual in a concrete mass is completely different from that of the person in a latent mass. In an active mob he is not required to test painstakingly what he can or must publicly express; here, the mainspring, the fear of isolation, is suspended. The individual feels himself to be part of a unit and has no fear of a court of judgment.

Public opinion, if flouted, may result in spontaneous crowds

A mob—or concrete mass—may also arise out of the discharge of tension between a consensus and an individual or a minority group that opposes stubborn norms, instinctive reactions, or the adoption of new value systems. The spontaneous mass thus reflects the two-sided nature of public opinion. Its effects are directed both downward and upward; it may attack institutions or governments whose principles or behavior have damaged consensus, or it may attack those that will not accede to a demand for change. Social researchers have measured such tensions with representative surveys in order to be able to predict the outbreak of revolutionary disturbances. To do this, one uses a series of questions to find out what the situation *is* as the people understand it, and how they think things *should be*. When the gap between the two widens to beyond its usual limits, danger lies ahead.[9]

9. Leo Crespi, oral report at the 24th annual conference of the American Association for Public Opinion Research, Lake George, 1969.

In an abstract or latent mass, in contrast to a concrete mass, there exists a mutuality of thought and feeling that is not specific to one place but produces conditions favorable for the emergence of a concrete mass, or what Theodor Geiger called an "effective" mass. This is similar to Leopold von Wiese's "clandestine community" as he speaks of it in the following example.

In August 1926, a variety of outbreaks against strangers had occurred in Paris. After a certain period of quiet, another serious incident occurred. A bus full of foreigners was stopped near a fire by the police who instructed them to take another route, in view of the possibility that the fire might spread.

> The crowd apparently believed that the stangers had come to watch the blaze and immediately attacked the party. . . . Before the police could prevent it, a regular hail of stones poured down on the passengers of the bus, many of whom were injured. Only through the energetic efforts of the guards was it possible to free the strangers. Among those arrested was a well-known Parisian painter who was said to have taken active part in the stoning of the bus. . . . Was there an abstract mass here before the incident? There certainly was—the clandestine community of all those who were outraged at foreign exploitation of their monetary inflation. It was the unorganized, innumerable mass consisting of all those who hated foreigners. (Wiese 1955, 424)

Unstable crowds do not reflect public opinion

The role of emotional crowds in the public opinion process—a process which is always trying to establish a value—becomes increasingly clear the closer the situation comes to being an "organized group" (McDougall 1920–21, 48ff.). An organized group is one that has undergone a long-term development toward a particular goal and that has leading figures or a leading group who have deliberately originated the development of a concrete, "effective," mass or who have deliberately reshaped one. In contrast, one can imagine primitive, spontaneous, unorganized masses which arise under certain circumstances without any goal of established public opinion. These masses arise with the single purpose of reaching the emotional climax which comes with participation in a spontaneous crowd: the feeling of mutuality, the intense excitement, the impatience, the feeling of strength and irresistible power, the pride, the permission to be intolerant or sensitive, the loss of a sense of reality. To members of such a mob, nothing appears improbable; everything may be believed without inconvenient reasoning; it is easy to act without responsibility and without making demands on endurance. It is characteristic of this kind of a crowd that it is completely unpredictable in its shifts from one goal to another and that it cannot be steered or guided, as the swing from "Hosanna!" to "Crucify him!" testifies.

The accounts of unstable crowds passed down for centuries have been so impressive that these images have become fixed in our minds as the natural way in which opinions develop in large crowds. We come to expect sudden shifts in viewpoints. But neither the sum of individual opinions measured in survey research, nor single individuals' estimates of the climate of opinion shows the instability that these accounts lead one to expect from "mass man." The abstract, latent masses and the concrete, effective masses follow different laws. They are composed in the one instance of people possessed by, and in the other of people without, a fear of isolation. The sense of mutuality is so penetrating in the concrete mass that individuals no longer need to assure themselves about how to speak or how to act. In such a dense union, even dramatic swings are possible.

13 Fashion Is Public Opinion

*P*eople find any situation exciting, and often inspiring, when they are part of a crowd. Today the resources of survey research allow us to observe the elation that occurs when an olympiad or a football championship takes place, or when a three-part television crime series empties the streets, or when a whole population rivets its attention on the exploits of a national hero. Even an election campaign produces elation.

Does this feeling of belonging arise from phylogenetic roots, from a state of security and strength, because the individual is briefly liberated from fears of isolation?

Statistical intuition as a link between the individual and the collective

"No one has succeeded in making clear how the relation of the individual consciousness to the collective consciousness is to be conceived," wrote the British social psychologist William McDougall in *The Group Mind* (1920–21, 30). Sigmund Freud thought that collective structures like the "group mind" and the juxtaposition of individual and society were unnecessary constructs. To Freud, placing the individual on the one side and society on the other seemed "the rupture of a natural relationship." According to Freud, things do not depend on a large number of people who seek to affect the individual from the outside, as it were. The individual has no relation to groups of people; his world consists of those few decisive and representative relations he has with certain other persons. These relations determine the individual's affective attitudes, and they determine his relation to the whole. Therefore, for Freud, even the scientific specialty of "social psychology" is a fiction.

Through the methods of survey research today we recognize the highly sensitive human capacity of a quasistatistical sense organ to perceive—without using statistical techniques—frequency distributions and changes of opinion in the environment, a capability Freud's ideas could not explain. What is peculiar about these environmental perceptions, these assessments of what *most* people think, is that they change simultaneously in practically all population groups (see figs. 11–13; see also chapter 24). There must be something beyond the individual's actual personal relations, an intuitive faculty perhaps, for permanently monitoring a multitude of people, just as there is a sphere that is aptly termed "public." McDougall expressly assumed that there was such a thing as an awareness of public sentiment, and we find more and more indications of such an awareness today. As McDougall wrote, in public each individual acts on the basis of a knowledge of public opinion (1920–21, 39–40).

We can see this statistical sense organ as the link that connects the person with the collective. We need not assume any mysterious collective consciousness, only the individual's capability, with regard to persons, behavior patterns, and ideas, to perceive environmental relations of approval and disapproval, to perceive their shifts and changes, and to react accordingly so as to avoid isolation as far as possible. McDougall states the motive thus: During "the formation of a crowd, . . . that isolation of the individual, which oppresses every one of us, though it may not be explicitly formulated in his consciousness, is for the time being abolished" (1920–21, 24).

In the nineteenth and twentieth centuries, two views have repeatedly clashed—the view that stresses instinctual behavior and sees man as determined by herd instincts; and the view that assumes man reacts rationally to the experience of reality, something much more in line with humanistic ideals. From one historical perspective it can be said that behaviorism has supplanted two different instinct theories, the one by the British biologist Wilfred Trotter (1916) and the other one by McDougall. Adding to the confusion is the fact that an important and manifest kind of human behavior, imitation, has two different roots, two different motives, which cannot be distinguished by outward appearances. We return here to the distinction between imitation as learning with the intent to gain knowledge; imitation of proven behavior patterns in order to profit from the experience and knowledge of others; the adoption of arguments because we assume they derive from good judgment, from what we take to be good taste; and the other kind of imitation: that arising from an effort to be similar to others; imitation stemming from a fear of isolation. The schools of thought that emphasized the rationality of man regarded imitation as a purposeful learning strategy. Because these schools clearly prevailed over the instinct theories, the subject of imitation out of fear of isolation fell into neglect.

Why must men wear beards?

All along, there were enough puzzling phenomena to have drawn attention in the right direction. But like everything else that is all too common, they scarcely appeared puzzling. In a conversation with de Gaulle, held in the last year of the general's life, André Malraux said: "I have never decided exactly what I think of fashions . . . the centuries when men must wear beards, the centuries when they must be clean shaven" (1972, 101).

Can learning or gaining knowledge motivate imitation, motivate wearing beards or shaving? The answer to Malraux should be: fashions are ways of behaving which, when they are new, one *can* exhibit in public without isolating oneself but at a later stage one *must* show in public to avoid isolation. In this manner, society safeguards its cohesion and ensures that individuals will be sufficiently ready to compromise. One may be sure that the style of beards will never change without a deeper reason, without its preparing people of a particular period for some other decisive change.

Plato considered "hairstyles, clothing, the shoes people wear, the entire outward physical appearance," as well as the kind of music in a state, part of the unwritten laws upon which it is founded (*Republic*, book 4). "As to receiving a new kind of music one should be specially cautious, as endangering the whole: for never . . . are the measures of music altered without affecting the most important laws of the state." In the guise of a diversion and by appearing to be harmless, novelty sneaks in. Adimantus, who shares the dialogue with Socrates, elaborates: "It does nothing . . . but by gradually insinuating itself into it, insensibly flow[s] into their manners and pursuits; and afterwards in a greater degree it finds its way into their contracts with each other; and from contracts it enters with much boldness into the laws and political establishments . . . till at last it overturns everything, privately as well as publicly" (Plato 1900, 108).

Fashion's playful character makes it easy for us to overlook its great seriousness, its importance as an integrating social mechanism. In this context, it does not matter whether a society maintains its cohesion with or without elaborate hierarchies, whether the public visibility of clothes, shoes, hair, and beard styles is used to show differences in rank, or whether—as in American society, for instance—the converse attempt is made to produce the impression that there are no such differences. That fashion's playful methods are well suited to mark hierarchical rank is widely acknowledged. This is because fashion as the expression of a striving for distinction and prestige—Hume's "love of fame," Veblen's "theory of the leisure class"—has received much more attention than the pressure to conform, which affects people more generally and which John Locke kept emphasizing when he talked interchangeably of the law of opinion, or reputation, or fashion.

Attending to fashion trains the ability to compromise

Discontent with fashion's disciplinary power shows itself in many negatively charged expressions: "the whims of fashion," "fad," or "clothes horse," "dandy," "swell." They imply shallowness, superficiality, transience, and a kind of imitation that borders on aping.

It is always touching to read in market analyses how wistfully consumers answer the question of what, above all, they are looking for when they buy a new dress: "It should not go out of style." Here, if anywhere, we witness a genuine resentment against the "coercion to consume," an anger about having to compromise one's own inclinations to the demands of fashion in order not to be ridiculed or rejected by contemporary taste as a scarecrow clad in the clothes of yesteryear. But the reasons for this "coercion to consume" are misjudged. It is not the storekeepers who pull the strings of these processes, as angry consumers tend to believe. They don't set the stage, steering the trend of fashion in one direction or the other. If they are successful, it is because like good sailors they know how to trim their sails to the wind. The outward garment is too good a means for expressing the signs of the time, too good a medium for the individual to exhibit his obedience to society.

In Bendix and Lipset's famous anthology *Class, Status and Power* one article finds fault with the all too general use of the word "fashion" in the social sciences, complaining that it is an "over-generalized term" (Barber and Lobel 1953, 323). As a deterrent, the article mentions that one author alone uses the term "fashion" with regard to painting, architecture, philosophy, religion, ethical behavior, dress, and the physical, biological, and social sciences. What is more, "fashion" is also used in reference to language, food, dance music, recreation, "indeed, the whole range of social and cultural elements." Basically, these many different applications of the word "fashion" are designed to express "changeful." "But," the authors say, "it is unlikely that the structures of behavior in these different social areas and the consequent dynamics of their change are all identical. 'Fashion' . . . has too many referents; it covers significantly different kinds of social behavior" (ibid., 323–24).

A strict pattern

Are these in fact entirely different patterns of social behavior? Anyone looking carefully will find, underlying them all, that layer Locke called the unwritten law of opinion, or reputation, or fashion. We find everywhere the strict pattern that, for Locke, justifies using the term "law": rewards and punishments following not from the act itself—as overindulgence leads to an upset stomach—but from the approval or disapproval given by the social environment at a certain time in a certain place. If we get to the bottom of things, it becomes clear that the general use of the term "fashion" is appropriate as a way of calling attention to common characteristics. In all kinds of areas considered to have no connection with one another, a person is liable to be either "in" or "out";

he must watch any change or be exposed to the threat of isolation. The threat of isolation is present wherever individual judgments manage to become prevailing opinion. Fashion is an excellent means of integration, and only this function of implementing the integration of society can explain why something as foolish as the height of heels or the shape of shirt collars can form the content of public opinion, the signal for being "in" or "out." The seemingly disparate areas in which fashion can be observed are not unconnected at all. To be sure, their synchronization has scarcely been explored; but, along with Socrates, we may presume a connection between tastes in music and hair styles and not miss the fact that, by this movement, laws can be overthrown.

---

14 The Pillory

Systems of punishment developed by various cultures have taken ruthless advantage of man's delicate social nature. This is true of those punishments which are difficult to hide from public view, such as cutting off the left hand, which is the Koran's penalty for theft, or cutting off the left foot for the second offense, or branding; but it is even more plain in the case of so-called "honor penalties," which are aimed at one's self- esteem, and, at least in principle, do not harm a hair of one's head. We have absolutely no difficulty in understanding the idea behind the penalties of the pillory.[10] That these penalties have existed at all times and in all cultures, in ours since the twelfth century (Bader-Weiss and Bader 1935, 2) testifies to a constant in human nature. The pygmies knew what man is most vulnerable to: ridicule or disparagement in front of others, so that all may see and hear of his folly (see chapter 11 above).

Honor penalties take advantage of man's delicate social nature
John Locke quoted Cicero's dictum: "Nihil habet natura praestantius, quam honestatem, quam laudem, quam dignitatem,

---

10. For a thorough presentation of the punishment of the pillory, see Nagler 1970; Bader-Weiss and Bader 1935; Hentig 1954–55.

quam decus" (There is nothing better in the world than integrity, praise, dignity, and honor). Cicero was well aware, Locke adds, that these were all names for the same thing (Locke 1894, 1:478). Depriving people of what is most valuable to them, their honor, is the substance of honor penalties. The pillory tears "a man's honor apart,"[11] as was said in the Middle Ages. People thought this experience so agonizing that, immediately with the first humanizing tendencies, it was decreed that young people under eighteen and—as in a law in Turkey—old people over seventy could not be put to the pillory (Bader-Weiss and Bader 1935, 130). The pillory was ingeniously contrived to attract the greatest possible public notice. It was erected in the marketplace or at a busy crossroads. The delinquent was bound to the pillory by an iron collar and "exposed" or "exhibited" at the busiest times, during the early hours of market days, or on Sundays, or holidays; or he was chained by leg irons to the church door as in "church pillory." Drums and bells were used to make noise, and the pillory was painted in a garish color, red or orange, to make it as visible as possible. Pictures of unclean animals decorated it. The delinquent's name and offense were written on a slate, which he had to wear around his neck. The passing rabble who derided and castigated him, or threw filth at him (ignoring, here, those who cast stones, which is not in line with the character of the punishment), were anonymous, outside the ordinary rules of social control. The delinquent alone was identified.

The pillory was not imposed for grave offenses, only for less conspicuous ones upon which the full light of the public view was to be shed. It was used in cases of fraud (if a baker used crooked weights, for example), or fraudulent bankruptcy; prostitution, pimping; and especially when libel or slander were involved—the point being that he who robs someone of honor shall be deprived of his own (Bader-Weiss and Bader 1935, 122).

Gossip can reveal a society's rules of honor
The boundary between slander and gossip is fluid. When does talking with disapproval about someone who is absent cease to be mere opinion? Reputations are destroyed, characters assassinated,[12] honor brought into disrepute and disgrace; it becomes

11. Fehr, *Folter und Strafe im alten Bern*, 198; cited in Bader-Weiss and Bader 1935, 83.
12. Brian Stross, "Gossip in Ethnography," *Reviews in Anthropology*, 1978, 181–88; Stross discusses Haviland 1977.

taboo to be seen in that person's presence. This is what the worldly Marquise meant in *Les Liaisons Dangereuses*, when she attempted to dissuade a young lady from continuing to keep company with her ill-reputed lover: "Would not public opinion persist in remaining against him, and would this not suffice to make you adjust your relationship with him accordingly?" (Choderlos de Laclos 1926, 1:89).

Character assassination, disrepute, outcast, loser, pariah—the language bubbles over with expressions from the sphere of social psychology that convey the individual's sense of being defenseless, abandoned. "Whoever said such a thing?" people ask, whenever they hear a damaging piece of gossip, eager to defend themselves. But gossip is anonymous. An American anthropologist, John Beard Haviland, elevated gossip to a subject of research. He set out to observe and describe gossip among the tribe of Zinacanteco, expecting to derive the society's rules of honor from its scientific investigation and analysis. He found that gossip persists until a misdemeanor is finally brought to light. Where an infraction of the rule against adultery is publicly recognized, the couple is subjected to an honor penalty similar to the pillory. In the midst of a public festival, the two must do hard labor (Haviland 1977, 63). This is a most imaginative way of effecting isolation because hard work, though not in itself dishonorable, obviously isolates the pair on festive days in the midst of celebrating people.

People have contrived many schemes to make disgrace conspicuous: "exhibiting" someone with a tall paper hat on his head, sending a girl with shaven head to make the rounds of a village, tarring and feathering. Think of the hapless Cephu among the pygmies and how they sneered, "You are not a human being; you are an animal!"

Even an emperor could be humiliated by being denounced and exposed to a contemptuous public. While Emperor Rudolf II resided in Prague in 1609, artisans and deliverymen waited in vain for payment of their bills, which the emperor could scarcely afford because the Bohemian Diet had blocked his tax revenues. The workers finally turned to a public audience and found their protest carried to a public far outside the limits of Prague by what might have been the first newspaper in the world, the *Aviso*. The *Aviso* reported that on the evening of 27 June 1609, as the emperor was sitting down to his evening meal, a great shouting and whistling arose in the darkness in front of his residence, people howling like dogs, wolves, and cats. The emperor was said to be more than a little shocked (Schöne 1939, afterword 2–3).

The pillory can be found even in a child's room or a schoolroom—being sent to stand in the corner as punishment. That red or orange stage for disgrace set up in the marketplace may seem as far removed from our times as the iron maiden of the medieval torture chamber, yet we live with it every day. People in the closing decades of the twentieth century are pilloried in the press and on television. The *Aviso* of 1609 was a harbinger of the mass media.

Even during the twentieth century, when at least fifty different definitions of public opinion drained the concept of any meaning, its original sense was and is still preserved in the German penal code. Sections 186 and 187 state that, where calumny or slander is charged, the most trifling fact suffices as evidence as long as it is calculated "to reduce the individual's reputation in public opinion." Just as one can derive rules of honor from gossip, so they can be derived from today's defamation and libel suits. A suit of 23 November 1978, decided by the German regional court in Mannheim, may serve as an example. We follow an extract from the *Neue Juristische Wochenschrift* 10 (1979):504. "If a woman complains of being called a 'witch,' a suspension of the case on the grounds of insignificant fault on the defendant's part is not justifiable on the grounds that the persons involved in the case are foreigners (Turks, in this instance) and that belief in witchcraft is widespread in the Near East. In order to protect the party involved, a vigorous punishment is required in the nature of a strong judicial reproach for such action." In explaining the reasons for its judgment, the court reasoned:

> Doubtless, belief in witchcraft is at present extremely widespread in the Near East . . . but things are scarcely better in this country. According to the last pertinent survey (1973), 2 percent of the population in the Federal Republic of Germany firmly believe in "witches," and a further 9 percent believe in the possibility of witchcraft. According to the estimates of the best-informed specialists, there is hardly a village in southern Germany without women who are rumored to be witches. . . . Hence there is no reason to judge similar superstitious ideas "way off in Turkey" differently or more mildly. As the counsel for the plaintiff correctly explained, suspecting someone of being a "witch" gravely and negatively affects that person's reputation, even for a foreign worker from Turkey, who in the

eyes of her close and superstitious environment may gradually become a despised outcast, exposed to permanent hostility and persecution which may eventuate in her being the victim of frequent and serious maltreatment or even in death, should no vigorous and effective action be taken against the slander by this court.

15 The Law and Public Opinion

*I*n its account of the trial in a case of a late-night robbery in the inner city of Zurich, the *Neue Zürcher Zeitung* (6 May 1978) gave the following commentary on the verdict: "The superior court should also reexamine its judgment to see if its relatively mild punitive measures for such offenses concur with national feelings and public opinion." Must the laws and the sentences of the courts concur with public opinion? Must they be suited to public opinion? What relation does public opinion bear to the legal arena?

The most pressing question is to what extent the three laws of John Locke—the divine law, the civil law, and the law of opinion—may contradict each other. Locke dealt with the question, for his time and his country, using the duel as an example. In the Federal Republic of Germany of the 1970s and 1980s, the question arises in the matter of abortion. A high dignitary of the church called abortion murder and refused to dissociate himself from the comments of a doctor who compared the massive number of abortions with the mass murders in the concentration camp at Auschwitz. The civil law allows abortion, said the cardinal, but *he* still calls it murder (*Frankfurter Allgemeine Zeitung*, 26 September, 6 October 1979). This is not a conflict of terms; the two views are irreconcilable. The prelate's view is much more than a facade concealing very different modern perceptions. The differing convictions with respect to abortion are virulent; the Christian belief in protection of life, including unborn life, confronts an equally strong emotional belief, the one Rousseau first called "religion civile" (1962a, 327)—a secular, civil religion, in which emancipation, or a woman's right of self-determination over her own body, has greater value. Here we are dealing with one of those conflicts that move people to set their paths so as to avoid acquaintances who think differently from themselves.

Polarization as divided public opinion

In attempting to avoid those who think differently from themselves, people lose their quasistatistical ability to assess correctly the views of their environment. The term "pluralistic ignorance," introduced by American sociology, could be applied to this ignorance of how "people" think. It is the condition known as polarization. Society splits; one can speak of divided public opinion. The distinguishing feature is that each camp greatly overestimates itself in what is called a "looking glass perception." We can measure this statistically: the farther apart estimates of how "most people think" are, the more polarized the question is; the adherents of the opposing views simply don't talk to each other anymore and therefore misjudge the situation. Tables 16–19 give some examples from the

Table 16. Polarization of opinion about Chancellor Brandt, January 1971

The two camps, the supporters and the opponents, differ greatly in their estimation of the opinion of the majority. This is because the two groups are moving apart. They don't talk to each other anymore and so they perceive the climate of opinion quite differently. *Question:* "Do you think that most people want to keep Willy Brandt as chancellor, or that most would rather have a different chancellor? Which do you think is the case?"

	Supporters of Chancellor Brandt (%)	Opponents of Chancellor Brandt (%)
Most people—		
want to keep Brandt as chancellor	59	6
prefer a different Chancellor	17	75
Undecided, impossible to say	24	19
	100	100
	N = 473	290
Discrepancy in perception of environment according to Osgood, Suci, Tannenbaum	D = 78.7	

Source: Allensbach Archives, survey 2068

1970s. Sometimes this ignorance is one-sided; one camp perceives the environment correctly whereas the other overestimates itself. This pattern suggests that integration will eventually favor those who overestimate themselves.

One may take the difference of opinion over the new German Ostpolitik of the early seventies as an example of this situation (table 17). The winners, those favoring Ostpolitik, are depicted as a solid block with 70 percent: "Most people think as we do." The opposition shows a split. They don't note the majority who are in favor of the treaties with the East, nor do they give themselves the majority. Instead, they remain noncommital with a lukewarm "half and half" answer. For the person making a prognosis and analyzing the state of public opinion, symmetry and asymmetry in estimating the environment are important elements. If symmetry predominates—more polarized, each camp seeing itself superior in strength—the result is a serious conflict. With asymmetry, there is great hesitation on one side—undecided answers, responses that

Table 17. Polarization of opinion about the treaties with the East, May 1972

In the case of treaties with the East there is also a wide gulf between the perception of those favoring and those opposing the treaties. *Question:* "Without taking your own opinion into consideration, what do you think: Are most people in the Federal Republic of Germany for or against the treaties with the East?"

	Persons favoring the treaties (%)	Persons opposing the treaties (%)
Most people are—		
for the treaties with the East	70	12
against the treaties with the East	3	30
About half and half, impossible to say	27	58
	100	100
	N = 1079	293
Discrepancy in perception of environment according to Osgood, Suci, Tannenbaum	D =	71.1

Source: Allensbach Archives, survey 2082

opinion is divided or the opinion of the environment impossible to ascertain—and the ability of this camp to defend itself is small. The measure of discrepancy used in the following tables was developed in the 1950s by three American social psychologists, Osgood, Suci, and Tannenbaum (1964). The following formula is used:

$$D = \sqrt{\sum_i d_i^2}$$

where d_i is the difference between the two groups being compared.

Barriers against change and against blind conformity to current trends: two extremes

Modern sociology has replaced the old-fashioned vocabulary of John Locke's three laws with more precise descriptions. Instead

Table 18. No polarization on the question of whether a member of the Communist Party should be employed as a judge, April 1976

Those favoring and those opposing agree to a great extent in their perception of the opinion of the majority. *Question:* "Apart from your own opinion, what do you believe that most people think? Are most people here in the Federal Republic of Germany for or against the employment of a member of the Communist Party as a judge?"

	Persons favoring employment of a communist as judge (%)	Persons opposing employment of a communist as judge (%)
Most people are—		
for the employment of a communist as a judge	6	1
against the employment of a communist as a judge	79	88
Undecided, impossible to say	15	11
	100	100
	N = 162	619
Discrepancy in perception of environment according to Osgood, Suci, Tannenbaum	D =	11.0

Source: Allensbach Archives, survey 3028

of what Locke called divine law we now speak about ethical ideals, tradition, basic values. Emphasis is on the "ideal"; the disparity between this and actual behavior is often considerable. We find John Locke's law of opinion, reputation, and fashion, that which determines behavior most strongly, under sociological terms such as custom and public morality. The law which the state determines splits in two directions. René König (1967) described them in his essay "The Law in the Context of Systems of Social Norms." The guardians of public morality expect the state to use the law as a barrier against changing worldviews. The spokesmen for public opinion or public morality, on the other hand, demand that law and jurisprudence continue to develop in accordance with the spirit of the times. They do, in fact, have strong arguments on their side. If one understands the process of public opinion, which is observable in all cultures, as a means of integration, a means of keeping a society viable, then law and jurisprudence cannot resist public

Table 19. Intermediate amount of polarization on the question of abortion for psychological or economic reasons, October 1979

Question: "What do you think: Are most people in the Federal Republic of Germany for or against allowing abortion for psychological or economic reasons?"

	Persons in favor of abortion for psychological or economic reasons (%)	Persons opposed to abortion for psychological or economic reasons (%)
Most people are—		
in favor of an abortion based on psychological or economic reasons	48	19
against it	17	44
half and half, undecided	35	37
	100	100
	N = 1042	512
Discrepancy in perception of environment according to Osgood, Suci, Tannenbaum	D = 39.7	

Source: Allensbach Archives, survey 3074

opinion for any length of time. Certainly, the time factor plays an important role on both sides. For the sake of public confidence in the legal system, fashionable tendencies must not be followed too readily. In his paper "Have We Lost Our Security of Orientation?" Reinhold Zippelius discusses this question:

> Under the specific aspect of the law, the need for reliable, normative structures of behavior appears as the need for legal security. . . . The need for legal security first of all implies an interest in establishing what the decisive norms should be for interpersonal behavior. . . . To this interest . . . add, secondly, the interest in a continuity of law. This continuity creates security of orientation for the future and thereby also provides the basis for planning and disposition. The demand for the greatest possible stability in the system of norms and for consistency in the development of the law is valid for yet another reason: the traditional law has stood the test of its ability to function. That is why, as Radbruch says, the law must not be subject to change too easily, must not fall victim to legislation based on the needs of the moment, which would permit each individual case to become law without any restrictions. (Zippelius 1978, 778–79)

Of course, the goal of political campaigns is precisely *not* to allow time for reflection up to the moment of decision; instead, they attempt to arouse public opinion to the extent that the excitement will not abate until the goal is achieved and permanently set, until the regulation that was sought has become the binding order of law. Niklas Luhmann describes the process in his essay "Public Opinion." A given political issue "reaches the culminating point of its career. The opponents must then resort to delaying tactics, to limited approval, to reservations in order to gain time; the supporters must try to fit it into the budget or into the administration's platform. The time for all this is brief. There the first signs of boredom, of reservations, of negative experiences appear. . . . If nothing happens with the issue, it is also taken as a symptom of future difficulties. Soon thereafter the issue loses its appeal" (Luhmann 1971, 19).

This description admittedly fits only a certain short-lived, fashionable movement of public opinion. Others continue over years, decades, and centuries—the movement for greater equality, for example, which Tocqueville traced for over a thousand years. However, the stages by which a great issue progresses may occur according to the model that Luhmann described.

An example of how judges and public administrators some-times precipitously react to public opinion, in the form of social conceptions or tendencies toward certain attitudes, is the campaign against smoking in the presence of nonsmokers. This issue had its ups and downs, which were described, as seen through survey research, in chapter 3. Nevertheless, by 1975 the campaign had gained enough ground for ministerial ordinances in the sphere of public administration to recommend or require that smoking be given up in the presence of nonsmokers. In 1974 the Stuttgart Regional Court, dissenting from previous decisions, ruled that a passenger who smoked in a taxi showed lack of consideration for the cab driver. The highpoint was reached when the Berlin Higher Administrative Court determined that smokers were "a nuisance in the legal sense." Joseph Kaiser, a Freiburg lawyer, commented: "Without further ado, the smoker is thus relegated to the category of those who are subject to definition for police purposes, namely the category of those who fall under police jurisdiction and may represent a concrete danger; he is thus subjected to definite police disapproval and exposed to the legally determined consequences of this sentence. The necessary conceptual prerequisite of this is suf-ficient proof that smokers represent a concrete threat to nonsmok-ers. Yet this is exactly what is lacking" (Kaiser 1975, 2237). Because legal facts are created here without support from factual evidence, this can be characterized as a process of public opinion; the com-mentator also chooses the appropriate fashion-related terminology when he says that the protection of nonsmokers is "en vogue."

The law must be supported by custom
Seen in reverse, a highly critical situation arises if the "prevail-ing opinion," public opinion, deviates too far from the legal norm and the legislative branch does not react. This situation arises above all when legal norms are in agreement with traditional moral values but customs or public morality are obviously deviating from both. Survey research today undeniably has the effect of speeding up this process. In 1971, the magazine *Stern* published an Allensbach finding according to which 46 percent of the population aged sixteen and over demanded that abortion be made easier. Just five months later, when the survey was repeated, the percentage had climbed from 46 to 56 (*Stern*, 4 November 1971, 260). This was one of the situations that Tocqueville had in mind when he spoke of a mere "facade," where public opinion still supports some view although the values behind it, which used to maintain it, have long since

crumbled away (Tocqueville 1948, 2:262). As long as this loss of value is not publicly expressed, the facade remains intact; it collapses, however, if—as today often happens through public opinion polls—its hollowness is suddenly exposed. The result can be a legally intolerable demonstration; in this concrete case, for example, many women publicly confess to violating the law: "I have had an abortion" (*Stern*, 3 June 1971, 16–24).

In the long run, the law cannot be maintained if it is not supported by custom. Behavior is influenced more effectively by fear of isolation, fear of disapproval from the environment, or any such implicit signal, than by explicit, formal law. What John Locke described as "law of opinion" and, two hundred years later, Edward Ross described as "social control," social scientists have substantiated in our century through experiments. One of these experiments had to do with traffic lights. The number of pedestrians crossing the street when the light is red were observed under three different circumstances: (1) if no one is setting a bad example; (2) if a man who, judging by clothing, seems to be from the lower class crosses the street when the light is red; (3) if a well-dressed man from the upper class does it. Assistants played the roles of the lower and upper class men crossing the street when the light was red; a total of 2,100 pedestrians were observed. Results: without a traffic offender as a model, only 1 percent crossed the street when the light was red; when the model from the lower class ignored the red light, 4 percent followed; when the model appeared to be from the upper class, 14 percent did so (Blake and Mouton 1954).

Changing public opinion through laws

The relation between law and public opinion can also proceed in the opposite direction; laws can be enacted or changed in order to influence public opinion in the desired direction. In his *Lectures on the Relation Between Law and Public Opinion in England During the Nineteenth Century* (1905), a classic on the issue of law and public opinion, Albert V. Dicey observed something that public opinion research later confirmed: the passing of a law itself increases approval of that law. At first glance, this is a very peculiar event, and even more unusual is that Dicey recognized it without any empirical means of support. He found it hard to explain. Armed with the idea of the spiral of silence, we would argue today that the fear of isolation one faces when giving approval diminishes when something becomes law. The sensitive relation between public opinion and legitimation finds expression in this tendency. Dicey proposes the following theorem: Laws foster and create opinion (Dicey 1962, 4; Lazarsfeld 1957).

That public opinion can be produced by laws aimed in the desired direction seems alarming, an invitation to manipulate, an exploitation of the political mandate by the ruling majority. It is also questionable whether, after a matter has become law, the approval effect will be strong enough to maintain it, or whether the necessary integration by which a society remains viable will be too much at cross-purposes with it.

Legal regulations have gone much further than public opinion desired—for example, in the penal reform of the Federal Republic of Germany in 1975, and in the new divorce law, introduced in 1977. Similarly, even among the 17–23-year-olds, only a minority approved the new laws needed to regulate parental custody issues, in order to strengthen the right of the child as the weaker party in an adult relationship. The question read: "Do you believe that the state must ensure that young people receive more rights in relation to their parents by passing laws, or don't you consider this necessary?" Twenty-two percent of the young people thought it necessary; 64 percent, not necessary.[13] The new divorce law threw the majority of the population into a much greater conflict between law and public morality. In July 1979 an Allensbach survey found a very lively moral opinion on the reality of guilt and of people's duty to be conscious of their own guilt. The new divorce law, however, demanded people to accept the view that in a divorce the question of guilt is not important and thus should have no financial consequences. The majority of the population could not go along with this. Among four legal reforms evaluated, the new divorce law was considered the least successful (table 20).[14]

One is reminded of the way Rousseau saw the relation between law and public opinion: "Just as an architect, before erecting a great edifice, observes and sounds out the ground to see if it can support the weight, the wise legislator does not begin by drawing up laws which are good in themselves, but first investigates whether the

13. Allensbach Archives, survey 1299 (August 1979); N = 843.
14. Allensbach Archives, survey 3062 (November/December 1978); N = 2033. The following topics were presented for discussion: improvement in the training of apprentices; tax reform for 1979; equal participation by employees and investors in the decision making of large companies; reform of the divorce law (incompatibility rather than adversary proceedings).

Table 20. The relationship between public opinion and law

Example: Reform of the divorce law. *Question:* "Do you believe that there is such a thing as moral guilt, that is, that someone can be at fault? Or is the idea of guilt outdated?"

	Population 16 years and over (%)
There is guilt	78
Idea is outdated	12
Don't know, no opinion	10
	100
	N = 1015

Question: "Here are two people talking about whether people should have feelings of guilt. Please read their statements. With which of the two would you tend to agree, the upper or the lower?" (Presentation of an illustration)

	Population 16 years and over
"People should have a sense of guilt, because otherwise it doesn't matter to them if they hurt other people or make other people unhappy."	72
"I think that people should not have feelings of guilt because that only makes them unhappy and embarrassed and doesn't help anyone."	18
Undecided	10
	100
	N = 1016

Question: "In divorce, nowadays, it no longer matters who is at fault. Do you think that this is good or not?"

	Population 16 years and over
Think it is good	24
Don't think it is good	57
Undecided, don't know	19
	100
	N = 495

Table 20—*continued*

	Population 16 years and over (%)
Question: "How satisfied are you with the reform of the divorce law?"	

	Population 16 years and over
As regards the reform of the divorce law (introduction of no-fault divorce), I am—	
very satisfied	7
fairly satisfied	20
not so satisfied	23
not at all satisfied	35
No reply	15
	100
	N = 2033

Source: Allensbach Archives, surveys 3071, July 1979, and 3062, November/December 1978

people for whom they are intended is capable of bearing them" (1953, 46). For Rousseau, laws are no more than "authentic acts of the general will" (1953, 98). Along the same lines as David Hume's statement "It is . . . on opinion only that government is founded," Rousseau said: "Opinion, queen of the world, is not subject to the power of kings; they are themselves her first slaves" (Rousseau 1967/1960, 73–74).

16 *Public Opinion Creates Integration*

We have merely touched on the question of societal integration—what public opinion accomplishes and what the relationship between public opinion and the law ought to be. Is the concept clear enough to be used this casually?

Empirical research lags behind

In 1950, a balanced assessment of integration was published in the United States; it has not yet been superseded.

> Ever since the days of Comte and Spencer, sociologists have been concerned with the integration of smaller units into social wholes. . . . What constitutes the difference between a group and a mere sum of total individuals? In what sense is it one single entity? . . . How can integration be measured? . . . Under what conditions does social integration increase? Under what conditions does it decrease? What are the consequences of a high degree of integration? What are the consequences of a low degree of integration? Sociology is in need of basic research oriented toward this kind of problem. (Landecker 1950, 332)

Werner S. Landecker, whose work has just been cited, stands out among the leading theorists who, in the tradition of Talcott Parsons, have concerned themselves with integration and its role in human social systems. Landecker, in contrast to the dominant school of the twentieth century, sought primarily empirical research and measurement procedures. He offered a variety of standards of measurement. Up to this point, he said, we still know so little about social integration that we cannot propose a simple, general measure. "Know," for Landecker, meant empirically supported knowledge. He identified four kinds of integration and four ways to measure them.

1. Cultural integration: To what extent does the value system of a society allow consistent behavior, or how loaded with contradictions—not logical but practical—are the demands made on the members of the society? As an example of contradictory demands in Western society, Landecker named altruism and the readiness to assert oneself competitively (1950, 333–35).

2. Normative integration: To what extent do the prescribed

rules of behavior for a society and the actual behavior of its members diverge? (335–36).

3. Communicative integration: To what extent do subgroups in a society shield themselves from each other by the appropriate ignorance, negative evaluation, or prejudice, and to what degree do they enter into communication with each other? (336–38).

4. Functional integration: To what degree are members of a society led to act together through division of labor, role specialization, and mutual assistance? (338–39).

This overview does not mention the integration that occurs through joint experience: world championships in baseball or soccer; a three-part television series which unites more than half the population in front of the television set; or (to use a 1965 example) a journey by the English queen through the Federal Republic, which gave rise to a shared sense of festivity and national pride. Further, there is no mention at all of fashion as a means of integration.

Rudolf Smend's doctrine of integration

A completely different approach to integration was taken by Rudolf Smend (1928), a legal scholar who has sought to find acceptance for his "doctrine" since the end of the twenties.

> The integration process is far from being conscious, but it may proceed with an unintentional lawfulness or "cunning reason." Consequently, it is not, for the most part, a subject of conscious constitutional regulation . . . and only in exceptional instances is it the focus of theoretical reflection . . . *personal* integration seems to be brought about by leaders, rulers, monarchs, and public officals of every kind. . . . *Functional* integration occurs through greatly varying, collectivizing forms of life: from the primitive, sensuous rhythm of mutual activity or movement . . . to the complicated and indirect forms, e.g. elections . . . the meaning of which, on the surface, is known not as consciously, but with at least equal urgency, as the meaning of creating a political society through the development of opinion, groups, parties, majorities. . . . *Substantive* integration refers to all those aspects of the life of the state which convey its purpose and promote integration of the community. This would be the logical place, for example, for a theory of the symbols of political value—flags, coats of arms, heads of state, political ceremony, national celebrations . . . the factors of political legitimization. (Smend 1956, 299–300)

The vicissitudes in the meaning of "integration"

Since Smend sketched his "integration doctrine" and Landecker wrote his plea for more empirical research into integration, no progress has been made in this area—surely not by accident but as a concomitant to the lack of research into the individual's fear of isolation. In Edward Ross's essay on social control (1969), there is a remark suggesting that the concept of "integration" was regarded with as much contempt at the end of the nineteenth century as "conformity" is today. Social scientists in the twentieth century were interested in erecting comprehensive, theoretical structures that would clarify the way in which integration stabilized human society, and in working out structure and function; but they perceived empirical investigations as strictly secondrate. Still, the empirically oriented, social-scientific reflection on the subject of integration that we do encounter—and an extensive treatment would have to look particularly into the work of Emile Durkheim—supports the assumption that public opinion has an integrative function.

Expressed in Landecker's terminology, the connection is particularly clear between normative integration and the role of public opinion as "guardian of public morality," as it has been understood for centuries; it follows that norms and actual behavior agree, and that deviation will be punished with isolation.

Zeitgeist: **the fruit of integration**

The term "communicative integration" recalls Tocqueville, who regarded public opinion as first arising at the end of the segmented feudal society. As long as segmentation lasted, there was, as he saw it, no comprehensive communication. The quasistatistical capacity demonstrable in modern Western society—the ability to register increases and decreases of approval and disapproval of ideas or persons reliably—could well be regarded as a sign of greater communicative integration. By the same token, the sense of general euphoria that can be empirically demonstrated before general elections may be linked with Smend's thinking: besides a manifest function of reaching decisions, elections also have a latent function, that of integration. Landecker asked, "What are the consequences of a high degree of integration?" Apparently, integration fills most people with a sense of well-being. But not everyone. Who is left out? The question points to the members of the avant-garde. We were very close to making this point earlier in speaking of Socrates' discussion about the way music changes, and the way these changes indicate in advance that the times are going to change. The times—how much more this phrase means than what is represented in clocks and calendars. Public opinion is surfeited with a sense of time, and what is generally regarded as the spirit of the times may be hailed as a great achievement in integration. Goethe made it clear that the process of successful integration involves a kind of spiral of silence in his famous description: "If one side now especially stands forth, seizes possession of the crowd, and unfolds itself to the degree that those who are opposed must pull back into a corner and, for that moment, at least, conceal themselves in silence, then one calls this predominance the spirit of the times (*Zeitgeist*) and indeed, for a period, it will have its way" (Goethe 1964, 705).

The first measure of integration identified by Landecker, cultural integration, could be the subject for research during periods of crumbling and rising value systems, when people find their old and new requirements irreconcilably mixed. Do the processes of public opinion cease to function at such times?

In times of danger to a society, public opinion exerts an even stronger pressure

Survey research is still too young in its explanations of the processes of public opinion to answer this question. There is an indication, however, that points to the reverse relationship; when society is in a crisis, pressures toward conformity increase. Again, one thinks of Tocqueville's description of American democracy and his stirring complaint about public opinion's unmerciful tyranny of it. This is due, he explains, to the domination of a belief in equality and to the loss of recognition of authority; authority at least always provides orientation. Given these factors, he thought, people would have to cling to the majority opinion. On the other hand, the delicate situation that arose from mixing several different cultures together in a single society might also explain the sharpness of the public opinion mechanisms that Tocqueville observed in America. With a lower degree of cultural integration, which we can well assume in a melting-pot society, the need to achieve integration is all the greater. Applying the argument to our current situation, we could project that, in view of the changes in value systems, there is a lower level of cultural integration and, therefore, an imminent need for greater integration. With this need would come an appropriate tightening of the reins of public opinion, a sharper threat of isolation for the individual. There are, then, conditions in which the working of public opinion becomes visible; as noted earlier, all the important observations about public opinion were made during revolutionary times.

Meanwhile, we find ourselves reflecting on the connection between integration and public opinion in territory which has not been secured by research. In chapter 3, we reported that Stanley Milgram, seeking to determine whether other people would react with levels of conformity similar to those of the Americans in the Asch experiment, selected for his investigation two countries whose societies struck him as contrasting—France, in which individualism is highly valued, and Norway, where he sensed a particularly high level of cohesion (Eckstein 1966). Although in both countries the research subjects showed a preponderant fear of isolation, there was a more pronounced conformity in the more integrated Norwegian sample. This confirms the observation Tocqueville never wearied of stressing: the more equality, the more pressure can be expected from public opinion. Under conditions of greater equality one might have to adhere to the opinion of the majority because there are no other clues to the best judgment; there is no hierarchical principle to be used. With the present empirical means of observation, we see that the pressure stems less from a mathematical majority than from one side's aggressive assurance that its beliefs are correct and the other side's fear of isolation.

We cannot hope for a simple relationship between the degree of integration and the pressure of public opinion. Is it the "equality" of Norwegian society that permits such a powerful pressure for conformity, or, conversely, does the pressure for conformity have other roots and itself lead to equality? Might the rugged natural setting have effects on the integration of a society similar to those that endanger a tribe living in the jungle and relying for survival on the hunt? Perhaps the degree of danger to which a society is exposed, whether the danger comes from within or without, is the key: greater danger demands greater integration, and greater integration is enforced by heightened reactions of public opinion.

17 Avant-garde, Heretics, and Outsiders: Challenging Public Opinion

*I*s public opinion, as described here—a social-psychological event growing out of the roots of the individual's fear of isolation—simply a pressure for conformity? Does the spiral of silence explain only how public opinion emerges and grows strong, not how it changes?

Those who do not fear isolation can change public opinion

Up to now, we have focused on people who are frightened or cautious, who fear isolation; now we shall look in the other direction, at those who do not fear isolation or are willing to pay its price—a more colorful group. These are the people who introduce the new music; painters like Chagall, who, in a 1917 painting, *The Stable*, has a massive cow break through the roof of a house and peer out into the open; or scholars like John Locke, who claimed that men are hardly concerned with God's commandments or the laws of the state—but they are at pains to follow the law of opinion. A little earlier, this teaching could have had him sentenced to the stake. In this circle we find the heretics, those human figures answering the needs of their time and yet timeless, who constitute the correlate to tightly united public opinion. The deviants. To use the title of an American study: "Heroes, Villains, and Fools as Agents of Social Control" (Klapp 1954)—in modern terms, stars and bums. The relationship between conforming members and outsiders is not, however, to be understood only as an accentuation of the value system and the going rules of society by those who injure them and by their "exhibition" at the pillory.

The concept of the spiral of silence reserves the possibility of changing society to those who either know no fear of isolation or have overcome it. "I must learn to bear ridicule and blame," Rousseau wrote (cited in Harig 1978). A high level of consensus, which is a source of happiness, a place of refuge and safety for the vast majority of mankind, fills the avant-garde, those who prepare the way into the future—the artists, scholars, and reformers—with horror. In 1799, Friedrich Schlegel offered the following description of a monster:

It seemed swollen with poison, its transparent skin shimmered with every color, and its entrails could be seen squirming like worms. It was large enough to instill fear, and it opened and closed crablike claws in all directions about its whole body. Now it hopped like a frog, now it crawled with loathsome agility on a countless swarm of little feet. I turned away in terror; because it wanted to follow me, however, I took courage, threw it onto its back with a powerful blow, and it immediately appeared to me as nothing but a common frog. I was not a little astonished, and even more so when, suddenly, someone immediately behind me said: "That is public opinion . . ." (Schlegel 1799, 40–41)

On the other hand, upright citizens were quite correct to be shaken when long-haired young men appeared during the sixties: whoever does not fear isolation can overthrow the order of things.

Trailblazers mind the public as little as sleepwalkers

A typology of innovators would have to make distinctions according to their relations with the public. There are artists and scientists who prepare the way for the new; whether they are received with understanding or with hostility scarcely influences what they do. Reformers are different. If they want to change the ways society thinks or behaves, they have to put up with a hostile public, since they need it in order to proselytize. Nevertheless, they suffer from the hostility. There seems to be a second type of reformer—in both a larger and a smaller format—for whom the provocation of the public becomes almost a purpose in itself, an intensified existence. There at least they find attention, and even public outrage is better than being ignored. The extraordinary spread of public opinion through the mass media of the twentieth century provides a wealth of contemporary examples. The Arab terrorist leader Wadi Hada was characterized by the Israeli secret service as one who experienced almost mystical satisfaction from being isolated from the rest of the world and, for that reason, held only his own laws and precepts valid (*Die Welt*, no. 189 [1976]:8). Rainer Werner Fassbinder says about one of his films: "Certainly I must have the right to realize myself in a manner appropriate to my sicknesses and my despair. I need the freedom to reflect about myself in public" (Limmer 1976, 237). It is no longer a matter of approval or disapproval; we are talking about the fiery stimulation that comes from contact with the public, from being torn out of the

narrowness of individual existence. Intoxicated with public exposure, public exposure as a drug: what releases the excitement? It
could be danger—the knowledge that fooling with the public can be
dangerous, even deadly, if it culminates in expulsion from society.

To suffer or to enjoy: two ways to lead a public life
   One can draw examples just as easily from the sixteenth century, and, for instance, contrast Martin Luther with Thomas Müntzer. Luther clearly suffers from public exposure but can see no
other way than to expose himself to the condemnation of the public.
He faces what he is unable to avoid: "Even if some will immediately
despise me . . ." "Others do not speak at all," he says, ". . . yet
even because they are silent, I must do it."[15] He describes the speed
with which his message spreads through the land. "In scarce four-
teen days it had traversed the whole of Germany," he writes, almost
breathless at this experience with the public; it was like "a traveling
storm." And then, too well described for him not to actually have
experienced it: "I did not want the fame, for as I said, I myself did
not know what the cause might be, and the song was pitched too
high for my voice."
   Thomas Müntzer represents the other side of the picture. He
too is a sharp observer of the processes of public opinion. "It goes
about and around the land, no less than in the thoughts . . . thus it
flies to establish order. And where does one begin? Where the inner
is turned to the outside, with fashion. If it has become customary to
change one's opinion like a shirt, then one simply forbids the
changing of shirt and coat, and, perhaps, the undesired changes in
opinion will be repressed."
   Just as we know that no one can restrain innovation in music,
so, when we hear the keys of his compositions, we know that
Thomas Müntzer is sure that shirts and coats will be changed
whether it is desired or not. In contrast to Luther, he does not suffer
from the public glare; he loves it—even though, or because, he
perceives its danger. "The fear of God must indeed be pure, without any fear of men or of any creature. . . . For the times now are
dangerous and the days are evil" (Streller 1978, 186). Is it characteristic of a libidinous relation to the public to be able to express the
spirit of the time, to be able to give it tongue, but not to be able to

   15. The Luther and Müntzer quotations in this passage are taken from Petzolt
1979.

sketch any program with constructive elements to it? Historians conclude that Thomas Müntzer's music could only have had destructive effects (Dülmen 1977).[16]

No typology examining the individual's relation to the public has been developed. Without empirical research, the colorful group that either has no fear of isolation or has overcome it remains spectral. We only know that this group drives society toward change, and that the spiral of silence is useful to those who are not shy of isolation. If public opinion for others equals pressure to conform, it is for them the lever for change.

Why and when does the music change?

That which remains in the air, whichever way the wind is blowing, so that one can no longer hold out against the stream of public opinion, "a tidal volume and sweep" (Ross 1969, 104)—such language reveals that we are dealing with fateful movements that have the power of natural forces. But to the question "How does the new begin?" we can provide no answer. Like Niklas Luhmann, in his essay on public opinion, we can point to some triggers, crises, or symptoms of crises (Luhmann 1971, 9), such as a stream that has always been clear but suddenly turns brown. At first it is only a personal alarm; but then the crisis finds its voice in a book, even in its title, *Silent Spring* (Carson 1962). Or, again according to Luhmann (1971, 17), it may be a threat or an injury to values that have transcendent priority. The radical eruption of public opinion against the Adenauer government in August 1961, right after the Berlin wall was built, could not have been foreseen because the ultimate value of the "nation" had been ignored. Unexpected events are releases: "Novelty implies importance." Pain, or any of civilization's surrogates for pain, is a release. Luhmann mentions "financial loss, budget cuts, status loss, particularly if they are measurable and of a comparative nature" (Luhmann 1971, 17).

But no crises, no threat explains why the topic of women's liberation became such a pressing issue in the public opinion of the sixties and seventies.

Why and when does the music change?

---

16. See also Martin Brecht's review of Dülmen in *Frankfurter Allgemeine Zeitung*, 3 August 1977, 21.

18 The Stereotype as a Vehicle for Spreading Public Opinion: Walter Lippmann

When the twentieth century was well on its way, and all sense of the meaning of public opinion had been lost, two works appeared, both containing the words "public opinion" in their titles. One was the essay by Luhmann (1971), which I have cited frequently. The other was the book Walter Lippmann published in 1922. Both works revealed unknown aspects of the dynamics of public opinion, and both called attention to the connection between public opinion and journalism.

Walter Lippmann's book has no precursor. Although it bears the title *Public Opinion*, it has remarkably little to do with public opinion directly. In fact, Lippmann's definition of public opinion is one of the few weak passages of the book. "The pictures inside the heads of these human beings, the pictures of themselves, of others, of their needs, purposes, and relationships, are their public opinions. Those pictures which are acted upon by groups of people, or by individuals acting in the name of groups, are Public Opinion with capital letters" (Lippmann 1965, 18). One could say, after reading the book and laying it aside, "Now I still don't know what public opinion is."

An exposé

What is so unusual about this book that, almost fifty years after its original publication, it was reprinted in paperback in the United States (1965), and in a German paperback edition at almost the same time (1964)? Without being at all sensational, it is in fact an exposé. But it is an exposé that runs so contrary to people's natural inclinations about how they wish to see things that now, long after its original publication, it still seems new and, for all practical purposes, still has not been incorporated into intellectual thought. Lippmann unmasks our rationalistic self-deception about how people in the modern world inform themselves and develop the judgments that guide their actions—with maturity and with tolerance, observing, thinking, and judging like scientists in a ceaseless effort to fathom reality objectively, all the while supported in this effort by the mass media. He contrasts this illusion with a completely different reality, showing how people in fact develop their conceptions; how they snatch things from the messages transmitted to them; how they process them and pass them along. Lippmann, almost in passing, describes phenomena that empirical social psychology and communication research will establish only decades later, item by item. I have not found in Lippmann's book a single idea about the functioning of communication that has not later been substantiated again and again by painstaking work in laboratories and in the field.

Like storm clouds, which blow over

At the same time, Lippmann has no conception of what is understood here as public opinion in relation to the spiral of silence. Lippmann says nothing about the role of pressure to conform in establishing a consensus, and nothing about people's fear of isolation and their fearful observation of their environment. Under the tremendous influence of the First World War, however, Lippmann identified the cornerstone of public opinion, the crystallization of conceptions and of opinions, in emotionally loaded "stereotypes" (1965, 85–88, 66). A journalist himself, Lippmann knew the expression was taken from the familiar technological world of newspaper printing, where text is poured into rigid form in offset or stereotype printing so that it may be reproduced as often as desired. A public opinion process is enhanced by stereotypes; stereotypes spread quickly in conversation and immediately convey negative or, in some cases, positive associations. They guide perceptions; they draw the attention to certain—usually negative—elements and lead to selective perception.[17] Stereotypes may also cause the political demise of candidates for national leadership. Governor George Romney, a presidential contender, once used the term "brainwashed" to describe his acceptance of certain statements about the Vietnam war, and was thereafter stereotyped as being too easily influenced. In the 1980 presidential race, Governor Brown of California ceased to be a serious contender after the press began to call him "Governor Moonbeam" because of his futuristic attitudes and interests in space exploration. Lippmann wrote: "He who captures the symbols by which public feeling is for the moment contained, controls by that much the approaches of public policy" (1965, 133).

---

17. The examples from German political life used in the German edition are replaced in the following passage by American examples.

Like storm clouds, stereotypes hover over the public opinion landscape for a certain time and then may disappear completely, never to be seen again. The behavior of people, of politicians, who have ducked under these storm clouds will be unintelligible to those who come later; and even someone who once ducked will later be unable to describe what happened, what pressures there were, and will have to seek a substitute explanation.

From Walter Lippmann's book we learn how, through stereotypes, public opinion penetrates into everything—"like the air all around, from the innermost recesses of the house to the steps of the throne" was Ihering's description (1883, 180). We also learn how the creation of public opinion could totally dissolve with time—something Lippmann could describe for his readers from his own experience after the First World War. First he tells how positive and negative stereotypes were shaped: "Beside hero-worship there is the exorcism of devils. By the same mechanism through which heroes are incarnated, devils are made. If everything good was to come from Joffre, Foch, Wilson, or Roosevelt, everything evil originated in the Kaiser Wilhelm, Lenin and Trotsky" (Lippmann 1965, 7). But then, a little later: "Think . . . of how rapidly, after the armistice, the precarious and by no means successfully established symbol of Allied Unity disappeared, how it was followed almost immediately by the breakdown of each nation's symbolic picture of the other: Britain the Defender of Public Law, France watching at the Frontier of Freedom, America the Crusader. And think then of how within each nation the symbolic picture of itself frayed out, as party and class conflict and personal ambition began to stir postponed issues. And then of how the symbolic pictures of the leaders gave way, as one by one, Wilson, Clemenceau, Lloyd George, ceased to be the incarnation of human hope, and became merely the negotiators and administrators for a disillusioned world" (Lippmann 1965, 8).

The pictures in our heads—a pseudoworld whose reality we swear by

Lippmann's great advance over other twentieth-century writers on public opinion was his realism, his down-to-earth assumptions about human understanding and human emotions. That he was a journalist helped considerably: he keenly saw the difference between the perceptions that a person obtains firsthand and those that come by other means, especially through the mass media; and he saw how this difference is blotted out because people are not conscious of it. People, he saw, tend to adopt indirect experience so completely and to adjust their conceptions to it so well that their direct and indirect experiences become inseparable. As a result, the influence of the mass media also remains largely unconscious.

> The world that we have to deal with politically is out of reach, out of sight, out of mind. It has to be explored, reported, and imagined. Man is no Aristotelian god contemplating all existence at one glance. He is the creature of an evolution who can just about span a sufficient portion of reality to manage his survival, and snatch what on the scale of time are but a few moments of insight and happiness. Yet this same creature has invented ways of seeing what no naked eye could see, of hearing what no ear could hear, of weighing immense masses and infinitesimal ones, of counting and separating more items than he can individually remember. He is learning to see with his mind vast portions of the world that he could never see, touch, smell, hear, or remember. Gradually he makes for himself a trustworthy picture inside his head of the world beyond his reach. (Lippmann 1965, 18)

"How small our proportion of direct observations is when compared to those observations that are conveyed to us through the media!" Lippmann makes his readers reflect. This, however, is just the beginning of a chain of circumstances, all of which in one way or another are liable to distort the picture of the world that people carry in their heads. To form a picture of reality is a hopeless task, "for the real environment is altogether too big, too complex, and too fleeting for direct acquaintance. We are not equipped to deal with so much subtlety, so much variety, so many permutations and combinations. And although we have to act in that environment, we have to reconstruct it on a simpler model before we can manage with it" (Lippmann 1965, 11). Fifty years later, Luhmann treated this subject under the caption "Reduction of Complexity."

The journalist's uniform rules of selection

How does this reconstruction happen? A rigorous selection takes place: what will be reported and what should be perceived is organized in graduated steps, like locks on a river, according to the image introduced at the end of the forties by the social psychologist Kurt Lewin (1947), who coined the term "gatekeeper." The gatekeepers decide what will be admitted to the public and what will be withheld. As Lippmann says, "Every newspaper when it reaches the reader is the result of a whole series of selections" (1965, 223). Circumstances—strict limitation of time and of attention (59)—necessitate selection. The reader devotes something like fifteen minutes a day to the paper, Lippmann found, using the results of early studies of readership (37). With a journalist's keen nose for the future, he scented the significance of the representative survey more than a decade before the American Gallup Institute was founded (95–97). Anticipating a major research branch of the science of communication in the fifties, sixties, and seventies, Lippmann explained what journalists consider "news values" in their selection (220; see also Schulz 1976): clear subject matter that can be conveyed without contradictions; conflicts; superlatives; the surprising; something a reader can identify with because it is close in either a physical or a psychological sense; the personally affecting; that which has consequences for the reader (Lippmann 1965, 223, 224, 230).

Insofar as all journalists use largely the same rules of selection, they create a certain consensus in reporting, which affects the audience like a confirmation. A pseudo-environment, as Lippmann calls it, thus emerges (16).

Lippmann berates no audience, scolds no journalists; he merely provides convincing evidence that a pseudo-reality must arise. Arnold Gehlen (1965, 190–91) later called it *Zwischenwelt*, the "in-between world."

People with different attitudes see the same events differently

Social psychology and communication research, starting in the mid-1940s, have discovered the concept of selective perception (Lazarsfeld et al. 1968; Heider 1946; Festinger 1957). People actively try to avoid cognitive dissonance and to maintain a harmonious picture of the world. Second only to the need to reduce cognitive complexity, selective perception becomes another unavoidable source of distortion in the perception of reality and in its reporting.

> I am arguing that the pattern of stereotypes at the center of our codes largely determines what group of facts we shall see, and in what light we shall see them. That is why, with the best will in the world, the news policy of a journal tends to support its editorial policy; why a capitalist sees one set of facts, and certain aspects of human nature, literally *sees* them; his social-

ist opponent another set and other aspects, and why each regards the other as unreasonable or perverse, when the real difference between them is a difference of perception. (Lippmann 1965, 82; emphasis added)

Lippmann bases all of this on observations of the press alone. How much more valid his observations would have to be in the age of television! Now the proportion of reality that is transmitted to people through the media, as compared to the original observations, has grown by a considerable factor (Roegele 1979, 187), and the distant, complex world, through increased visibility and audibility, flows together with one's own firsthand observations even more strongly. The emotional content—what is good and what bad—is grasped directly through picture and sound. These emotional impressions are resistant; people retain them long after the rational arguments have slipped away, as one can read in Lippmann.[18]

After the German federal election of 1976, an anachronistic debate arose as to whether television can influence the climate of opinion before elections. It was not a question of manipulation, for the journalists reported only what they really *saw*. The apparent consensus arising out of a one-sided media reality can only be avoided if reporters of various political persuasions present their points of view to the public. I call the 1976 debate anachronistic because it could have been carried on *before* the appearance of Lippmann's book. That it took place at all, more than fifty years later, was only because Lippmann and all the subsequent confirming evidence provided by communication research had been ignored. "We just report it as it is." This phrase, which journalists use even today to describe their activities, should really not be admissible more than fifty years after Lippmann's book. By the same token, the famous slogan of the New York Times, "All the News That's Fit to Print," should be honored only because of its historical associations. It would be a good idea if from time to time, among the foregone conclusions of the journalists, the facts and the opinions conveyed should be made to recede into the background and that which is not conveyed should become the central figure, as in those well-known perceptual psychology pictures illustrating the relation of figure to background. This change of perspective should be possible at least occasionally, and it needs to be practiced. Then

---

18. The correctness of this observation has been confirmed by Sturm et al. (1972, 42–44).

journalists no longer mislead themselves about the effect of their profession with the argument: "But what I presented is really true," and "the public found it interesting."

What usually gets left out from the reports of the media? Lippmann concludes that very different consequences can follow, depending on what aspect of the complex reality is left out in the picture the public receives. He does not pass an adverse moral judgment on this state of affairs; far from it. In fact, he evaluates stereotyping positively—a detail that those who have repeated his ideas immediately lost—for only substantial simplification allows people to distribute their attention among a good many subjects and not to have to content themselves with a very narrow horizon.

Whatever is not reported does not exist

Lippmann with great persistence seeks to clarify the consequences of this process of selection. What arises from the simplified pictures of reality *is* reality as people actually experience it; the *"pictures in our heads" are* reality (1965, 3). Whatever reality may actually be does not matter, for only our assumptions about reality count; only they determine expectations, hopes, strivings, feelings; only they determine what we do. These actions, however, are themselves real and have real consequences, creating new realities. One possibility is that the prophecy will fulfill itself, that our expectation of reality will be actualized through what we do. The second possibility is a collision. Actions governed by false assumptions lead to effects that are completely unexpected yet undeniably real. Reality at long last reasserts itself, but the later this happens the greater the risk; eventually we are forced to correct the pictures in our heads.

From what materials is Lippmann's "pseudo-environment" constructed? What are the building blocks that derive from the powerful processes of crystallizing reality? "Stereotypes"—"symbols"—"images"—"fictions"—"standard versions"—"the current way of thinking about things"—Lippmann engulfs his readers with words coined to make these materials intelligible. "By fictions I do not mean lies," he writes (1965, 10). He enthusiastically grasps the Marxist concept of "consciousness" (16). Journalists can only report what they from their consciousnesses are able to perceive; the reader can only complete and explain the world by making use of a consciousness which in large measure has been created by the mass media. Some people, on learning that television influenced the

"Dad, if a tree falls in the forest, and the media aren't there to cover it, has the tree really fallen?"
Drawing by Robert Mankoff; reprinted from the *Saturday Review*

climate of opinion for the 1976 election campaign, conclude that television newsmen had been telling lies, "manipulating us"; but these people haven't advanced beyond the beginning of the century in their understanding of the effects of the media. One must admit, however, that the conclusions Lippmann reached so effortlessly, are now being approached by communication researchers only one step at a time, amid numerous difficulties.

"Dad, if a tree falls in the forest, and the media aren't there to cover it, has the tree really fallen?" Father sits in the easy chair reading, son bothers him with superfluous questions—this cartoon suggests that communication research and the general public have gradually caught up with Walter Lippmann.

What does not get reported does not exist, or, stated somewhat more cautiously, its chances of becoming part of ongoing, perceived reality are minimal.

A German communication researcher, Hans Mathias Kepplinger, used the objective reality, which exists outside our consciousness, and the perceived, imagined "pseudo-reality" of Lippmann as complementary concepts in the title of his 1975 book, *Realkultur und Medienkultur* (Actual Culture and Media Culture). Media culture is what the media select from the world and offer us; insofar as the actual world lies outside one's reach, outside one's sight, the former one is usually our only view of the world.

Stereotypes transmit public opinion

Why did Lippmann title his book *Public Opinion*? Perhaps unconsciously, certainly without stating it, he, like other journalists, was convinced that *published* opinion and *public* opinion are basically the same thing; at least his descriptions of the two often blend together. At a certain point, however, when the book is already well under way, the recollection of the original meaning of public opinion breaks through and he adds a second definition to the stale one in the opening chapter (18): "The orthodox theory holds that a public opinion constitutes a moral judgment on a group of facts. The theory I am suggesting is that, in the present state of education, a public opinion is primarily a moralized and codified version of the facts" (81–82). The moral nature of public opinion— approval and disapproval—has retained its central place. But Lippmann varies the traditional perspective by applying to it the discovery that so fascinates him: how the observation of facts is filtered even in a moral sense by selective viewpoints, viewpoints guided by stereotypes or "Codices." One gets to see what one expects to see, and moral evaluations are channeled through emotion-laden stereotypes, symbols, fictions. The limited viewpoint within which every person lives is Lippmann's theme. For us, however, his greatest achievement was to show how public opinion is transmitted, how it can be forced upon us. So concise and so unambiguous is the stereotype, whether positive or negative, that it lets everyone know when to speak and when to keep quiet. Stereotypes are indispensable in getting conformity processes in gear.

19 Public Opinion Selects the Issues: Niklas Luhmann

*I*t is almost beyond belief that the perspectives Luhmann brought to light eluded Lippmann entirely, for both were working on more or less the same issues. Both describe how societal consensus takes form; the reduction of complexity that makes communication and action possible. Highly similar in their contents, the two differ often only in their selection of words: instead of "stereotypes," Luhmann speaks of the necessity of finding "word formulas" to get the public opinion process started (1971, 9). As he sees it, attention is short-lived (15), and persons or issues must establish themselves in the public awareness against strong competition. The media create "pseudo-crises" and "pseudo-novelty" (25) in order to beat competing topics out of the field. These stimuli must be timely, they must have a burning reference to the moment. The relevance of fashion is indicated in many ways (18); an issue is created like the latest style in sleeves, and then, after everything about it has been said, it becomes "old hat"; the issue is obsolete (24), just like a style in sleeves becomes obsolete. Those still wearing it show that they are not "in." The vocabulary of fashion deceptively understates what really goes on.

Making issues worthy of discussion

Luhmann holds himself aloof from his predecessors who wrote about public opinion—Machiavelli, Montaigne, Locke, Hume, Rousseau, and even Lippmann. Morality based on approval and disapproval is not his topic. The "formulas" are not used to label clearly that which is good or evil; they are required, instead, to make a topic worth discussing or negotiating (Luhmann 1971, 9). For Luhmann the function of public opinion is fulfilled when it brings an issue to the negotiating table. The social system cannot deal with many subjects at once, but at the same time it may be a matter of life and death for it to take up topics that have become pressing. Therefore the processes of public opinion must regulate the focus of public attention. For brief periods, the general attention is turned to a pressing topic, and within this short space of time a solution must be found, for in the field of mass communication one must reckon with quick changes of interest (12).

Selecting issues is Luhmann's idea of what public opinion achieves, and this proceeds according to "rules of attention" that can be analyzed. First the issue is brought up, and formulas that make it suitable for discussion are found; only then will positions be taken for or against various "options"—to use the favorite term of modern planners—and, if the process goes forward without a hitch, it will finally be considered ready to come up for decision (12). Luhmann supposes "that the political system, insofar as it rests on public opinion, is integrated not by rules governing decision but by rules governing attention" (16), that is, by rules that determine what reaches the table and what does not.

This version of public opinion only applies to short-lived events, fluid aggregational situations, as Tönnies called them. The steady historical processes that take place over decades or, if we credit Tocqueville, over centuries—striving for equality, or attitudes toward capital punishment, to take two examples—are scarcely touched on, and the "general weather conditions" are not taken into account at all. "After everything has been said, the issue is obsolete" Luhmann writes (24). Journalists would say that the issue is dead. "After everything has been said" expresses a very journalistic point of view, one scarcely appropriate to the lack of interest that an overburdened population takes in the process of public opinion.

Luhmann envisions a regular order of events: first, a pressing issue is brought to general attention; then, positions pro and con are drawn. Surveys of public opinion show that this order rarely exists. Usually what happens is that one party kicks the topic, as it were, into the social field of play—a process that Luhmann disapprovingly calls "manipulation" and regards as the result of one-sided communication, in particular the technically determined one-sidedness of communication from the mass media (13–14). When only one opinion is presented about a particular issue, when issue and partial opinion merge, so to speak, we have what Luhmann calls "public morality" (14). "Public morality" refers to those opinions that must be publicly affirmed if one is not to isolate oneself. Luhmann, drawing from systems theory, has given "public opinion" a new and different content.

The agenda-setting function of mass media

Just as we found no problems in recognizing the significance of Walter Lippmann's stereotypes as vehicles of public opinion in the sense used here, so we can also appreciate Luhmann's contribution to the understanding of public opinion without adopting his conception of its functions within the social system. He highlights the importance of structuring attention, of selecting issues, as a phase in the public opinion process, and he leaves no doubts about the significance of the mass media, which, more than any court, take it upon themselves to select these issues.

American communication researchers have arrived at a result similar to Luhmann's quite independently, and by a completely different path.[19] Their goal was to investigate the effects of the mass media. By comparing, over a period of time, the subject matter emphases of the mass media with actual social developments reflected in statistics and with the views of the population about

19. McCombs and Shaw 1972; Funkhouser 1973; McLeod et al. 1974; Beniger 1978; Kepplinger and Roth 1979; Kepplinger and Hachenberg 1979; Kepplinger 1980b.

pressing political tasks, they found that the mass media were usually ahead of the other two trends. Thus it seems that they bring up the issues and place them on the table. To describe this process, American researchers have invented the expression: "agenda-setting function."

20 The Journalist's Privilege: Conferring Public Attention

"I have experienced the spiral of silence in my club." "I've seen it at work in my volleyball team." "That's just the way things are in my business." In this way people often confirm the concept of a spiral of silence. This is as it should be, for there are varied opportunities to observe this all too human conforming behavior. Experiences such as we all have in small groups are parts of the process. When public opinion is forming, identical or similar experiences across various groups lead observant individuals to suppose that "everyone" will think the same way. Something unique happens, however, as soon as the spiral of silence starts to develop in public; it is this blending with publicity that gives the process its irresistible force. The element of public attention is brought into the process most effectively through the mass media. In fact, mass media objectify publicity—shapeless, faceless, unreachable, immovable public attention.

Feeling powerless facing the mass media

Communication may be classified as one-sided or two-sided (a conversation, for example, is two-sided); as indirect or direct (a conversation is direct); as public or private (a conversation is generally private). The mass media are one-sided, indirect, public forms of communication, thus contrasting threefold with the most natural form of human communication, the conversation. This is why individuals faced with the mass media feel so helpless. In every survey where people are asked, who in today's society has too much power, the mass media are ranked right there at the top.[20] This powerlessness is expressed in two ways. The first occurs when a person tries to gain public attention (in Luhmann's sense) and the media, in their selection processes, choose not to give that person attention. The same thing occurs if there are unsuccessful efforts to gain public attention for an idea, a piece of information, or a perspective. This may result in a desperate outbreak in the presence of the guardians who have denied access to public attention— someone throws a bottle of ink at a Rubens in an art museum in Munich; a bottle of acid is thrown at a Rembrandt in an Amsterdam museum; someone hijacks an airplane in order to borrow public attention for some message or cause.

The second aspect of powerlessness comes into play when the media are used as a pillory; when they draw faceless public attention to an individual who is surrendered to them as a scapegoat to be "exhibited." He cannot defend himself; he cannot deflect the slings and arrows. The means of rebuttal are grotesque in their comparative weakness, in their awkwardness compared to the polished objectivity of the media. Those who freely consent to appear on a television talk show or to give a television interview without belonging to the inner circle of media gatekeepers are putting their heads into the jaws of a tiger.

A new start for research on media effects

Public attention can be experienced from two viewpoints, from that of the individual who is exposed to it or who is ignored by it—which we have just described—and from the perspective of the collective event, when hundreds of thousands, when millions of people observe their environment and either speak or keep quiet, thereby creating public opinion. Observation of the environment has two sources; public opinion is nourished from two springs: the individual undertakes direct observation in his or her environment, and receives information about the environment through the mass media. Today, television with its color and sound creates extensive

20. Allensbach Archives, surveys 2173 (January 1976) and 2196 (February 1977): "Would you please take a look at this list. Among the items on the list, which do you think exercise too great an influence on the political life of the Federal Republic?" "Television" ranked third in both surveys, named by 31 percent and 29 percent respectively. "Newspapers" was found in ninth and tenth place with 21 and 22 percent. There were eighteen possible answers on the list.

confusion between one's own observation and mediated observation. "Good evening," the weatherman said at the start of his
television weather report. "Good evening," answered the guests in
a hotel in which I was spending my vacation.

People have long been questioning the effects of the mass
media, expecting a very simple, direct relationship between cause
and effect. They have assumed that the statements in any one
medium cause changes in opinion, or—also to be considered as an
effect—reinforce opinion in the audience. The relationship between mass media and audiences is somehow likened to a private
conversation between two persons, one saying something and the
other being strengthened or converted. The reality of media effects
is much more complex, and differs considerably from the individual
conversation model. Walter Lippmann taught us this when he
showed how the media imprint stereotypes through innumerable
repetitions, and how these become building blocks in that "in-
between world" which intervenes between people and the objective
external world to serve as their pseudo-reality. This is the implica-
tion of Luhmann's agenda-setting function, the selection of what
the public must attend to, of indicating what is urgent, which
questions everyone must be concerned with. All of this is decided
by the media.

Moreover, the media influence the individual's perception of
what can be said or done without danger of isolation. And finally we
encounter something that could be called the articulation function
of the mass media. This brings us back, then, to the starting point of
our analysis of the spiral of silence, the train test as a paradigm
situation for a small group in which public opinion is created
through talk and reluctance to talk. For the moment, however, we
will remain with the topic of how persons experience the climate of
opinion through the mass media.

Public notice legitimates
Everyone who read reprints of the purported "memorial
address" that was put out by a group of students on the occasion of
the death of Buback, a federal prosecutor murdered by terrorists in
1977, knew that more was involved in the reprint than mere docu-
mentation. The text, brought out under the pseudonym "Mes-
caleros," was reissued, ostensibly, to let the widest possible circles
have the opportunity to read the original and thereby form their
own judgment of it. The active publicity attending its republication

increased the text's impact. Despite mildly disapproving editorial comments that barely concealed an underlying approbation, the publicity created the impression that one might secretly be pleased to hear that a federal prosecutor had been murdered, and might publicly express oneself to that effect without running the risk of isolation. Something like this occurs whenever a tabooed behavior receives public notice—for whatever reasons—without being painted as evil, something to shun or pillory. It is quite easy to sense whether we are dealing with publicity that stigmatizes or condones the behavior. To publicize behavior that violates norms without strongly disapproving of it makes it more fit for polite society, more acceptable. Everyone can see that engaging in this behavior no longer makes one isolated. Those who break social norms are often eager to receive the merest hint of sympathetic publicity; and their eagerness is well founded, for the rule, the norm, is thereby weakened.

21   Public Opinion Has Two Sources—One, the Mass Media

*E*arly in 1976, half a year before the German federal election, the full resources of survey research instrumentation and observation were for the first time set up to trace the development of a climate of opinion and the resulting formation of voting intentions according to the spiral of silence theory. The principal method was the repeated interviewing of a representative sample of voters, technically called a panel study. In addition, normal representative surveys were used to keep track of developments. Two surveys among journalists were carried out, and the political broadcasts of the two national television networks were recorded on videotape.[21] We will examine only a small segment of the complete effort here in order to indicate how the theory of the spiral of silence guided the empirical research (Noelle-Neumann 1977b; 1978; Kepplinger 1979; 1980a).

21. The research program was made possible by the close cooperation between the Allensbach Institut für Demoskopie and the Institut für Publizistik at the University of Mainz.

We had developed pertinent questions starting with the federal election of 1965. These involved the voting intentions of the respondents, their beliefs concerning who was going to win the election, their willingness to demonstrate publicly their political preferences, their overall interest in politics, and their level of media use (newspapers and magazines read and television watched), with special attention to political broadcasts.

Before the 1976 election, a sudden change in the climate of opinion

In July, during the height of the vacation season, a set of completed questionnaires arrived at the Allensbach Institute. They constituted the second wave of questioning of a panel of around 1,000 voters, representative of the total West German population. I was staying in Tessin, Switzerland, at the time, enjoying the cloudless summer days, and I vividly remember the contrast between the broad green leaves in the vineyards and the granite table with the computer output spread upon it. It was a few months before the election and not the right time to forget about work altogether. One thing was emerging clearly from the printouts. The most important measurement, the question concerning people's perceptions of the climate of opinion, showed a dramatic deterioration for the Christian Democrats. The question was: "Of course no one can know for sure, but what do you think: Who is going to win the coming federal election? Who will receive the most votes: the Christian Democratic Union or the Social Democratic Party/Free Democratic Party?" In March of 1976, panel respondents gave a 20 percent advantage to the Christian Democratic Union, expecting that they would triumph at the polls, but now the sentiment had changed and the estimates for the Christian Democratic Union and the Social Democratic Party/Free Democratic Party were only 7 percent apart. A little while later the Social Democratic Party/Free Democratic Party overtook the Christian Democratic Union (table 21).

My first guess was that the supporters of the Christian Democrats had behaved about as they had done in 1972, remaining publicly silent and not indicating, even before the election campaign began, what their convictions were. I knew that the campaign leadership of all the parties, including that of the Christian Democratic Union, had tried to make clear to their supporters how important it was to affirm their position publicly; but, as we know, people are cautious and afraid. I telephoned Allensbach and asked

Table 21. Early in the election year 1976, the climate of opinion favoring the Christian Democratic Union deteriorated

Question: "Of course no one can know for sure, but what do you think: Who is going to win the coming federal election? Who will receive the most votes: the Christian Democratic Union or the Social Democratic Party/ Free Democratic Party?"

		Population 18 and over		
		March 1976 (%)	July 1976 (%)	September 1976 (%)
Christian Democratic Union		47	40	36
Social Democratic Party		27	33	39
Impossible to tell		26	27	25
		100	100	100
	N =	1052	925	1005

Source: Allensbach Archives, surveys 2178, 2185, 2189

for the results of the questions about willingness to stand up for a party publicly. The finding was puzzling; it did not fit the theory. Compared to the results for March, the supporters of the Social Democratic Party tended to be lazier than those of the Christian Democratic Union. In answer to the question of what they were willing to do for their party, and given a list of possible activities including the answer "none of these," between March and July, supporters of the Social Democratic Party saying they would do nothing increased from 34 to 43 percent, while supporters of the Christian Democratic Union stayed almost constant (38 percent in March and 39 percent in July said they would do nothing). The Christian Democratic supporters' declining willingness to stand up for their party could not explain the change in the climate of opinion (table 22).

With the eye of television

I then thought of the two sources we have for obtaining information about the distribution of opinions in our environment: firsthand observation of reality and observation of reality through the eyes of the media. So I ordered a tabulation from Allensbach recording the data according to who had read much or little in the

Table 22. The supporters of the Christian Democrats do not appear to be remiss in their readiness to affirm their support between spring and summer of 1976: therefore the reduced expectation of the chances for a Christian Democratic victory cannot be explained by a poor public showing of Christian Democratic supporters

Question: "Now a question about the party that comes closest to your views. If you were to be asked whether you would like to do something for the party that you regard as the best, for example, some of the things on these cards here, is there anything at all that you would do for this party? Could you pull out the cards that apply?" (Cards are given to the respondent)

	Christian Democratic Supporters		Social Democratic Supporters	
	March 1976 (%)	July 1976 (%)	March 1976 (%)	July 1976 (%)
I would take part in a meeting of this party	53	47	52	43
I would stand up in a meeting of this party and contribute something to the discussion if it seemed important to me	28	25	31	23
I would put a bumper sticker on my car	18	25	26	24
I would also represent the standpoint of this party in the meetings of another party	22	20	24	16
I would wear a campaign button	17	17	23	22
I would help distribute campaign literature	17	16	22	14
I would contribute funds to this party's campaign	12	12	10	11
I would take part in a discussion on the streets and stand up for this party	14	11	19	15
I would put up posters for this party	11	9	13	10
I would put a poster for this party on my home or in my window	10	9	8	6
I would ring the doorbells of strangers and discuss the advantages of this party with them	4	4	5	3
None of these	38	39	34	43
	244	234	267	230
N =	468	444	470	389

Source: Allensbach Archives, surveys 2178, 2185

press, and watched much or little television. When the results were spread out on the table, they looked as simple as a primer. Only those who had more frequently observed the environment through the eyes of television had perceived a change in the climate; those who had observed their environment without television's eyes had noticed no change in climate at all (table 23).

The several checks we ran to determine whether the filtering of reality through television changed the climate of opinion in the election year of 1976 are described in detail elsewhere (Noelle-Neumann 1977b; 1978). Still, we cannot help being curious about the way this impression of a changed climate of opinion was brought about. Once again we enter into territory barely touched by research.

Reporters did not manipulate; they presented what they saw

In order at least to approach the solution to this riddle, we analyzed the surveys of journalists and the videotapes of political broadcasts during that election year. If one starts with Walter Lippmann's thesis, it was not at all surprising that television viewers saw the Christian Democratic Union's chances disappearing. The journalists themselves saw no chance for the Christian Democrats to win the 1976 federal election. In reality, the two political camps were of almost identical strength, and the Christian Democratic Union would have won on election day, 3 October 1976, if 350,000 persons from among about 38 million voters (0.9 percent) had switched their votes from the Social Democratic Party or the Free Democratic Party to the Christian Democratic Union. An objective assessment of the situation before the election should have led journalists to answer the question, "Who do you think will win the election?" with "It's completely up in the air." Instead, more than 70 percent answered that they thought the Social Democratic/Free Democratic coalition would win, while only 10 percent expected a Christian Democratic victory. Journalists saw the world quite differently than the electorate, and, if Lippmann is right, they could only show the world as they saw it. In other words, the audience had two views of reality, two impressions of the climate of opinion—an impression from their own, firsthand observations, and an impression from the eyes of television. A fascinating phenomenon arose: a "dual climate of opinion" (table 24).

Why did the population and the journalists see the political situation so differently? After all, the electorate still believed (in

Table 23. **Concerning the second source of public opinion, impressions from the eye of television, regular TV viewers perceived a worsening of the climate of opinion for the Christian Democrats, but persons who saw little TV between spring and summer noticed no worsening of the climate for the Christian Democrats**

Question: "Of course, no one can know for sure but what do you think: Who is going to win the coming federal election? Who will receive the most votes—the Christian Democratic Union or the Social Democratic Party/Free Democratic Party?"

	Frequent viewers of political TV broadcasts		Persons who seldom or never view political TV broadcasts	
	March 1976 (%)	July 1976 (%)	March 1976 (%)	July 1976 (%)
Total				
Christian Democratic Union	47	34	36	38
Social Democratic Party/				
Free Democratic Party	32	42	24	25
Impossible to tell	21	24	40	37
	100	100	100	100
N =		175		118
Politically Interested Persons				
Christian Democratic Union	49	35	26	44
Social Democratic Party/				
Free Democratic Party	32	41	26	17
Impossible to tell	19	24	48	39
	100	100	100	100
N =		144		23
Politically Disinterested Persons				
Christian Democratic Union	39	26	39	37
Social Democratic Party/				
Free Democratic Party	32	45	23	26
Impossible to tell	29	29	38	37
	100	100	100	100
N =		31		95

Source: Allensbach Archives, surveys 2178, 2185

Table 24. Journalists see the political situation differently than the Electorate. Is their manner of seeing things transmitted to the television viewers?

Question: "Of course, no one can know for sure, but what do you think: Who is going to win the coming federal election? Who will receive the most votes: the Christian Democratic Union or the Social Democratic Party/ Free Democratic Party?"

	July 1976	
	National sample 18 years and older (%)	Allensbach's survey of journalists (%)
Predictions:		
Christian Democratic Union	40	10
Social Democratic Party/Free Democratic Party	33	76
Impossible to tell	27	14
	100	100
	N = 1265	1235
	National sample August 1976 (%)	Journalists in July 1976 (%)
Voting intentions:		
Christian Democratic Union	49	21
Social Democratic Party	42 ⎱ 50	55 ⎱ 79
Free Democratic Party	8 ⎰	24 ⎰
Other parties	1	x
	100	100
	N = 1590	87

Source: Allensbach Archives. Upper half of the table: surveys 2185, 2187. A survey of journalists run parallel to this one by the Institut für Publizistik at the University of Mainz resulted in 73 percent expecting a Social Democratic/ Free Democratic win, 15 percent a Christian Democratic win, 12 percent "impossible to say." N = 81. Lower part of the table: surveys 3032, 2187. It presents the answers of persons who gave a specific party preference. x = less than 0.5%.

the summer of 1976) that a Christian Democratic victory was a little more likely than a Social Democratic/Free Democratic one.

One reason was that the population and the journalists diverged substantially in their political convictions and party preferences. And, of course, as Lippmann makes clear, convictions guided their views. Supporters of the Social Democratic Party and the Free Democratic Party (Liberals) saw many more indications of a victory for their own parties, whereas supporters of the Christian Democratic Union thought their party more likely to win. This is true in general, and it was true for the population and for the journalists in 1976. Since the national sample was split about evenly between the Social Democratic Party/Free Democratic Party on the one hand and the Christian Democratic Union on the other, whereas the journalists were split about three to one in favor of the Social Democratic Party/Free Democratic Party, it was only natural that they perceived the reality differently.

Decoding the language of visual signals

So began the expedition into the unresearched territory of the way television journalists transmit their perceptions to the viewers through pictures and sound. First we looked to America and England, to Sweden, to France in hopes that the communication researchers in these countries had already solved this problem. But we found nothing. Then we sat in a seminar—students, assistants, professors—and tested ourselves. Without discussion, we watched video recordings of political rallies, or interviews with politicians, and immediately afterward completed questionnaires about how the manner in which the persons we had seen had affected us. Where we found ourselves largely in agreement in our decoding of the visual message, we sought to ferret out which clues we had used to obtain the particular impression. Finally, we invited well-known communication researchers, such as Percy Tannenbaum from the University of California at Berkeley and Kurt and Gladys Engel Lang from the Stony Brook University in New York, to come to Mainz to the Institut für Publizistik. We played the video recordings of the political broadcasts for them and asked for their advice. Percy Tannenbaum suggested that we do a survey of cameramen and ask them what visual techniques they employed when they wanted to achieve a particular effect. Or we might ask it the other way around: what effect did they feel particular shots and techniques had on viewers. We carried out this suggestion in 1979 (Kepplinger 1983;

Kepplinger and Donsbach 1982). A majority of the cameramen, 51 percent, answered our written questions, and we received back 151 questionnaires. Seventy-eight percent of the cameramen thought it "very likely indeed" and 22 percent "quite possible" that "a cameraman through purely visual means could cause persons to be seen in a particularly positive or particularly negative fashion." What techniques can have these effects?

The cameramen we surveyed agreed overwhelmingly on one point. For a politician they particularly liked, two-thirds of the cameramen would take a frontal shot at eyelevel, since, in their view, this would tend to strike a sympathetic note and establish the impression of calmness and spontaneity. None of them, on the other hand, would use a high shot (bird's eye view) or a low shot (frog's eye view), since these positions would tend to be unsympathetic and to convey the impression either of weakness or of emptiness.

Professor Hans Mathias Kepplinger and a working group subsequently studied videotapes of the television election campaign as covered by the two German television systems, the ARD and the ZDF, between 1 April and the election of 3 October 1976. Among the many findings they reported: Helmut Schmidt was seen only 31 times in shots taken from a frog's or a bird's perspective while Kohl was presented this way 55 times. But due to ongoing protests by journalists and cameramen who were opposed to analyzing the effects of camera angles, the research was not continued.

Today, more than a decade later, we are still exploring how television journalists transmit their perceptions to the viewers through images and sound. But the indignation over the scientific study of cameramen and film editors has meanwhile subsided. Experimental studies published subsequently have provided definite confirmation of the influence exerted by camera and editing techniques on viewers' conceptions of reality. These studies were so dispassionately written, however, that they are unlikely to stir up further excitement (Kepplinger 1987, 1989b).

Also, there has not been a federal election in Germany with an outcome as close as the election of 1976. Bitter accusations about the effects of the media on the climate of opinion will not be made, of course, unless there is a potential for decisive influence, with the outcome depending on a few hundred thousand votes. For communications research seeking to determine the influence of television images on the viewers, this absence of public excitement has actually proved favorable. Michael Ostertag devoted his dissertation (1992) at the Institut für Publizistik in Mainz to the subject of how journalists' party preferences affect politicians being interviewed on television and how this effect in turn shapes the impression politicians make on the public. In analyzing 40 television interviews with the top candidates—Schmidt, Kohl, Strauss, and Genscher—during the federal election campaign of 1980, Ostertag and his collaborators worked with the sound turned off. They wanted to avoid being influenced by the arguments put forward and the language used, as well as by the elements connected with speech, such as voice pitch, intonation, and deliberate pauses—in other words, by what are considered "paralinguistic" or "paraverbal modes of expression." Their sole concern was the visual content.

Ostertag's research included a comparison of the facial expressions and gestures of the four leading German politicians, depending on whether they were being interviewed by a journalist with similar political views or by one tending to the opposing side. It appeared that the typical facial expressions and gestures of the four leading politicians remained essentially unchanged in all the interviews. There was, however, a change of degree. When speaking with a journalist of a different political persuasion, the politicians' rhythmic nodding became more emphatic while they were speaking; and the process of looking away from or staring at the other person was prolonged. This intensity seemed to have an unfavorable effect on the viewer. When interviewed by journalists with whom they seemed to be in agreement, each of the four leading politicians was, for the most part, given a positive rating by the viewers, while politicians who argued with the interviewing journalist got a negative rating (Ostertag 1992, 191ff.).

Nonetheless, although we are now in a position to identify some of the visual signals that influence opinion about politicians appearing on television, research still has far to go before it can really determine how television transmits the climate of opinion.

22 The Dual Climate of Opinion

*In Germany at the Polls: the Bundestag
Election of 1976*, an American political scientist, David P. Conradt,
reported to those Americans interested in politics that

> Union strategists . . . sought to make the spiral of silence work
> to the benefit of the Union in 1976. At the party's convention in
> Hamburg in December 1973, [the] findings were presented to
> the party leaders. In 1974 simplified summaries of the spiral-of-
> silence concept were given to the party's activists . . . Finally,
> the decision to begin the Union's nationwide advertising and
> poster campaigns before those of the Social Democratic Party
> was also a result of the [spiral-of-silence] thesis, which, in
> operational terms, meant that the party had to become visible
> before the Social Democratic campaign could get into full
> swing. (Conradt 1978, 41)

Struggle against the spiral of silence

As a matter of fact, in 1976 the people at the grassroots acted
differently than they had in 1972. There was no spiral of silence.
Supporters of the Christian Democrats gave public evidence of
their convictions, wore buttons, and fastened signs to their cars to
no less a degree than the supporters of the Social Democrats. They
argued where they could be heard and they canvassed for their
cause. Five or six weeks after the election, when people were asked
which party's supporters had been most active in campaigning, 30
percent named the Christian Democratic supporters and only 18
percent the Social Democratic supporters.

The "dual climate of opinion"—the climate the population
perceives directly, in contrast to the climate as portrayed by the
media—was strong enough in 1976 to prevent a bandwagon effect in
the direction of the expected winner. This was probably the first
time in a modern election campaign that any group has consciously
fought the bandwagon effect. For months, the two political camps
had run neck and neck in terms of their strength (figure 22). And
they stayed neck and neck as the election results were being
counted on the evening of 3 October 1976, until the Social Democratic Party/Free Democratic Party managed to cross the finish a
scant margin ahead. We need more experience before we can say
whether the Christian Democratic Union might have won if the

Figure 22

1976: The Dual Climate of Opinion

Conscious struggle against the spiral of silence: in contrast to 1965 and 1972, there is no last-minute bandwagon effect favoring the expected winner of the election.

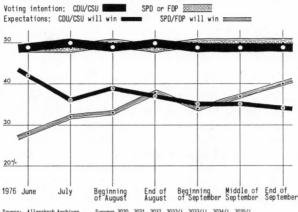

Source: Allensbach Archives,   Surveys 3030, 3031, 3032, 3033/I, 3033/II, 3034/I, 3035/I

media climate had not been against it. The dual climate of opinion is a fascinating phenomenon. It is as exciting as an unusual weather situation or a distant vista; it is like the warm spring wind that occurs only once a year, a double rainbow, the northern lights, for it can only arise under very special circumstances. It only happens when the climate of opinion among the people and that dominant among media journalists diverge. From this observation, however, it is also possible to develop a worthwhile instrument. Whenever one stumbles upon a divergence between opinions or intentions as they are actually expressed by the individuals and an assessment of how most people feel or—which is very much the same—who will win, it is worthwhile checking the hypothesis that the error in judgment was caused by the mass media.

Pluralistic ignorance: the people misjudge the people

The longer one has studied the question, the clearer it becomes that fathoming the effects of the mass media is very hard. These effects do not come into being as a result of a single stimulus; they are as a rule cumulative, following the principle that "water dripping constantly wears away stone." Further discussions among people spread the media's messages further, and before long no difference can be perceived between the point of media reception and points far removed from it. The media's effects are predominantly unconscious; people cannot provide an account of what has happened. Rather, they mix their own direct perceptions and the perceptions filtered through the eyes of the media into an indivisible whole that seems to derive from their own thoughts and experiences, as Walter Lippmann predicted. Most of these media effects occur indirectly, on the rebound, as it were, to the extent that the individual adopts the eyes of the media and acts accordingly. All of these conditions make it seem particularly necessary to find systematic procedures for researching media effects. What American sociologists have called pluralistic ignorance,[22] a condition whereby the people have a mistaken idea about how most people feel, will serve as a kind of guide for tracking down the media's effects.

You may remember an observation reported in chapter 3 of this book. It had to do with a test that failed—a picture of several persons sitting together in a friendly way, and one person sitting apart, segregated, isolated. We were trying to find out whether respondents were conscious of the relationship between representing a minority opinion and being isolated, so that they would implicitly assign a clear minority opinion to a person who appeared isolated.

As a minority opinion we used in this test the view that members of the German Communist Party should be able to serve as judges. In April 1976, at the time of the test, only 18 percent of the population agreed with this statement while 60 percent opposed it. Only 2 percent imagined that the majority of the population favored the measure, while 80 percent assumed that the majority was opposed. The test, as we said, did not work. An almost equal proportion of respondents saw the isolated person as either opposing or as favoring Communist Party members as judges. Did this indicate a dual climate of opinion? Did some respondents attribute the minority opinion to the loner while others, who saw with the eyes of the media, attributed to this isolated figure the majority view that the media currently scorned as utterly conservative and incorrigibly antiliberal?

22. Merton 1968; Fields and Schuman 1976; O'Gorman and Garry 1976; Taylor 1982; Katz 1981.

23   The Articulation Function: Those Whose Point of View Is Not Represented by the Media Are Effectively Mute

Scientists tend to be very vulnerable people. When I saw for the first time the results of the train test asking whether members of the Communist Party should be allowed to be appointed as judges, I had to rub my eyes. It looked like a clear refutation of the spiral of silence. The supporters of the majority opinion, in full awareness that they were the majority, wanted to keep quiet. The supporters of the minority opinion were happy to enter into conversations to the tune of more than 50 percent (table 25).

The hard core

Even the earliest tests of the spiral of silence, run in 1972, had shown that there were exceptions to the rule. An important part of the empirical examination of theories consists in determining where their boundaries lie, finding the conditions under which a theory is not confirmed and thus must be modified. Right from the first tests, we had found that the minority that followed Franz Josef Strauss in the early seventies was much happier to enter into conversation in the train test than the overwhelming majority of Strauss opponents (table 26) (Noelle-Neumann 1974/1979, 189–90).

At that point, for the first time, we encountered the hard core—the minority that remains at the end of a spiral of silence process in defiance of the threats of isolation. The hard core is, in a certain sense, related to the avant-garde; it regards isolation as a price it must pay. Unlike the members of the avant-garde, a hard core can turn its back to the public, can close itself completely off when it finds itself in public with strangers, can encapsulate itself like a sect and orient itself to the past or to the most distant future. The other possibility is that the hard core simultaneously feels itself to be an avant-garde. We discern this from its willingness to speak up, a willingness that at least equals that of the avant-garde. A hard core that is counting on the future is encouraged by a condition which an American social psychologist, Gary I. Schulman (1968), has empirically demonstrated; the supporters of a majority opinion that becomes large enough will, with time, be unable to argue well

Table 25. The majority, knowing well that it is the majority, is effectively silenced. The minority, knowing well that it is a minority, is quite willing to talk. Does the majority lack arguments because the media have insufficiently formulated them?

	The majority: Persons who are against having members of the Communist Party appointed as judges and meet someone in a train compartment who—	
	thinks differently than they do (%)	shares their view (%)
In a conversation during a train trip about appointing members of the Communist Party as judges—		
would willingly join in	27	25
would not join in	57	67
no opinion	16	8
	100	100
	N = 169	217

	The minority: Persons who are in favor of having members of the Communist Party appointed as judges and meet someone in a train compartment who—	
	shares their view (%)	thinks differently (%)
In a conversation during a train trip about members of the Communist Party as judges—		
would willingly join in	52	52
would not join in	40	42
no opinion	8	6
	100	100
	N = 48	54

Source: Allensbach Archives, survey 3028, April 1976

Table 26. At the end of a long spiral of silence process, a hard core remains that is willing to isolate itself by talking

Question: "Suppose you had a five-hour train journey ahead of you, and someone in your compartment began to talk strongly *in favor of* (in every second interview, *against*) Franz Josef Strauss gaining more political influence among us. Would you gladly hold a conversation with this person, or would you not think it worth your while?"

	1972	
	Majority: Strauss opponents (%)	Minority: Strauss supporters (%)
Would gladly converse	35	49
Would not think it worth my while	56	42
No opinion	9	9
	100	100
	N = 1136	536

Source: Allensbach Archives, surveys 2087/I + II, October/November 1972

for it, since they no longer meet anyone who has a different opinion. Schulman found supporters of the viewpoint that one should brush one's teeth daily completely lacking in assurance when they were suddenly confronted by someone with the contrary opinion.

In any event, Strauss's supporters were in no sense inclined to turn their backs to the public; they didn't crawl into a hole or turn themselves into a sect; they certainly didn't write off the possibility that they would win ground again in the near future. They were a hard core that saw themselves as an avant-garde, and, for this reason despite their representing a minority opinion, they were prepared to engage in direct conversation.

If the mass media fail to provide them, there will be no words

In the issue of allowing members of the Communist Party to become judges, however, something else was happening. Those who were in favor of allowing such appointments were no hard core, and the great majority of the opponents had not fallen asleep in their opposition. In fact, the fear that communism might gain ground was as strong as ever. If they kept quiet in the train test with both fellow believers and opponents in strikingly large numbers, then it must have been for a reason that was not yet known. Could it be that words failed them because opposition to communists as judges had scarcely ever been articulated in the mass media, in particular on television?

If we accept this hypothesis, we will have to add yet another item to the known ways in which the media work: the articulation function. The media provide people with the words and phrases they can use to defend a point of view. If people find no current, frequently repeated expressions for their point of view, they lapse into silence; they become effectively mute.

In 1898, Gabriel Tarde wrote an essay titled "Le public et la foule" (The public and the crowd). We close our discussion of public opinion and the effects of the mass media with Tarde's concluding reflections:

> A private telegram addressed to the editor-in-chief results in a sensational new story of intense immediacy, which will instantaneously arouse crowds in all the great cities of the continent; from these dispersed crowds, in intimate though distant contact through their consciousness of their sumultaneity and their mutual action born of the news story, the newspaper will create an immense, abstract, and sovereign crowd, which it will name opinion. The newspaper has thus finished the age-old work that conversation began, that correspondence extended, but that always remained in a state of a sparse and scattered outline—the fusion of personal opinions into local opinions, and this into national and *world* opinion, the grandiose unification of the public mind. . . . This is an enormous power, one that can only increase, because the need to agree with the public of which one is a part, to think and act in agreement with opinion, becomes all the more strong and irresistible as the public becomes more numerous, the opinion more imposing, and the need itself more often satisfied. One should thus not be surprised to see our contemporaries so pliant before the wind of passing opinion, nor should one conclude from this that characters have necessarily weakened. When poplars and oaks are brought down by a storm, it is not because they grew weaker but because the wind grew stronger. (Tarde 1969, 318)

What would Tarde have written during the age of television?

"*E*lisabeth," my friend said mockingly to her other guests, "now goes from door to door and asks: 'Do you agree or do you disagree with Adenauer?'"

It was in Munich, the winter of 1951/52, and I had ended up at this party of intellectuals merely by chance. "Do drop by," she had said on the telephone. We had been school friends. When was the last time we had seen each other? It was in 1943 or 1944 on the Limonenstrasse in Berlin-Dahlem, by the botanical gardens, southwest of the city, on the approach path for the bombers that came in from the west. The house was collapsing; the walls were cracked; the room was half-empty; the furniture, rugs, and pictures were all stored away.

Her question brought me back to the issue of research on public opinion: What on earth were such opinions worth? It could not be explained to this circle of literati, artists, and scholars, even if it had not already been so late, and they had not already drunk so much, and the room had not been so dark and full of smoke.

Yes, it was precisely this question "Do you, by and large, agree with Adenauer's policies or do you disagree with them?"—through which, in 1951, I first encountered the force of that which I would gradually learn to understand as the public and public opinion. At that time, I regularly pretested our questionnaires in Allensbach before they were sent out to hundreds of interviewers through the whole of Germany. In fact, I had frequently interviewed the young wife of a railroad signalman with questions that repeated themselves, and I knew her answers, I had already heard at least eight times that she did not agree with Adenauer. But acting conscientiously and strictly according to the rules—the whole interview had to be tested, and the length needed to be determined, too—I once again read to her: "Do you agree with Adenauer . . . or do you disagree . . .?" "Agree," she said. I tried to hide my surprise, since interviewers are not supposed to show surprise. Then, about four weeks later, the results of our new survey lay on my desk before me, and I saw that within one month, from November to December, the level of agreement with Adenauer in the Federal Republic had jumped 8 percentage points to a total of 31 percent, after long having remained stationary at 24 and 23 percent. From then on, it continued to climb until 57 percent "agreed" during the parliamentary election year of 1953,[23] "a tidal volume and sweep," as Ross called it (1969, 104). By what means had the wave of pressure in the Federal Republic reached this railroad signalman's wife? And what was such an opinion worth?

Destiny, not reason

Vox populi—vox dei? If we trace this phrase backward in time, we find it being used as a maxim as early as 1329 (Boas 1969, 21; Gallacher 1945). In 798 a learned Anglo-Saxon, Alcuin, referred to it in a letter to Charlemagne, using it as if it were a common, well-known expression. It can ultimately be traced back to the eighth century before Christ with the prophet Isaiah, who proclaimed: "Vox Populi de civitate vox de templo. Vox domini reddentis retributionem inimicis suis." "A voice of noise from the city, a voice from the temple, a voice of the Lord that rendereth recompense to his enemies."[24]

Over the centuries, the pendulum had swung between disdain and something akin to reverence on the part of those who have evoked this formula. Hofstätter, in his *Psychologie der öffentlichen Meinung*, thought that "equating the voice of the people to God's voice is a blasphemy!" (1949, 96). The German Chancellor of the Reich, von Bethmann Hollweg (1856–1921), thought it might be more correctly stated as "Voice of the people—voice of cattle," and with this he was merely copying what a pupil of Montaigne's, Pierre Charron, suggested in 1601 as a more appropriate version: "Vox populi, vox stultorum" (Voice of the people—voice of stupidity). Charron drew his inspiration from Montaigne's *Essay Concerning Fame*, in which the crowd's inability to appreciate the character of great men and their towering achievements is discussed.

> Is it reason to make the life of a wise man depend on the judgment of fools? . . . Is there anything more foolish than to think all together they are oughts, whom every single one you would set at noughts? Whosoever aims to please them has never done. . . . No art, no mildness of spirit might direct our steps to follow so straggling and disordered a guide. In this

23. Neumann and Noelle 1961, 44–45; see also Institut für Demoskopie Allensbach, "Die Stimmung im Bundesgebiet" (chart), October 1952.

24. The Vulgate, Isaiah 66:6 (Latin translation done by Hieronymus in the fourth century after Christ). English from the King James version.

breathy confusion of brutes, and frothy chaos of reports and of vulgar opinions, which still push us on, no good course can be established. Let us not propose so fleeing and so wavering an end unto ourselves. Let us constantly follow reason. And let the vulgar approbation follow us that way, if it please. (Cited in Boas 1969, 31–32)

Alcuin writes in the same spirit in his note of 798 to Charlemagne: "Nor are those to be listened to who are accustomed to say, 'The voice of the people is the voice of God.' For the clamor of the crowd [*vulgi*] is very close to madness" (ibid., 9).

Thus do all those express themselves who, over the centuries and the millennia, translate "vox dei" as the "voice of reason" and who seek that reason in vain in the voice of the people, public opinion.

But a second, completely different theme runs alongside this one. "A voice of noise from the city, a voice from the temple, a voice of the Lord that rendereth recompense to his enemies," said the prophet Isaiah. About 700 B.C., Hesiod, though lacking the later words, described "public opinion" as a moral tribunal, as social control, and indicated that it could become destiny: "So do: and avoid the talk of men. For Talk is mischievous, light, and easily raised, but hard to bear and difficult to be rid of. Talk never wholly dies away when many people voice her: even Talk is in some ways divine" (Hesiod 1959, 59).

The Roman philosopher Seneca was reverential: "Believe me, the people's tongue is divine" (*Controversae* 1.1.10) and about a millennium and a half later, Machiavelli: "Not without reason is the voice of the people called the voice of God, for *una opinione universale* predicts events in such a wonderful manner that one might believe in a hidden power of prophecy" (cited in Bucher 1887, 77).

It is not reason that makes public opinion worth noticing, but precisely the reverse—the irrational element it contains, the element of the future, of destiny. Machiavelli once again: "Quale fama, o voce, o opinione fa, che il popolo comincia a favorire un cittadino?" "What fame, what voice, what movement of opinion brings it about that the people begin to turn toward a citizen?" (ibid.)

"Voice of the people, voice of destiny" was Karl Steinbuch's contribution to the interpretation, when he compared the results of a question Allensbach asked annually toward the end of the year with the gross national product for the following year. The question

Figure 23
Hopes Before the Beginning of a New Year Precede Economic Development

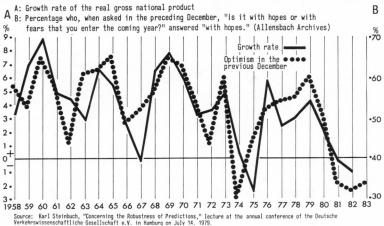

A: Growth rate of the real gross national product
B: Percentage who, when asked in the preceding December, "Is it with hopes or with
fears that you enter the coming year?" answered "with hopes." (Allensbach Archives)

Source: Karl Steinbuch, "Concerning the Robustness of Predictions," lecture at the annual conference of the Deutsche
Verkehrswissenschaftliche Gesellschaft e.V. in Hamburg on July 14, 1979.

reads: "Do you look forward to the coming year with hopes or with fears?" The high or low level of hopes at the end of the year did not correspond to greater or less economic growth during that year; instead, it correlated with the economic development of the *following* year (figure 23).

Hegel moves between the two camps "Voice of the people, voice of cattle" and "The people's tongue is divine" in his reflections on public opinion.

> Public opinion, therefore, deserves to be as much *respected* as *despised*, the latter for its concrete consciousness and expression, the former for its essential basis, which shines rather dimly in that concrete expression. Since public opinion, in itself, neither has a criterion of discrimination, nor the ability to turn the substantive aspect into precise knowledge, being independent of it is the first formal condition of achieving anything great and rational—in life as in science. Great achievement can be assured that public opinion will, in due course, accept it, recognize it, and make of it one of its own prejudices. *Corollary:* Public opinion contains everything that is false and everything that is true, but it is only the great man who can find the truth in it. He who is able to express what his times are saying and to carry out what they want is the great man of the times. He does what is intrinsic and essential to the times; he embodies them—and anyone who does not know how to despise public opinion, as he may hear it here and there, will never rise to greatness. (Hegel 1970, 485–86, § 318)

Toward the end of the eighteenth century, Wieland made the expression "public opinion" popular in German. In the ninth of his "Confidential Conversations," "Concerning Public Opinion" (1794), the two participants conclude their dialogue thus:

> Egbert: Every declaration of reason has the strength of a law and does not need first to become public opinion.
>
> Sinibald: Please say rather, *should* have the strength of a law and surely will attain it as soon as it is proclaimed as the opinion of the majority.
>
> Egbert: That will be something for the nineteenth century to determine.

Lothar Bucher, who cites this dialog of Wieland's, closes his essay with the words: "Sinibald and Egbert consider at length how reason and public opinion behave toward one another, adjourning the decision to the nineteenth century; let us leave it to the twentieth century to conclude this discussion" (Bucher 1887, 80). Shall we now carry it over to the twenty-first?

Operational definitions for empirical investigations of public opinion

When one reflects on how much effort over how long a period of time has been spent on defining public opinion, it becomes necessary to explain why in the present book I have purposely kept the supply of definitions meager. Harwood Childs provided more than fifty definitions, including some confusing descriptions of characteristics, forms, origins, functions, and innumerable categories of content. The superabundance and the density of his definitions moved me to seek a new beginning; an economical definitional statement that, in contrast to the arsenal of definitions that so discourages us in Childs's work, allows empirical analysis. I sought an operational definition. One should be able to lay out investigations with it and use it to derive testable propositions. That goal has led me to offer the following: "Public opinions are attitudes or behaviors one *must* express in public if one is not to isolate oneself; in areas of controversy or change, public opinions are those attitudes one *can* express without running the danger of isolating oneself." This definition can be tested with the methods of representative survey research and representatively distributed observations. Are all injunctions, morals, and traditions of our time so shaken that public opinion in this sense does not exist any longer, that people can say or do anything without isolating themselves? We argued about this in a seminar at the University of Mainz. One of the participants in the seminar said that all you need do is go to a funeral in a red suit and you will be taught that public opinion in this sense still exists today. One can also describe opinions and ways of behaving in a survey interview and then ask which of these opinions and ways of behaving would be so disturbing to you that you would not want to live in the same house with someone who engaged in them, or meet him or her at a party, or work in the same place. There is still a large number of attitudes and behaviors that can isolate a person, as this test shows.

A second definition that provides a starting point for empirical work from which testable propositions can be derived goes as follows: "Public opinion is an understanding on the part of people in an ongoing community concerning some affect- or value-laden question which individuals as well as governments have to respect at least by compromise in their overt behavior under the threat of being excluded or losing one's standing in society." This second definition emphasizes the correlate of the fear of isolation: social agreement.

From either of these definitions, propositions can be derived concerning the significance of talking or keeping quiet, and concerning the intuitive statistical human ability to observe people and the language of cues that belongs to that ability—a language yet to be decoded systematically, although we already understand it intuitively. It is possible to theorize about how this quasistatistical, unconscious frequency-registering organ atrophies in periods of stability and becomes highly alert in periods of instability and change; or how the threat of isolation increases in intensity with the danger a society experiences in holding its own. Propositions can be derived concerning the effects of the mass media, how publicity is given or held back, how arguments are put into words or left unformed, so that the vocabulary that can spread an issue and bring it to the agenda of public discussion will be lacking. Propositions can be derived concerning the two sources of public opinion and how a dual climate of opinion can result from them. On the basis of these definitions it is possible to develop instruments—in particular, survey questions—to measure the amount of isolation connected with a certain position or behavior, the degree of affect, the extent of agreement and rejection; to measure signals of the public readiness to admit viewpoints or to be silent; and to measure the indices of polarization.

The emperor's new clothes. Public opinion is bound to a particular place and to a particular time

When, in the first half of this century, the thicket of definitions for public opinion became too impenetrable, voices multiplied calling for the concept to be abandoned because it had outlived its usefulness. After such demands, nothing happened. Despite all its lack of clarity, the concept received more rather than less use. This was the surprised conclusion W. Phillips Davison reached in his article on public opinion in the 1968 *International Encyclopedia of the Social Sciences.*

In December 1965, I began my inaugural lecture at the University of Mainz with these words:

> Public opinion: in some mysterious way, this concept has retained its excitement. At the same time, it has been the fate of writers or scholars who dared to take up the subject to disappoint their audiences. When they prove that there is no such thing as "public opinion," that we are dealing with a fiction, they are not convincing. "The concept simply refuses to die," Dovifat lamented. . . .
>
> What does this stubbornness with which the concept hangs on mean? Why this sense of disappointment when one has tried to analyze its definitions? It means that the concept of public opinion reflects a reality that these conceptual efforts have not yet been able to capture. (Noelle 1966, 3)

Reflects a reality—that does not help us at all; we must determine this reality. Then, suddenly, we see that traces of this reality are spread throughout the language, among simple words, words without sense unless we take increasing account of the sensitivity of our social skin, unless we temporarily repress our ego ideal, the reasonable person we believe ourself to be. What are some of these words? To lose face; publicity as the sphere in which one can lose face, make a fool of oneself, commit a faux pas; to find something embarrassing; to slander someone; to brand someone. Unless we face this reality, how can we understand what the poet Max Frisch meant by the formula he used in his opening address at the Frankfurt Book Fair: "Publicity—it's loneliness turned inside out"? (Frisch 1976, 56). There is the individual, and there are the many in their invisible cloak of anonymity who pass judgment on him—this is what Rousseau described and called public opinion.

We must come to grips with this reality of public opinion, this creation that is tied to a space, tied to a time. Otherwise we shall deceive ourselves into supposing that we would not have kept quiet like everyone else around when the emperor entered in his new clothes. The Andersen fairy tale is about public opinion dominating a scene, reigning at a certain place. If a stranger had happened to enter, he could scarcely have contained his surprise.

And there is this matter of time. As those who have come later, we shall judge as unjustly and as ignorantly as people in the Middle Ages judged on the causes of sickness. We shall make judgments about words and acts of the past as if they had been spoken or had occurred in our times, but, in doing so, we shall become ignoramuses who know nothing about the fervor of an age. In Sweden, a press agent for the Ministry of Culture said: "We wish to have the school system look like a well-cut lawn. We do not want to have an isolated flower sticking up here and there; rather everything should be a single well-mown lawn" (*Die Welt*, 12 October 1979, 6). That is the zeitgeist boiled down to a formula, as Lippmann described it. He also described how, later, formulas crumble and then become incomprehensible to those who follow. Even that sentence about the well-mown lawn may someday appear incomprehensible.

To sharpen one's feelings for the times and, simultaneously, one's understanding of public opinion would be a goal worth reaching and training for. What does it mean to be a "contemporary"? What does "timelessness" mean? Why did Hegel urgently point to the element of time: "He who is able to express what his times are saying and to carry out what they want is the great man of the time"? We should understand what the German author Kurt Tucholsky described when he said: "Nothing is harder and nothing requires more character than to find oneself in open conflict with one's time and loudly to say 'NO'" (1975, 67); and what Jonathan Swift caricaturized in 1706 when he wrote: "Reflect on Things past, as Wars, Negotiations, Factions, and the like; we enter so little into those Interests, that we wonder how Men could possibly be so busy, and concerned for Things so transitory: Look on the present Times, we find the same Humour, yet wonder not at all. . . . No Preacher is listened to, but Time; which gives us the same Train and Turn of Thought, that elder People have tried in vain to put into our Heads before" (Swift 1965, 241).

In October 1979, when a statement of the Nobel prize winner Mother Teresa immediately became world famous, I asked myself whether our times had begun to perceive and respect the sensitive social nature of mankind. The statement ran: "The worst sickness is not leprosy or tuberculosis, but the feeling of being respected by no one, of being unloved, deserted by everyone." Perhaps a short time from now people will not be able to understand why such a self-evident statement could have aroused such attention.

Two meanings of social skin

To be despised, to be expelled—that is the leper's curse. A person can be a leper in many ways—physically, in emotional relations with other persons, and socially. As we better understand public opinion, we better understand the social nature of human beings. We cannot insist that those who fear becoming social lepers should resist all pressures toward conformity, all invitations to go along with the crowd. Perhaps, instead, we could ask with Marie Jahoda (1959), a social psychologist, just how independent a person should be? Really, how independent do we want good citizens to be? Would it be best for society if people were not in the least concerned about the judgments of others? Jahoda questions whether we can consider a radical nonconformist who behaves with complete independence normal at all. Should we suppose that such a person is mentally ill? She goes so far as to indicate that only after such a person has shown an ability to conform can independent, nonconforming behavior be recognized as a civic virtue. Nor should one simply condemn a society as intolerant or illiberal when it threatens the deviant individual with isolation to protect the value of its mutually held convictions.

"Public Opinion—Our Social Skin" characterizes both of these aspects. On the one hand it refers to our society, which public opinion protects like a skin, holding it together. On the other hand it refers to individuals, for they who suffer at the hands of public opinion suffer from the sensitivities of their social skin. Did not Rousseau, who introduced the concept of public opinion into modern language, in fact express what was most important about it when he described it as the enemy of the individual and the protector of society?

25 *New Discoveries*

*D*id Erasmus of Rotterdam know Machiavelli? The name Erasmus did not appear in the index of the first German edition of the *Spiral of Silence* of 1980. But in the spring of 1989, while preparing my lectures for the University of Chicago, I began to investigate the question of whether Erasmus knew Machiavelli.

Historical perspectives

To arrive at new insights, a scholar needs to be lucky as well as clever. I certainly was lucky during the initial work on the theory of the spiral of silence. It was sheer luck that I found a quote from Tocqueville in Tönnies describing the spiral of silence almost as precisely as a botanist would describe a plant (Tönnies 1922, 394). It was lucky that Kurt Reumann, a research assistant in Allensbach at the time, called my attention to chapter 28, "On other relations," from Book II of John Locke's *Essay Concerning Human Understanding*. That chapter, which had gone largely unnoticed in professional circles, contains a description of the law of opinion, of reputation, and of fashion. We then decided to systematize the search for important texts, rather than continuing to depend on chance and serendipity. At the Institut für Publizistik of the University of Mainz we designed the questionnaire addressed to books rather than people (see above, p. 66). Over the years we have used this questionnaire in seminars at Mainz to study about four hundred authors in order to find out everything we could about public opinion.[1] Thus, for example, we found that in a speech inaugurating the Book Fair in Frankfurt in 1958, Max Frisch stated: "Öffentlichkeit ist Einsamkeit außen" ("Facing the public, facing the multitudes, is loneliness directed outwards"—Frisch 1979, 63). These words were a key to the fear of isolation that sometimes overcomes people in public. Many years later, when Michael Hallemann began to study embarrassment and demonstrated that this feeling increases in proportto the size of the public (Hallemann 1990, 133 ff.), I was reminded of Max Frisch's formulation and realized how writers have a way of anticipating scholars.

To return to Erasmus: using the questionnaire on public opinion during the summer term of 1988, Ursula Kiermeier analyzed

---

1. The questionnaire is reproduced in the Appendix.

three texts by Erasmus, including "The education of a Christian prince," written in 1516 as advice for Charles of Burgundy, then seventeen, who was later to become Emperor Charles V. Reading Ursula Kiermeier's commentaries on the texts by Erasmus, I was struck by a similarity with Machiavelli's writings. Using the same questionnaire, Werner Eckert (1985) for his master's thesis had analyzed works of Machiavelli. Both Machiavelli and Erasmus advised their princes that it was impossible to rule against public opinion. In chapter 4 I cited a phrase of Shakespeare's King Henry IV: "Opinion that did help me to the crown." I assumed that his taking public opinion seriously could only be attributed to Machiavelli's influence (see above, pp. 64–65). But now I read in Erasmus that the ruler's power is essentially based on the *consensus populi*. It is the approval of the people that makes a king: "Believe me: He who forfeits the people's favor loses an important comrade-in-arms" (Erasmus [1516] 1968, 149). There are similarities between Machiavelli's and Erasmus' texts, right down to the details. In listing threats to the ruler, even the sequence is the same; first comes the hatred of his subjects, then their contempt.

Both writers emphasized that it was most important for the ruler to *appear* to be great and virtuous. They differed on an important point, however: Machiavelli thought the prince need not truly have these virtues; it was enough for him to appear to have them. Erasmus, a devout Christian, took the opposite stance. The prince had to have all these virtues and ought not be guilty of any crime, yet reality was not in itself enough: he also had *to appear* virtuous to his subjects (Erasmus [1516] 1968, 149ff.; Machiavelli [1532] 1971, chaps. 18, 19).

Did Machiavelli and Erasmus know each other, or were they familiar with each other's writings? I found that they had been born at about the same time, Erasmus in 1466 or 1469 in Rotterdam and Machiavelli in 1469 in the vicinity of Florence. But their respective situations were totally different. The son of a priest and of a doctor's daughter, Erasmus suffered all his life from being illegitimate. After the premature deaths of his parents, he entered a monastery as a young man. He quickly established a career as secretary to a bishop and later as a scholar at the Sorbonne. But his illegitimacy prevented him from receiving a doctorate at many universities. Eventually he was granted one by the University of Turin in Northern Italy, not far from Machiavelli's Florence.

Every scholar who has dealt with the threat of public opinion has experienced social isolation. Perhaps it takes experiences such as these to create an awareness of the pressure of public opinion. Erasmus, the "king of the humanists," who was at home all over Europe, had practice in enduring social isolation. He was attacked in a pamphlet for being a *homo pro se,* a self-sufficient person who did not need others. And Machiavelli had fallen from his powerful position of councillor in Florence, had been suspected of treason and tortured, and had then been banished to his minor country estate outside Florence.

Machiavelli's *The Prince* and Erasmus's *The Education of a Christian Prince* were written within a few years of each other. Machiavelli's book was written first (1513/14), but it was not published until 1532. Erasmus wrote *The Education* in 1516 and published it immediately after presenting it to Charles of Burgundy (later Emperor Charles V), for whom it was written. Machiavelli and Erasmus had a common source: both had based their writings on Aristotle's *Politics.*[2] However, they probably never met personally, according to several other authors who had already noted the odd similarity between Erasmus and Machiavelli and whom I came upon in the course of my research, much as a traveler unexpectedly finds traces left by previous visitors in a remote place.[3]

I was thus not surprised to learn of John of Salisbury, an English scholastic who used the expressions *publica opinio* and *opinio publica* twice in Latin in his *Policraticus* of 1159 ([1927] 1963, 39, 130). Although the English editor of *Policraticus* finds the use of those expressions in a twelfth-century writing remarkable (ibid., 39, 130), it is hardly to be wondered at, as John of Salisbury had also read the classics of antiquity during the early Humanist period and had encountered the idea of the power of *opinio publica.*

A great statesman is familiar with public opinion

The concept of public opinion is not articulated in the Old Testament, yet King David had an innate sense of how to deal with it.

2. The passages consulted by both Machiavelli and Erasmus are in 1312b18–20; 1313a14–16; 1314a38–40; 1314b14–19; 1314b38–39.
3. See Geldner 1930, 161. On the question whether Erasmus was familiar with the writings of Machiavelli, see for example Renaudet 1954, 178; Weiland et al. 1988, 71.

He tore his clothes and fasted until the sun set to demonstrate his grief over the murder of a powerful opponent, when it would have been logical to suspect that he had instigated or countenanced the murder. These symbolic actions were more effective than any words in winning over public opinion.

The great spectacle King David organized to accompany the transfer of the Ark of the Covenant to Jerusalem "with shouting and with the sound of the trumpet," to emphasize the common sacred center of Israel and Juda, the two kingdoms he ruled, was a masterful act of integration. But it is the part he played himself, the way he personally participated in the procession, leaping and dancing, wearing nothing but a loincloth, and humbling himself before the Lord, that shows that his approach to public opinion was far more than an elaborate ritual. His wife Michal, a king's daughter, mocked him: "How glorious was the king of Israel to day, who uncovered himself to day in the eyes of the handmaids of his servants, as one of the vain fellows shamelessly uncovereth himself!" And King David's response to the daughter of King Saul was: "And I will yet be more vile than thus, and will be base in mine own sight: and of the maidservants which thou hast spoken of, of them shall I be had in honour" (II Samuel 6:15, 20, 22). While the means used are different today, political leaders in our times also "rub shoulders with the crowd."

David's response to his wife demonstrates clearly that he knew what he was doing and what he wanted to achieve. The story of the two emissaries whom David sent to Ammon to express his grief over the death of the king of the Ammonites should also be studied in the context of public opinion. The new King Hanun suspected that the two emissaries were actually spies, and so Hanun "took David's servants, and shaved off the one half of their beards, cut off their garments in the middle, even to their buttocks, and sent them away." The story continues: "When they told it unto David, he sent to meet them, because the men were greatly ashamed: and the king said, 'Tarry at Jericho until your beards be grown, and then return'" (II Samuel 10:4, 5). David knew what the effect would have been if his emissaries had returned home amid ridicule and scorn, and if they had been isolated in public by appearing as fools; he knew that not only the messengers but also the reputation of the king who had dispatched them would suffer.

Erich Lamp, who has analyzed the phenomena of the public eye and public opinion in the Old Testament, states that the literature is not unanimous with regard to the meaning of certain events described in the Bible (Lamp 1988). If a clarified theory of public opinion is to be of service, however, it would cast certain events in a new light, leading to a better understanding of them. It is striking how much more adept David was in dealing with public opinion than his predecessor, King Saul, and his successor, King Solomon—not to mention the latter's unfortunate successor Rechabeam, during whose reign Israel seceded from Judah. Might it not be worth studying successful statesmen and politicians in terms of how accurately they judge public opinion?

John of Salisbury made an interesting remark about Alexander the Great: nothing had so convinced him of Alexander's true statesmanship, he said, as his behavior when a military court handed down a verdict against him. He thanked the judges because their legal convictions had been more important to them than his power, the power of the plaintiff (John of Salisbury [1927] 1963, 130). John of Salisbury also explained why he considered Trajan the greatest of all the pagan Roman emperors: it was said that when Trajan was accused of not keeping a sufficient distance from the people, he responded that he wanted to be the kind of king to his subjects that he would have wanted as king when he was still a subject (ibid., 38). A great ruler's relation to public opinion thus involves a mix of two antithetical elements—charisma and closeness.

In his study of Julius Caesar and public opinion, Zvi Yavetz, an Israeli historian, describes how comfortable Caesar felt in dealing with the masses, while his relationship to the senators was touchy. Yavetz writes that modern historical research has neglected the meaning of *existimatio*. According to Yavetz, *existimatio*—which the dictionary defines as "reputation," "estimation"—was the concept mainly used by the Romans in treating what we now call public opinion (Yavetz 1979, 186ff). *Existimatio* also suggests a statistical estimate, thus establishing a slight connection with the quasi-statistical sense in the theory of the spiral of silence.

My professional experience leads me to believe that successful politicians have a remarkable ability to judge public opinion without recourse to survey research. At the seminar in Mainz, we began to use the questionnaire about books to analyze the works of statesmen. We studied Richelieu, for example. In his "Political

Testament" for King Louis XIII, Richelieu (1585–1642) compares the power of the ruler to a tree with four branches—the army, current revenue, capital assets, and reputation. The fourth branch, reputation, is more important than the other three, for the ruler who enjoys a good reputation achieves more by his name alone than others do with their armies if they are not respected. He shows that his concern is the good opinion of the people. The source of the ruler's power, the root of the tree, is "the treasure of the hearts" (*le trésor des coeurs*) of his subjects. But Richelieu also warns of the "laughter of the world" (*la risée du monde*), which one ought to avoid. With regard to political decisions—like the prohibition of duelling or abolishing the sale of offices—he weighs the pros and cons of these measures with a view to public opinion. Richelieu shows that rational considerations have less weight when moral issues are involved—compared to the "laughter of the world."[4] The newest weapon of journalism—newspapers, which first appeared in 1609—was immediately grasped by Richelieu. He fought his opponents in the *Mercure Français* and later founded his own newspaper, *La Gazette de France*.

Bernd Niedermann concluded his presentation on Richelieu in the seminar at Mainz with the exhortation, "We must use our questionnaire to study Napoleon, Metternich and Bismarck!"

He who loses the support of the people is a king no longer (Aristotle)

Caesar might not have been murdered if he had retained his feel for public opinion. Zvi Yavetz asks, Why did he let his Spanish guards go? If he had been protected by them when he appeared in the Senate, his assassins would probably not have dared to attack him. Did Caesar spend too much time abroad? Did he lose his feel for public opinion as a result? Just three days after the assassination on the Ides of March, he had planned to set out to do battle against the Parthians. Erasmus comes to mind: Erasmus warned the prince that he should not spend too much time abroad lest he lose touch with public opinion. He also said that long absences might make him too different from his people. A successful ruler depends upon a sense of family resemblance between the ruler and his people. Erasmus even warned against the dynastic marriage

---

4. Richelieu [1688] 1947, 220, 236ff., 373–74, 450; the concept of a "world public" comes to mind with the use of "reputation du monde" (p. 104) or "l'opinion de la plus grande partie du monde" (p. 112). See also Albertini 1951, 1:185.

policies of the period: taking a wife from another ruling house creates a distance from one's own people. Would the French Revolution have taken a different course if Louis XVI had not married the Austrian Marie Antoinette? Although the people first greeted her ecstatically on the streets, they later turned their backs on her when her coach appeared.

Homeric laughter

We now go back to even earlier writings, to the *Iliad* and the *Odyssey*—considered the oldest literary texts in the West. They were myths passed on orally for many generations before being written down by Homer in the eighth century B.C. The following analysis is based on Tassilo Zimmermann's master's thesis, which examined the *Iliad* using the questionnaire designed in Mainz.

Homer starts his epic by describing a scene at the beach near Troy. In the second book of the *Iliad,* Agamemnon calls a meeting of the Achaean army and tries to test their morale. He provokes them by listing all the arguments in favor of ending the war, which has lasted almost nine years—the siege of Troy—and of going back home at last. Then the soldiers behave like the flocks of jackdaws described by Konrad Lorenz, which with loud cries suggesting "Off to the woods!" "Off to the fields!" fly back and forth until finally one group gains the upper hand and all fly off in the same direction (Uexküll 1964, 174). The soldiers jump up. Some call, "To the ships! Home again!" while others, especially the army command, the Gerontians, call, "Stop! Stay here! Sit down!" A chaotic scene ensues, with the first soldiers reaching the ships with the intention of pulling them into the water. Odysseus confronts the loudest of the soldiers and stops them with a good beating. He manages to isolate one of the leaders favoring departure, Thersites, and diverts all the anger onto him. Thersites is the perfect scapegoat: "This was the ugliest man . . . He was bandy-legged and went lame of one foot, with shoulders stooped and drawn together over his chest, and above this his skull went up to a point with the wool grown sparsely upon it" (Homer 1951, 2:216ff; See Zimmermann 1988, 72–83). Most of the others are also thinking just what Thersites is shouting and swearing. But now, as Odysseus begins to mock him, Homeric laughter takes hold among the soldiers and Thersites finds himself alone. The army of the Achaeans sits down again and the decision to continue the siege is made.

Although Homer does not say a word about public opinion, he does describe the role of laughter in creating a threat of isolation and determining the process of public opinion. The French medievalist Jacques Le Goff points out that both Hebrew and Greek have two different words for laughter; one is positive, friendly, and bonding, and the other is negative, derisive, setting someone apart. The Romans, whose language was not as rich, reduced laughter to one word (Le Goff 1989, N3).

Accordingly, we began to look for the means by which threats of isolation are perceived. How does an individual realize that he has moved away from the consensus of public opinion? And that he should return if he is not to be isolated and banished from the friendly community? While there are many signals, laughter plays a special part. We shall come back to this point in chapter 26.

Unwritten laws

That the Greeks took the effectiveness of public opinion for granted is evident from their open-minded attitude toward "unwritten laws." The following discussion is based on chapter 2 of Anne Jäckel's master's thesis: "Unwritten Laws in Light of the Social Psychological Theory of Public Opinion."

The earliest passage found thus far in which unwritten laws are mentioned is in Thucydides' (460–400 B.C.) *Peloponnesian War*. It is a speech by Pericles during the first year of the war (431–430 B.C.) that was to result in the demise of Athens. In order to show the grandeur of Athens at the height of its power, Thucydides has Pericles say:

> While we are thus unconstrained in our private intercourse, a spirit of reverence pervades our public acts; we are prevented from doing wrong by respect for authority and for the laws, having an especial regard for those ordained to protect the injured as well as for those unwritten laws which bring upon the transgressor the reprobation of the general sentiment. (Thucydides 1881, 118)

"Unwritten laws" are mentioned by many other Greek authors.[5] But Pericles' words say everything that needs saying: unwritten laws, rather than being less compelling than written laws, tend to be stronger, as John Locke was also to find when he categorized the three kinds of laws (Locke [1690] 1894, 476). Unwritten laws

5. See p. 117 above. See also Noelle-Neumann 1981, 883–88.

are not simply the laws of custom. Custom alone has no power to compel behavior. As John Locke stated, the effect is dependent on knowing that painful punishment will result from a transgression. While the punishment is not set down anywhere in the law, he who believes that this makes it less effective, according to Locke, does not know human nature. The disgrace Pericles speaks of, the loss of honor and reputation among one's fellow citizens, who mete out this punishment with all the force of their jointly held opinion, is among the worst things that can happen to anyone (Thucydides 1881).

Public contempt is the result of violating the moral norms contained in the unwritten laws. Plato states that the relationship between unwritten and written laws is comparable to the relationship between body and soul. Rather than just complementing the written laws, unwritten laws are the very basis of law.

Public opinion in the Nibelungenlied

Students in our seminar persisted in the belief that public opinion had involved only a small elite in past centuries and was therefore relevant only to the upper classes. And yet they had already read that this was not true in the 1588 edition of Montaigne's essays. As previously mentioned (p. 66), Montaigne cited Plato, who had developed a strategy for changing public opinion about pederasty. He specifically stated that following this strategy would ultimately change the opinion of one and all, including women, children, and slaves.

In our Mainz seminar, we not only found the workings of public opinion described by the ancient Greeks but also in the Nibelungenlied, the old Teutonic song cycle, which was set down in written form almost two thousand years after Homer. While the word "public" only appears once in this epic, the occasion is the scene which gives rise to the whole extraordinary tragedy (*Nibelungenlied* 1965, 138). It is the "14th adventure," in which Queen Kriemhild and Queen Brünhild argue at the gates of the church over who is to go in first. The church square is crowded, just as it would be today if two queens happened to be there. Queen Kriemhild reviles Queen Brünhild "in front of all the people" for having slept with Siegfried rather than her own husband Gunther on her wedding night. Who would claim that in former times reputation and public opinion were established only by the upper classes?

A cartoon from 1641

When David Hume stated, "It is . . . on opinion only that government is founded" (Hume [1739/1740] 1963, 29), he was merely repeating what Aristotle had said two thousand years before and what those who had studied Aristotle's *Politics,* such as Machiavelli and Erasmus, would later say. Hume must have taken the idea of the rule of public opinion very much for granted after everything that had occurred during the two English revolutions of the seventeenth century. An English cartoon entitled "The World is Ruled and Governed by Opinion" appeared in 1641, predating the beheading of Charles I by eight years (Haller 1965).[6] This cartoon provides a map, as it were, of how much of the nature of public opinion had been discovered at the time.

"What meaneth that Chameleon on thy fist / That can assume all Cullors saving white" the young nobleman asks public opinion, who is perched in the treetop. "OPINION thus can everie waie shee list / Transforme herself save into TRUTH, the right" is the answer. "And why those saplings from the roots that rise / In such abundance of OPINIONS tree?" asks the young nobleman. "Cause one Opinion many doth devise / And propagate till infinite they bee," he is informed. "And Ladie what's the Fruite, which from the tree / Is shaken of with everie little wind? / Like Bookes and papers this amuseth mee / Beside thou seemest (veiled) to bee blind?"

The response confirms the point made by Plato that public opinion includes everyone—slaves and free men, women and children, and the entire citizenry. For these fruits of public opinion, newspapers and books, certainly do not merely relate to the upper classes. They are found on all the streets and in all the shopwindows. And the last two lines of the dialogue emphasize that they are found everywhere—in every house, on every street.

And why is such a far-reaching matter as public opinion watered by a "sillie Foole"? Well, it is the fool who imbues it with real life. It is up to us to imagine what present-day fools who "water" public opinion look like.

Absence of the concept of public opinion in apolitical germany

German political culture has never been especially attentive to the concept of public opinion. It appears for the first time in Ger-

6. I would like to thank Dieter Reigber, the archivist at the Institut für Demoskopie Allensbach, for calling my attention to this cartoon.

THE WORLD IS RVLED & GOVERNED by OPINION.

Viator	Who art thou Ladie that aloft art set	*Viator.*	Cannot OPINION remedie the fame
	In state Maiestique this faire fpredding	*Opinio*	An no then should I perish in the throng
	Vpon thine head a Towre-like Coronet.		O'th giddie Vulgar. without feare-fhame
	The Worldes whole Compasse *resting on thy hand*		Who confure all thinges, bee they right -----
Opinio	I am OPINION who the world do swaie	*Viator*	But Ladie deare whence came at first *the beam*
	Wherefore I beare it on my head that *time*		Or why doth WISEDOME fuffer it to grow
	L BABELS meaning my confufed waie		And whats the reafon its farre reaching -----
	The Tree so shaken, my unfetled Bowre		Is water'd by a sillie Foole below
Viator	What meaneth that Chameleon on thy fist	*Opinio*	Becaufe that FOLLIE giveth life to thefe
	That can afsume all Cullors faving white		Ibut retaile the fruites of idle Aire
Opinio	OPINION thus can everie waie shee lift		Sith now all Humors utter what they *plede*
	Transforme her self save true TRVTH *she repels*		Toth loathing loading of each Mart *and faire*
Viator	And Ladie whats the Fruite, which from *the tree*	*Viator*	And why thofe faplings from the roote that *rise*
	L shaken of with everie little wind		In such abundance of OPINIONS tree
	Like Bookes and papers this amufeth mee	*Opinio*	Caufe one Opinion many doth devife
	Befide thou feemest (veiled) to bee blind		And propagate, till infinite they bee
Opinio	Tis true I cannot as cleare IVDGMENTS fee	*Viator*	Adieu fweete Ladie till againe wee meete
	Through felf CONCEIT and haughtie PRIDE	*Opinio*	But when shall that againe bee I *entr* Ladie *is te*
	The fruite thofe idle bookes and libells bee	*Opinio*	Opinions found in everie house and street
	In everie ftreete. on everie ftall you find		And going ever never in her waie

VIRO CLA: D: FRANCISCO PRVLEANO D: MEDICO. OMNIVM BONARVM AR
hum et Elegantiarum fautori et Admiratori summo. D. D. D.   *Henricus Peacamius*

Engraving by Wenceslas Hollar, 1641. British Museum Catalogue of
Satirical Prints, 272.

man much later than it does in English, French or Italian, and when it does appear, it is merely as a direct translation from the French *opinion publique*. For a while we thought that Klopstock had been the first to mention it in his ode "An die öffentliche Meinung" ("To public opinion") of 1798. By the time the 1980 German edition of the *Spiral of Silence* was completed, the earliest instance we had found was one of the "Gespräche unter vier Augen" ("têtes-à-tête") by Wieland: "Über die öffentliche Meinung" ("About public opinion") of 1798. It was not until later that we discovered Johannes von Müller, the Swiss who used the expression "public opinion" for the first time in German in 1777 (Müller [1777] 1819, 41). Johannes von Müller was a professional historian—today we would call him a political scientist and a journalist—who gave talks all over Germany and was invited to serve as a political consultant. He was probably instrumental in disseminating the concept of public opinion.

For all to see, for all to hear
There are still problems with translating the concept today, as there were in 1980. One example is the difficulty of capturing the social-psychological dimension of "public," a condition in which the individual is seen and judged by one and all, so that his reputation and popularity are at stake. The social-psychological meaning of public can be gathered only indirectly from linguistic usage. Saying that something happened "in the spotlight" tells us what is involved. No one would say that a concert took place "in the spotlight." The Latin expression *coram publico* already had the very same associations.

The French humanist and novelist François Rabelais, a contemporary of Erasmus, did not hesitate to use the terms "in front of everybody," "in front of the whole world," and *publicquement* (Rabelais 1955, 206, 260, 267). It was a great surprise to find that even in the twentieth century *in aller Öffentlichkeit*, or *publicquement*, could hardly be translated into English. I spent weeks trying to find a solution by talking with colleagues and students in Chicago. To no avail. One day I was in a taxi in New York and the driver was listening to the news. When I chanced to hear the newscaster conclude an item by saying, "The public eye has its price," I sat up—that was the translation. *In aller Öffentlichkeit*—in the public eye. This captured the social-psychological meaning of the German concept *Öffentlichkeit:* for all to see.

Gunnar Schanno, one of my students at the Mainz seminar, found that this usage originated with Edmund Burke in 1791 (Burke [1791] 1826, 79). Burke referred not only to the "public eye" but also to the "public ear," which we translated as *vor aller Ohren*. Both expressions hit the nail on the head. The context in which Burke used these expressions was also interesting. He was discussing what it was that made a natural aristocrat, for example getting accustomed to being subject to public criticism from an early stage: being in the public eye. Burke continued "to look early to public opinion" (Burke, 217). Erasmus and Machiavelli had already taught the princes that they were not to hide from the public but rather must learn to be visible (Erasmus [1518] 1968, 201; Machiavelli [1532] 1971, chap. 18).

Nietzsche as an inspiration to Walter Lippmann

Much of what nineteenth-century German writers wrote about public opinion and man's social nature seems not yet to have been discovered. It was almost by accident that Kurt Braatz found a reference in Harwood Childs to a German author of the mid-nineteenth century who had fallen into complete oblivion in Germany: he was mentioned neither by Ferdinand Tönnies, the leading theoretician of public opinion of the first half of the twentieth century, nor by Wilhelm Bauer, the leading historian. Childs's reference was to Carl Ernst August Freiherr von Gersdorff, a lifetime member of the Upper Chamber of Parliament in Prussia and a doctor of philosophy, whose "Ueber den Begriff und das Wesen der oeffentlichen Meinung. Ein Versuch" was published in 1846. Childs probably came across it when studying in Germany in the 1930s but did not mention it until he wrote *Public Opinion* in the mid-sixties.

It was only because Braatz took a special interest in Nietzsche that the similarity of the name to that of Nietzsche's friend and secretary Carl von Gersdorff struck him. In his research, he discovered that the young man who had helped Nietzsche, particularly in working on the *Unzeitgemäße Betrachtungen* ("Untimely Meditations") was the son of the man who had written about public opinion. And even though Nietzsche never mentions either these writings or the father's name, the fact that he began to take an interest in public opinion during these very years, frequently mentioning it in his writings, is striking. To verify that Nietzsche had taken a special interest in the phenomenon of public opinion, Braatz wrote to the Nietzsche Archives in Weimar, where Nietzsche's private library is stored, requesting the archivists to check whether important passages on public opinion were marked in books by certain authors or whether notes had been made in the margin. In a systematic study of the writings by the older von Gersdorff compared with Nietzsche's statements about public opinion, Braatz was eventually able to show that many of von Gersdorff's ideas in the field of social psychology were adopted by Nietzsche (Braatz 1988). Von Gersdorff describes public opinion as we see it today: "Public opinion, as I see it, must always exist in intellectual life . . . as long as people lead a social life. . . . It can thus never fail to exist nor be lacking nor be destroyed, *it is everywhere and always.*" It is not subject to any limitations by subject and it can "best be termed: 'the commonality of values a people assigns to the social subjects of its times, which is based in customs and history and is created, maintained and transformed by life's conflicts.'" "In addition, it is known that public opinion is the common property of an entire people" (Gersdorff 1846, 10, 12, 5).

Gersdorff suspects that much of the power of public opinion derives from the fearful silence of many individuals. He suggests "investigating the reasons for the silent abstention from making value judgments." Von Gersdorff also explicitly states that opinion-formation processes are hardly the result of rational considerations, but rather are of psycho-anthropological origin. He writes of "galvanic currents." For a modern public opinion researcher this immediately calls to mind the way a change in a population's attitudes takes place in all groups of a population within only a few weeks' time—in all geographic areas, in all age groups, in all social classes.

During his study of Nietzsche's ideas on public opinion, Braatz found a variety of connections which I had not been aware of at the time when the first edition of the *Spiral of Silence* was published. He discovered the first use of the concept of "social control" by Herbert Spencer in 1879 (Spencer [1879] 1966, 383), a term subsequently taken up by Edward Ross, who was responsible for establishing it in the social sciences.

Our admiration for the grand scale of Walter Lippmann's *Public Opinion* of 1922 is not diminished by the impression, based on a comparison of texts, that many of his ideas were probably anticipated by Nietzsche. This applies to the role of stereotypes as vehicles of public opinion as well as to his guiding principle that the point of view of the observer shapes what is observed. Nietzsche writes: "There is *only* seeing from a certain perspective, *only* 'understanding' from a certain perspective" (Nietzsche 1967, 383). Even the bizarre practice of distinguishing between *Public Opinion* (capitalized) and *public opinion* (not capitalized) goes back to Nietzsche's analysis rather than being Lippmann's own idea.

In the mid-thirties, after the method of representative population surveys had proved itself by accurately predicting the outcome of the U.S. presidential elections of 1936, expectations for the field of public opinion research were high. A few months later the first issue of the new journal *Public Opinion Quarterly* appeared. It contained an introductory essay by Floyd H. Allport titled "Toward a Science of Public Opinion." Twenty years later, in 1957, the same confidence was expressed in the title of Herbert H. Hyman's essay "Toward a Theory of Public Opinion," also published in *Public Opinion Quarterly.*

The next time this key word figured in a review article in *Public Opinion Quarterly,* in 1970, there were signs of impatience. The proceedings of the 25th Annual Conference of the American Association for Public Opinion Research had included a report on a session titled "Toward a Theory of Public Opinion." The main speakers were psychologist Brewster Smith and the political scientist Sidney Verba from the University of Chicago. The psychologist stated that research has "not yet faced the problem of how opinions of individuals articulate to produce social and political consequences. The problem of articulation implied in any conception of public opinion as a social fact is primary agenda for political science and for sociology" (Smith 1970, 454). The political scientist maintained: "Much political public opinion research is irrelevant for the development of macro-political theory dealing with the relationship between mass attitudes and behavior and significant political outcomes. The main reason for this irrelevancy is the focus in most public opinion research on the individual citizen as a unit of analysis" (Verba 1970, 455).

Basically, both speakers were seeking an answer to the same question: How does the sum of individual opinions as determined by public opinion research translate into the awesome political power known as "public opinion?"

No feel for public opinion

The answer took so long to find because nobody was looking for an awesome political power. Not one of the fifty definitions of public opinion compiled by Harwood Childs in the famous second chapter of his book *Public Opinion* explicitly focuses on the power of public opinion (Childs 1965, 12–41). Instead, several definitions confuse the barometer with the weather, so to speak. "Public opinion consists of people's reactions to definitely worded statements and questions under interview conditions" (Warner 1939, 377). Or: "Public opinion is not the name of a something, but a classification of a number of somethings, which, on statistical distribution in a frequency distribution, present modes or frequencies that command attention and interest" (Beyle 1931, 183).

How could frequency distributions statistically arranged topple a government or fill an individual with fear?

The spiral of silence is not compatible with the democratic ideal

It was to be expected that the spiral of silence theory was not hailed as progress toward a theory of public opinion when it was first presented at the 1972 International Congress of Psychology in Tokyo or in 1980 or 1984 when my book appeared in German and English respectively. There was no room here for the informed, responsible citizen, the ideal upon which democratic theory is based. Fear of public opinion—fear on the part of the government and of the individual—is not provided for by classical democratic theory. Democratic theory does not deal with topics such as the social nature of man, social psychology, or what creates cohesion in society.

A German-American research team consisting of Wolfgang Donsbach from the University of Mainz and Robert L. Stevenson from the University of North Carolina at Chapel Hill tested the hypotheses of the spiral of silence in the North Carolina Poll surveys conducted by the university's Institute for Communication Research. They were able to confirm the tendency for one side to remain silent on the controversial issue of abortion legislation. At the same time they were pessimistic about the possibilities of defending the spiral of silence. The theory consists, they wrote, of a long chain of theses, a chain of causal relations. "The chain begins in micro-sociological terms with the social-psychological variable of fear of isolation and with the tendency to speak out or remain silent, and in macro-sociological terms with integration into society" (Donsbach and Stevenson 1986, 14; see also 7). Every link in the chain offered points for criticism. The theory also linked theses from a variety of different social sciences which are traditionally viewed separately, namely hypotheses about behavior and attitude theory, from communication theory and from social theory (ibid., 8ff.). Perhaps they were right in maintaining that the theory's failure to respect the borders between the different disciplines put it at a disadvantage. At that time scholars were often not particularly interested in dialogues with related disciplines.

What one must know to analyze public opinion

Progress toward a theory of public opinion can only be achieved with a clear definition of the concept and knowledge of the conditions required for the empirical study of public opinion. To facilitate this endeavor, I have constructed a list of six basic questions, the answers to which provide the minimum of information necessary to test the spiral of silence theory (Noelle-Neumann 1989a, 20):

1. Using relevant representative survey methods, the distribution of public opinion on a given issue should be determined.

2. The climate of opinion must be assessed, the individual's opinion on "What do most people think?" This often results in an entirely new picture.

3. How does the public think the controversial issue will develop: Which side will gain strength, which side will lose ground?

4. The willingness to speak out on a particular issue or the tendency to remain silent, especially in public, should be measured.

5. Does the issue in question bear a strong emotional or moral component? Without such a component, there is no pressure of public opinion and therefore no spiral of silence.

6. What is the position of the media on this issue? Which side do the influential media support? The media are one of two sources from which people derive their assessment of the climate of opinion. The influential media lend words and arguments to other journalists and those who support their side, thus influencing the process of public opinion and the tendency to speak out or to remain silent.

The silent majority does not refute the spiral of silence

Some researchers who have tested the spiral of silence have suggested disregarding the media as a factor, at least initially, to simplify their studies (See Glynn and McLeod 1985, 44). Doing this would, however, refute the spiral of silence theory wherever the tone of the media diverges greatly from public opinion. Not in a single instance has the process of the spiral of silence run counter to the line taken by the media. The fact that an individual is aware that his or her opinion is supported by the media is an important factor in determining that person's willingness to speak out. One example of this in Germany was the question of whether or not members of the Communist Party could be judges (see above, p. 169). Although the minority in favor was certainly small enough and was also aware of its minority status, it was far more willing to speak out than the majority. The majority, which sensed that it lacked support from the media, evolved into a silent majority. The English cartoonist of 1641 (discussed in the previous chapter) had good reason for showing the tree of public opinion with newspapers and books hanging from it. As with many issues, the question of whether Communist Party members should be judges became almost incomprehensible after the passage of one or two decades. The pressure exerted by public opinion disappeared completely, like thunder clouds dispersing. Even by poring over newspapers of the time, yellowed with age, it would be impossible to develop a feeling for the tenor of the media against the so-called "decree on radicals," which forbade the appointment of avowed communists to civil service posts.

Assumptions of the theory

With the help of the six questions listed above we can design case studies and make predictions. On an issue such as nuclear energy with a clear-cut media position and a strong moral component regarding the safety of future generations, the opponents of nuclear energy might be expected to be more willing to speak out in public and to appear much stronger in the climate of opinion than the supporters (Kepplinger 1988, 1989a). This assumption was confirmed by Sabine Mathes in her master's thesis for the University of Mainz (Mathes 1989). Only after the supporters have been reduced to a hard core can they be expected to show a greater willingness to speak out in public than the opponents. (See the discussion of "hard core" near the end of this chapter.)

What is the theory behind the analysis of such a case study? Let us review the main points in brief. The theory of the spiral of silence is based on the assumption that society—and not just groups in which the members are known to each other—threatens with isolation and exclusion those individuals who deviate from the consensus. Individuals, in turn, have a largely subconscious fear of isolation, which probably is genetically determined. This fear of isolation causes people constantly to check which opinions and modes of behavior are approved or disapproved of in their environment, and which opinions and forms of behavior are gaining or losing strength. The theory postulates the existence of a quasi-statistical sense for making such assessments. The results of these assessments affect people's willingness to speak out, as well as their behavior in general. If people believe that their opinion is part of a consensus, they have the confidence to speak out in both private and public discussions, displaying their convictions with buttons and car stickers, for example, but also by the clothes they wear and other publicly visible symbols. Conversely, when people feel that they are in the minority, they become cautious and silent, thus reinforcing the impression of weakness, until the apparently weaker side disappears completely except for a hard core that holds on to its previous values, or until the opinion becomes taboo.

Testing the theory is complicated because it is based on four separate assumptions as well as a fifth one that deals with the interrelations between the previous four.

The four assumptions are:

1. Society threatens deviant individuals with isolation.
2. Individuals experience fear of isolation continuously.
3. Because of this fear of isolation, individuals are constantly trying to assess the climate of opinion.
4. The results of this estimate affect behavior in public, particularly the open expression or concealment of opinions.

The fifth assumption is that the above assumptions are connected and thus provides an explanation for the formation, maintenance, and alteration of public opinion.

Any empirical test of these assumptions requires that they be translated into observable indicators in situations which can be recorded in survey interviews.

Testing the threat of isolation

Does public opinion exert a threat of isolation? Does public opinion employ the threat of isolation to defend itself against individuals holding deviant opinions? Is it through the threat of isolation that public opinion gains acceptance? We view ourselves as a liberal society. "Liberal" has a nice ring to it according to 52 percent of the German population,[1] and "tolerance" is a virtue which 64 percent of today's German parents want to instill in their children.[2]

To threaten a person who deviates from the generally held public opinion is certainly intolerant. That is the reason it is so difficult to ask questions about this topic in an interview. Nevertheless, we were able to describe several forms of the threat of isolation in the 1984 edition of *The Spiral of Silence*. One example is the questionnaire item dealing with the slashing of the tires on a car that bears a sticker for a party disapproved of by the respondent (see above, pp. 52ff.). As part of our election surveys, we also use a question about a driver who is a stranger in a city and is refused information by a pedestrian. The question ends: "I should mention that the driver is wearing a political badge on his jacket. What do you think: which party did this badge support?" We also ask a question about which party's posters were most often defaced or torn down, which we regard as a measure of the public threat of isolation against supporters of this party (see above, pp. 55ff.).

In Mainz, we began to delve seriously into the topic of how the threat of isolation works. Sabine Holicki (1984) wrote a master's thesis titled "The Threat of Isolation—Sociopsychological Aspects of a Concept in Communications Theory." A second master's thesis, by Angelika Albrecht, (1983), was titled "Laughing and Smiling: Isolation or Integration?" We recalled that Stanley Milgram had resourcefully used acoustic signals such as whistling, booing, and derisive laughter as signs of the threat of isolation (see above, p. 40). But it was not until 1989 that the test we had sought for so long finally occurred to me. All one had to do was keep in mind the signals of conformist behavior described in the literature on the field and those dealing with laughter described in social psychology, even though there was no mention of public opinion in these studies (Nosanchuk and Lightstone 1974; Berlyne 1969).

We applied the new test immediately to the issue of nuclear energy, using the indicators of booing and derisive laughter. The text of the question read: "I would like to tell you about an incident which recently took place at a large public meeting on nuclear energy. There were two main speakers: One spoke in favor of nuclear energy and the other opposed it. One of the speakers was booed by

---

1. Allensbach Archives, IfD Survey 4005, question 21, February 1982.
2. Allensbach Archives, IfD Survey 5013, question 20B, November 1988.

Table 27. Testing the threat of isolation in Germany and England: Nuclear energy

Question: "I would like to tell you about an incident which took place recently at a large public meeting on nuclear energy. There were two main speakers: One spoke in favor of nuclear energy and the other opposed it. One of the speakers was booed by the audience. Which one do you think was booed: the speaker supporting nuclear energy or the speaker opposing it?"

	February 1989 Federal Republic of Germany (%)	March 1989 Great Britain (%)
Supporter of nuclear energy	72	62
Opponent of nuclear energy	11	25
Undecided	17	13
	100	100

Source: Germany: Institut für Demoskopie Allensbach, IfD Survey 5016, question 38, 2,213 respondents. Great Britain: Social Surveys (Gallup Poll) Limited, approximately 1,000 respondents.

the audience. Which one do you think was booed: the speaker supporting nuclear energy or the speaker opposing it?" Seventy-two percent of German respondents were of the opinion that the speaker in favor of nuclear energy had been booed; 11 percent assumed that the opponent of nuclear energy had been booed. Only 17 percent remained undecided (see table 27).[3]

There is no doubt that the threat of isolation exists and that the public knows which opinions run a high risk of triggering the threat of isolation when publicly expressed. Just a few weeks after we applied it, the same test was applied in England. Our colleague, Robert J. Wybrow, included the question in an omnibus survey with 1,000 interviews and released the results shortly thereafter. In England too, the climate of opinion was clearly against supporters of nuclear energy, though not to the same extent.

There can be no doubt that such a hostile climate of opinion influences an individual's willingness to speak out or remain silent. The fact that the respondents in England accepted the test question

3. Allensbach Archives, IfD Survey 5016, question 38, February 1989.

was important, however. Any theory of public opinion must be internationally applicable. While it may include points specific to the country in question, it must be possible to confirm the essence of these studies on an international basis.

Thus the tests must also be applicable in a variety of cultures. I thought of the civilized manner of social intercourse in Japan and had doubts about the new threat of isolation test being suitable for use in that culture. For even American students felt affronted when I described the test in which the tires on a car bearing a sticker for an unpopular party had been slashed.

When I discussed the test question with Hiroaki Minato, a Japanese student in one of my seminars at the University of Chicago, he rejected the feasibility of applying the boo test question in Japan. After we had discussed a wide variety of options, he said: "This is the way the situation would be in Japan." The revised text for Japan now reads: "There was a debate about nuclear energy at a neighborhood meeting. One person present spoke out in favor of nuclear energy, while another spoke out against it. One of the two later heard that there had been gossip behind his back condemning him. What do you think: Which of the two was condemned behind his back?"

Testing the fear of isolation

Many Americans were discomfited by the fear-of-isolation experiments conducted by Asch and Milgram (see pp. 37ff., above). Milgram repeated his experiments—with a modified design—in France and Norway, because he wanted to know whether conformist behavior was as prevalent in Europe as it seemed to be in America.

The thought that Americans could experience fear of isolation so offended the students during one of my lectures at the University of Chicago that many walked out of the auditorium. It was obviously impossible to ask in an interview, "Do you have a fear of isolation?" even though this same question had actually been asked in America in testing the spiral of silence. The theory had often been criticized for what was felt to be too great an emphasis on the irrational and emotional motives for conformity; it was claimed that I underestimated the good and rational reasons for it. This is, of course, a traditional area of contention between European and American social scientists, with Americans favoring rational explanations for human behavior.

One method for testing the fear of isolation is described in chapter 3 above (pp. 42ff.). In the "threat test," smokers were intimidated when confronted with a sketch showing one person saying angrily: "I think smokers are terribly inconsiderate. They force others to inhale their unhealthy smoke." But we were still far removed from being able to satisfy our American colleagues' demand that we find a method for actually measuring the fear of isolation (See Glynn and McLeod 1985, 47ff., 60).

We experienced a breakthrough while looking at research that went back to Charles Darwin in the nineteenth century and which led in the 1940s and 1950s to the flourishing area of research known as group dynamics.[4] The focus here was on questions relating to group cohesion: What is the stability of a group based on? What does the group do when individual members violate the rules and threaten the group's existence? Sabine Holicki (1984) came upon research in this area while tracking down material on the threat and fear of isolation. She found that experiments in the area of group dynamics had recorded a three-phase process. In the first phase the group uses friendly persuasion to try to win back the deviant member. If this does not work, the deviant individual is threatened with exclusion from the group. If this too fails, "the group redefines its boundaries" (in the idiom of group dynamics), meaning that the deviant individual is excluded from the group (Cartwright and Zander [1953] 1965, 145).

We are reminded here of Edward Ross's phrase, "until the dead member drops from the social body" (see pp. 95–96, above). One thing is strange: researchers in the field of group dynamics studied how groups maintain cohesion but stopped there. Why didn't they go one step further and investigate what holds society as a whole together? Had they taken this step, they would have had to deal with the phenomenon of public opinion as an instrument of social control.

But the term "public opinion" is never mentioned in connection with group dynamics. Nor does it appear in the writings of Erving Goffman, whose systematic research in the 1950s and 1960s took up where Montaigne left off around 350 years ago. According to Goffman, as soon as people are no longer alone—even with only

---

4. For examples of research conducted in the early stages of this field of research in the 1930s, see Moreno [1934], 1953; Lewin [1935–1946], 1948; Sherif [1936], 1965.

one other person present, and even more so when there are many—they are transformed by the awareness that others are forming an opinion about them. Goffman focused on the public from the point of view of social psychology, illuminating an area that had formerly been ignored. *Behavior in Public Places* was the laconic title of one of his pioneering works (Goffman 1963a). All of Goffman's books published between 1955 and 1971 (e.g., 1956, 1963b) reflect his preoccupation with the social nature of man and the suffering created by that social nature.

In the course of his studies on personality, Goffman found Darwin's description of the many physical symptoms pointing to the social nature of man. We too can usefully refer to Darwin's *The Expression of the Emotions in Man and Animals* (1873) in our search for evidence of man's fear of isolation. In chapter 13 of that work, Darwin turns his attention to the topic of embarrassment and describes the physical symptoms associated with it, such as blushing, turning pale, sweating, stuttering, nervous gestures, trembling hands, a tight, cracked or abnormally high or low voice, unnatural grinning, looking away—about which Darwin comments that people try to avoid noticing that they are being observed by reducing eye contact (Darwin 1873, 330).

Darwin distinguishes between two sides of human nature, one oriented outward and the other inward. When the individual orients himself outward, he conforms to his social nature; this is confirmed by objective signs, such as blushing, which is not found in animals. Darwin makes a distinction between feelings of guilt, shame, and embarrassment: a person may be deeply ashamed of a minor lie without blushing, but he will blush as soon as he believes that his lie has been detected. Shyness, Darwin states, leads to blushing. But shyness is merely a sensitivity to what *others* may think of us.

Darwin never uses the term "public opinion." Although he never mentions the fear of isolation, his observations clearly indicate that man's social nature causes him to reflect upon the opinions of others, to consider how he is seen by the outside world and to hope that he creates a favorable impression so that no one can point a finger at him, whether explicitly or implicitly. Even the public attention created by good deeds is embarrassing to many people.

Erving Goffman, to the contrary, assumed that embarrassment was a form of mild punishment, forcing people to abide by certain rules of conduct in public (Goffman 1956, 265, 270ff.). This assumption was refuted by Michael Hallemann in his doctoral thesis written at the University of Mainz. Hallemann showed embarrassment to be a reaction to any situation in which an individual feels isolated, even if he is thrust into the limelight as a hero for having saved a child from drowning (see table 28 below).

Table 28. Cross-Cultural Comparison of Embarrassing Situations in Germany, Spain, and Korea

Question: "These cards describe some situations people might find themselves in at one time or another. Could you please distribute the cards onto this sheet according to whether you would find the situation embarrassing or not? Just put aside the cards with situations you have no opinion on."

(Presentation of a set of cards and a list with the categories: "Would find embarrassing;" "Would not find embarrassing.")

"Would find embarrassing"	Federal Republic of Germany (%)	Spain (%)	South Korea (%)
Somebody slaps you in public	79	83	92
You are unjustly accused of being a shoplifter by an employee in a store	78	89	88
In a department store you accidentally knock over and shatter a valuable crystal glass	76	84	92
While at a restaurant, you spill soup on your pants	70	73	74
You are at the cash register in the supermarket with a cartful of groceries when you discover you don't have any money with you	69	65	84
You are at the theater and have a cold, but you don't have a handkerchief with you	68	66	41
You are attending a concert with a friend. Your friend falls asleep and starts to snore	63	59	63
In a group you're standing with, someone is being discussed who is listening all the while and then joins the group	56	51	64

(continued)

Table 28. (*Continued*)

"Would find embarrassing"	Federal Republic of Germany (%)	Spain (%)	South Korea (%)
Someone makes fun of you in front of others	56	68	76
In the middle of a busy street you suddenly slip and fall down flat on your face	56	76	75
In the train, you open the door to the toilet in the restroom, and someone is sitting there who has forgotten to lock the door	55	71	88
You address someone by the wrong name	52	37	65
You are at a friend's house when you happen to enter a room where someone is undressing	50	73	94
You find yourself in the same room as an old friend you're eager to say hello to, but he walks out without so much as a glance in your direction	49	46	64
You meet an old friend whose name you can't think of	45	41	66
You feel sweaty after doing some work, but you have to go shopping before you can wash up	44	44	22
You are planning to spend a vacation with friends. When you arrive at your destination, you discover that what is involved is a nudist beach	43	59	-
You are in a train and the ticket collector comes, but you can't find your ticket	-	-	92
You tell a joke to friends and no one laughs	40	41	46
The plumber comes and your apartment is messy	36	43	36

(*continued*)

Table 28. (*Continued*)

"Would find embarrassing"	Federal Republic of Germany (%)	Spain (%)	South Korea (%)
Because you did your laundry too late, it's still hanging on the line to dry on Easter Sunday (Korea: on New Year's Day)	33	17	28
You have to make an important telephone call that takes a bit longer than usual from a public phone booth. There are two or three people in line behind you	31	49	69
You are approached by a television reporter with his TV camera on	28	39	74
By chance you succeed in saving a small child from drowning. As a result, a reporter absolutely insists on taking your picture for the local paper	27	37	62
You run out of butter or margarine at the weekend and have to go to the neighbors to borrow some	27	27	40
You notice around noon that your shoes haven't been cleaned	26	25	11
In a hotel room you can hear what is going on in the room next door through the thin walls	24	33	35
You run into someone on the street and don't know whether you should greet him	23	37	48
In a train compartment that is half empty, one of the other travelers suddenly begins talking to himself	15	31	23
You dial the wrong number when phoning	12	16	26
You are addressed by the wrong name	12	18	28
	1343	1498	1766
n =	2009	1499	352

- = not asked

Sources: Germany: Allensbach Archives, IfD Survey 4031, August 1983. Population 16 and over.
Spain: DATA, S.A., June 1984. Population 15 and over.
South Korea: Tokinoya, September 1986. Population 20 and over.

Van Zuuren (1983) describes a group of young Dutch social scientists conducting self-experiments about embarrassing situations. Stopping to chat in the midst of a busy pedestrian zone, for example, the group was able to experience what it felt like to be the target of angry, disapproving looks. In a half-empty cafe they joined another couple at a table and observed their own reactions at this infringement of an unspoken rule. They went into a store twice and purchased the same item within a short period of time. One task involved taking the elevator up to the top floor in an unfamiliar apartment house and just looking around. One of the participants in the experiment said that she was afraid she would not know what to say if someone were to ask her what she was doing there. "Suddenly I realized how grotesque I must look with my pink slacks and my pink blouse."

These self-experiments showed that there is a type of internal personal control which filters behavior prior to social control, anticipating the threat of isolation. The mere thought of how unpleasant a situation *could* be causes an individual to correct behavior divergent from the public consensus before external social control is exercised by the collective, and even before the collective learns of the intended infraction. Indeed, many of the participants in the Dutch self-experiments did not go through with the actions they had planned. This is the area of "symbolic interaction" described by George Herbert Mead of the University of Chicago. The "symbolic interaction," the thought of what others would think or how they would react, influences the individual as if it were reality. But this world of silent debates held within one's own mind, with the fear created by man's social nature, was so foreign to Mead's contemporaries in the social sciences that he never published a second book. One of his main works, "1927 Class Lectures in Social Psychology" (in Mead 1982), which is today read and used in seminars on public opinion, is based on notes compiled by Mead's students.

Embarrassment as a manifestation of man's social nature

How does the individual recognize the threat of isolation? What are the signals? How does the individual experience the fear of isolation and how can it be measured? A group of students in a Mainz "workshop seminar" planned a self-experiment. In Germany the carnival in Mainz is an important event which may be assumed to be supported by a public consensus. The students set up a stand on a busy street and hung a banner to drum up membership in a newly founded organization—an organization opposed to money being wasted on the annual carnival in Mainz. The leaflets argued that the money would be better spent in helping the Third World. The leaflets were piled in big stacks on the stand and the students tried to distribute them to passersby and to gather signatures for their cause. One of the students filmed the event from a neighboring house, making it possible to analyze the types of behavior exhibited (Ewen et al. 1981–82). Even the shop owners on the adjacent streets participated. They tried to detour passersby around the stand with gestures clearly indicating they thought the students were crazy.

The experience of having people turn their backs when he approached and of seeing others immediately go out of their way to avoid him, made such a strong impression on Michael Hallemann that he devoted his master's and doctoral theses to the subject (Hallemann 1984, 1989; see also 1986).

In a representative survey, the Allensbach Institute presented respondents with a drawing. Male respondents were shown the picture of two men, and females the picture of two women. In each, one person is saying to the other: "Can you imagine what happened to me yesterday—it was so embarrassing: I . . . " The interviewer then says: "Here are two people talking. Unfortunately, the man/woman got interrupted in mid-sentence. But what do you think he or she wanted to say, what could have happened to him or her?" After analyzing the replies from approximately 2,000 respondents, Hallemann designed thirty situations. During the next Allensbach survey, interviewers presented these situations, written on separate cards, to respondents, with the question: "These cards describe some situations people might find themselves in at one time or another. Could you please distribute the cards on this sheet according to whether you would find the situation embarrassing or not?"[5]

The various embarrassing situations are listed in table 28, along with the findings from the Federal Republic of Germany, Spain, and Korea. In June 1989, researchers replicated the series of questions.[6] There appeared to be hardly any change in what people find embarrassing. The results of the replicated survey were almost identical to those of the first survey. Until this test, we had

5. See Allensbach Archives, IfD Survey 4031, August 1983.
6. See Allensbach Archives, IfD Survey 5021, June 1989.

Figure 24

Ascertaining embarrassing situations

Illustration for sentence completion test used in interview. By projecting themselves into the situation of the portrayed individual and by being compelled to complete the sentence, respondents are more easily able to associate with an embarrassing situation

Figure 25

Ascertaining embarrassing situations

Illustration for sentence completion test used in interview. By projecting themselves into the situation of the portrayed individual and by being compelled to complete the sentence, respondents are more easily able to associate with an embarrassing situation

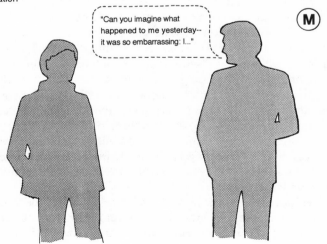

assumed that embarrassment depended largely on cultural traditions and would vary greatly from country to country. At least in Germany, Spain, and Korea, there is a surprising similarity between the situations perceived as embarrassing.

Goffman (1956, 270) wrote that if we want to learn more about man's social nature, we must study the situations that cause embarrassment. Because we cannot ask people directly about their social nature—most people would much rather ignore their social nature (the majority of Germans maintain: "I don't care what others think of me")—we must search for indicators, as Emile Durkheim stated in *The Rules of Sociological Method* (1895). Indicators are not identical with what one is looking for but they provide insight into what we want to study.

Measuring the fear of isolation

The publication of *The Spiral of Silence* raised a host of difficult questions. Social research had focused on the area of group dynamics since the 1930s, and so one criticism was that the various groups to which an individual belongs are much more influential than the undefined public the theory focused on. People place far greater importance on what their neighbors, colleagues, fellow club members, and reference group members say and think than on what strangers in an anonymous public do.

Donsbach and Stevenson tried to refute this objection (1986, 10ff). They stated that the spiral of silence was not meant to be a deterministic theory seizing upon one particular factor—for example, the fear of isolation—as the sole determinant of an individual's behavior, affecting all people in the same manner. The fear of isolation in public is one of several factors determining the process of public opinion. Reference groups also play a role. They cited a study conducted by the Dutch scholar Harm t'Hart, showing that whether the opinions of the primary reference group are reinforced by or are in opposition to the pressure of public opinion, or whether the groups a person is involved with continue to defend views that are in the minority, is important in determining whether a person will speak out or remain silent in defense of his opinion on a controversial issue (t'Hart 1981).

After decades of successful social research in the area of group dynamics, the influence of groups on the process of opinion formation was self-evident. But researchers in the field of group dynamics did not go beyond the boundaries of the groups they were studying; they failed to consider the public element. Thus it seemed vital to direct attention to this area, which represents the key to understanding the term "public opinion." Without a clear understanding of the implications of the public as a jury for man's social nature, it is impossible to grasp the phenomenon of public opinion.

Using the indicator developed by Hallemann to measure embarrassment, the significance of the anonymous public can be demonstrated. When respondents are asked to spontaneously describe embarrassing situations, they seldom pick situations involving small groups of people familiar to them; 21 percent of the situations take place in the presence of a rather small group of strangers, and 46 percent involve a large, anonymous public (Hallemann 1989, 135: table 14). Hallemann regrouped his test situations into private settings and settings involving a small versus a large public. The results showed that the larger the public is, the greater the percentage of people who find the situation especially embarrassing (ibid, 137: table 15).

It seems perfectly logical that an unpleasant situation among acquaintances would be more embarrassing than with strangers one may never see again, that is, in the presence of an anonymous public. But the results refute this logic. The stigma attached to an embarrassing situation involving acquaintances is not final. There is always the opportunity to rectify the impression; but there is no recourse, no way to explain or excuse one's actions, when an anonymous public is involved. The stigma is indelible.

Hallemann has also come closer to the objective of measuring the fear of isolation than anyone else to date. He calculated a score based on the number of situations an individual considered embarrassing: the sensitivity of the respondent's social nature was rated as very exceptional, exceptional, average, limited, or very limited, with corresponding ratings for the fear of isolation. He then examined the respondents' willingness to speak up or remain silent. He found that individuals with a stronger sense of embarrassment—and, we may add, a stronger fear of isolation—also had a stronger tendency to remain silent on controversial issues. This was not, however, due to a shy or taciturn nature, for they were just as willing as anyone else to join in conversations about noncontroversial topics (ibid., 178ff.).

Testing the quasi-statistical sense

Is there really such a thing as the quasi-statistical sense, as described by the theory of public opinion? Can people determine the climate of opinion? Respondents in every country we studied readily supplied answers to questions such as: "How do most people think?" or "Do most people favor or oppose a particular issue?" One would expect the respondents to reply: "Why are you asking me? You're the opinion pollster!" But that is not what they say. The willingness to make an assessment is an indication that people continually try to assess the strengths of opposing sides on a given issue.

The assessments, however, are often incorrect. Opinions supported by the influential media are often overestimated. This phenomenon is what is now generally termed "pluralistic ignorance."[7] "The public misjudges the public." In his book *Social Psychology* (1924), Floyd Allport discussed this phenomenon, which had been analyzed extensively by R. L. Schanck in his community study (1932; cf. Merton 1949; Newcomb 1950). Allport pointed out that the individual has only three ways of making deductions about the opinions and views that prevail among the population: the press, rumor and "social projection." The concept of "social projection" is actually identical with the "looking-glass perception," a term introduced later in an effort to explain pluralistic ignorance (O'Gorman and Garry 1976; Fields and Schuman 1976) and to counter the assumption of a quasi-statistical sense (Glynn and McLeod 1985; Salmon and Kline 1985). In fact, tests have unanimously confirmed the looking-glass perception but at the same time they have shown that, regardless of individual points of view, the population as a whole does notice which opinions are gaining and which are losing ground, just as one notices whether it is getting warmer or colder (Noelle-Neumann 1985, 1991). What other explanation could there be for this if not that people have the ability to sense distribution frequencies? It is obvious that attempts have been made to influence such perceptions from the beginning of time and not just in recent years when social research has shed light on this phenomenon. This makes it all the more remarkable that the media, i.e. the press, cited by Allport as an additional source of orientation about prevailing opinion in the community at large, were not considered significant until well into the 1980s. To-

7. See Noelle-Neumann 1989b; Katz 1981, 28–38.

day we know that the media represent the most important source for the individual's constant observation of his or her environment. Whenever the frequency distribution of popular opinion on an issue deviates from the population's assessments of how most people think about that issue, we may suspect that media effects are involved—in other words, impressions about frequency distributions are conveyed by the media (Noelle-Neumann 1989).

Testing people's willingness to speak out or remain silent

It is unfortunate that so few countries have a well-developed railroad network. From the first publication of *The Spiral of Silence,* the "train test" has been used to measure willingness to speak out or remain silent (see pp. 16ff., above). As the theory spread internationally, however, there were more and more complaints that the test would not work in other countries, where a five-hour train ride was far too unusual a situation for respondents to imagine. We therefore developed a substitute: "Assuming you are on a five-hour bus trip, and the bus makes a rest stop and everyone gets out for a long break. In a group of passengers, someone starts talking about whether we should support . . . or not. Would you like to talk to this person, to get to know his or her point of view better, or would you prefer not to?" Donsbach and Stevenson designed another question where a television reporter asks people on the street for an interview on a controversial topic. Here, however, the public dimension is too large. Halleman found that the fear of isolation increases with the size of the public. The television audience, after all, constitutes the largest public today.

There are many other public expressions of an individual's willingness to show his or her convictions: hairstyles, beards, bumper stickers—used as symbols both in America and in Europe—or, in Germany, purple scarves symbolizing participation in large church conventions and rallies. All this could be translated into test situations to detect the readiness to show or to conceal one's convictions.

The hard core: A response from "Don Quixote"

There were some misunderstandings when the spiral-of-silence theory was put to the test after the first edition of this book appeared, in part because chapter 17 (on heretics and the avant-garde) and chapter 23 (on the hard core) were too short in that edition. Today we still know no more about the avant-garde than Plato did when he attempted to win over the poets to effect a change in values, as we saw in chapter 25.

Several commentators have assumed that the hard core is simply made up of people who are especially convinced of an opinion, or people with extremely stable voting behavior. Then there are critics who maintain that I invented the hard core to have an excuse whenever findings did not confirm the theory.

But Maria Elisa Chuliá-Rodrigo's Master's thesis for the University of Mainz, in which she examines public opinion in Cervantes' *Don Quixote de la Mancha,* has better defined the hard core. Reading Cervantes with public opinion theory in mind heightens the tragic dimension of this work. Don Quixote has become imbued with society's system of values by reading too many romances of chivalry. And now he is dying to fight and be rewarded for this, "to be viewed by the world with honor and respect." But everything he does, the clothes he wears and the peculiar weapons he carries, belong to a world that existed two hundred years before his time. He finds himself isolated, laughed at, defeated, and yet he remains true to the ideals of chivalry almost to the end of the novel (Chuliá-Rodrigo 1989).

Those who belong to the avant-garde are committed to the future and thus, by necessity, are also isolated; but their conviction that they are ahead of their time enables them to endure. The "hard core" remains committed to the past, retaining the old values while suffering the isolation of the present.

How the sum of individual opinions is transformed into public opinion

At the conference held by the American Association for Public Opinion Research in 1970, Sidney Verba, the political scientist, contended that political opinion research was making no progress toward a theory of public opinion because it "usually focuses on the individual as a unit of analysis" (Verba 1970, 455). I disagree. It was not the fact that the individual was the unit of analysis that kept a theory from being developed; it was that survey research neglected the social nature of the individual. Survey questions inquired about the individual's opinion, behavior, and knowledge: "Are *you* in favor of . . . ?" "Are *you* interested in . . . ?" "Are *you* concerned about . . . ?" "Do *you* prefer . . . ?" And so on.

What was lacking, especially in election research, were questions about the climate of opinion—"What do *most* people think?"

"Who is winning . . . ?" "What is IN, OUT?" "What might you argue about with even the best of friends?" "Who is jeered?" "Who is snubbed?"—questions oriented toward the social setting, and thus toward the individual's social nature.

It is not that man's social nature has been completely neglected in social research. In 1949, in *Psychologie der öffentlichen Meinung,* Peter R. Hofstätter wrote: "For an opinion to be public it must possess what at first glance appears to be a peculiar characteristic: its expression must be accompanied by an unclear— possibly even false—understanding of the opinions held by the other members of the group. . . . Our present definition of public opinion as the frequency distribution of individual opinions, is incomplete: The aspect of publicness demands that one's own position be localized somewhere along the assumed frequency distribution of expressed viewpoints" (Hofstätter 1949, 53). But no conclusions were drawn from this in opinion research. Thus the vital question of how the mighty structure known as public opinion develops from the sum of individual opinions, which survey research expresses in percentages, was not answered. Public opinion, which induces fear and trembling in governments, forcing them to take political action and "producing social and political consequences," as psychologist Brewster M. Smith stated at the conference in 1970, was ignored. So were the forces that kept individuals quiet if they did not share public opinion, as remarked by James Bryce.[8]

As far as we know, it is the constant interaction between people, due to their social nature, that accounts for the transformation of the sum of individual opinions into public opinion. The threat of isolation, the fear of isolation, the continual observation of the climate of opinion and the assessment of the relative strength or weakness of different sides determine whether people will speak out or keep silent.

8. See pp. 92–93, above; and Tönnies 1922, 138.

The Manifest and Latent Functions of Public Opinion: A Summary

> There is the tangled, matted field of opinion
> theory. It is a field cluttered with the stumps
> of the once mighty theoretical particularisms,
> a field in which a dense underbrush has
> grown, in which there are confusing brambles
> of terminological disputation and an infinite
> thicket of psychological descriptions.
>
> (WILLIAM ALBIG, 1939)

As I conclude this book, I want to come back full circle and ask: What is public opinion?

Consider the second chapter of Harwood Child's book *Public Opinion: Nature, Formation, and Role* (1965), in which Childs presents fifty definitions of public opinion. Or the first sentence of W. Phillips Davison's (1968) article on public opinion in the *International Encyclopedia of the Social Sciences:* "There is no generally accepted definition of 'public opinion.'" It seems that the fifty definitions cited by Childs all stem from just two different concepts of public opinion. In addition, there are a few definitions that are technical-instrumental in nature, in that public opinion is equated with the results of public opinion polls, defined as "the aggregation of individual attitudes by pollsters" (Beniger 1987, S54; cf. Gollin 1980, 448). Almost all the definitions compiled by Childs are related to the following two concepts:

1. Public opinion as rationality. It is instrumental in the process of opinion formation and decision-making in a democracy.
2. Public opinion as social control. Its role is to promote social integration and to ensure that there is a sufficient level of consensus on which actions and decisions may be based.

A comparison of the two concepts calls to mind a famous distinction which Robert Merton made in *Social Theory and Social Structure* ([1949] 1957):

> —*Manifest functions* are those objective consequences contributing to the adjustment or adaptation of the system

I would like to thank Wolfgang Donsbach and W. Phillips Davison for their suggestions on this chapter.

which are *intended and recognized* by participants in the system;

—*Latent functions,* correlatively, being those which are *neither intended nor recognized.* (ibid. 51).

The first concept of public opinion may be viewed as manifest function, intended and recognized, whereas the second concept of public opinion involves a latent function, neither intended nor recognized.

Given the vast differences between various concepts of public opinion, a number of scholars have urged that the term "public opinion" be abandoned, at least in scientific usage (Palmer [1936] 1950, 12; Habermas 1962, 13; Moscovici 1991, 299). However, a term that has been shown to exist as far back as antiquity and has been used throughout the centuries should not be discarded as long as no other equally comprehensive term has been found that is more capable of conveying the meaning of the concept, that is, a certain form of social control. Were we to abandon the term "public opinion," we would lose our age-old knowledge of the latent function of public opinion, by means of which a sufficient consensus is maintained within a society—and perhaps throughout the world (B. Niedermann 1991; Rusciano and Fiske-Rusciano 1990). We would no longer be able to recognize the connections between such different phenomena as the climate of opinion, the zeitgeist, reputation, fashion and taboos, and would thus revert to a level of knowledge prior to John Locke's "law of opinion, reputation and fashion."

The following discussion will first focus on the concept of "public opinion as rationality" and then turn to the concept of "public opinion as social control." Finally, I will present a list of arguments that support the contention that the concept of public opinion is more effective when viewed in terms of its latent function of social control, as in the spiral of silence concept.

Public opinion as a manifest function: The formation of opinion in a democracy

Late twentieth-century thinking is still dominated by the concept of public opinion that began to take hold in the late eighteenth century. According to this view, public opinion is characterized by rationality. Rationality here is taken to mean the conscious acquisition of knowledge by means of reason and the making of logical and rationally sound judgments based on that knowledge. Acquiring knowledge and making judgments involve the use of logical transformations and deductions. Rationality operates with unequivocally defined concepts that are included in a larger framework of concepts. Rationality thus apprehends different object areas where logical inferences may be drawn. A focus on such areas is hence shaped by logic, causality, and consistency. The products of rational thought are convincing, sensible, and intersubjectively comprehensible.

The concept of public opinion based on rationality is succinctly defined by Hans Speier: "opinions on matters of concern to the nation freely and publicly expressed by men outside the government who claim a right that their opinions should influence or determine the actions, personnel, or structure of their government" (Speier 1950, 376; see also p. 93, above). Here, the relationship between public opinion and rationality is straightforward: They are identical. In practice—provided there is freedom of the press—there is a high degree of agreement between public opinion and the prevailing published opinion in the media. The manifest function of public opinion is also incorporated in Hans Speier's definition. Public opinion is related to politics; it supports the government in the formation of opinions and decisions on political matters.

This notion of public opinion as a sort of political *raisonnement* in the public sphere, as a correlate to the government (Habermas 1962), appeared especially convincing thanks to the widespread belief that the concept of public opinion first emerged in the eighteenth century at the time of the Enlightenment. Even today, this claim is still found in encyclopedias and lexicons throughout the world. The term is frequently attributed to Jacques Necker, the French minister of finance who had tried to keep the government's finances stable despite growing public turmoil shortly before the French Revolution.[1]

The first attempts to explain the term "public opinion" were made in the nineteenth century. James Bryce (1888, 1889), who dealt with the different roles of public opinion in England and the

---

1. See for example: *International Encyclopedia of the Social Sciences*, 1968, vol. 13, 192; *International Encyclopedia of Communications* 1989, vol. 3, 387; *Staatslexikon Recht, Wirtschaft, Gesellschaft* 1988, vol. 4, 98; cf. Bucher 1887, 77; Bauer 1930, 234f.

United States in the fourth section of *The American Common-wealth*, limited the concept to the rational discussion of controversial political issues in a democracy. Robert Ezra Park, studying in Germany at the start of the twentieth century, found himself torn between Tönnies, his professor at the University of Berlin, who was trying to clarify the concept of public opinion theoretically, and Oswald Spengler, the author of *Decline of the West* (1918–22), another of his teachers at the University of Berlin, who introduced him to the field of mass psychology. Mass psychology was then a relatively new field; it had been founded in the last few decades of the nineteenth century by the Italian criminologist Scipio Sighele, and by Gustave Le Bon and Gabriel Tarde. In his dissertation, *Masse und Publikum* (1904), published in English in 1972 as *The Crowd and the Public*, Park attempts to find a way out by attributing feelings to the crowd and reason to public opinion. Public opinion is the product of *raisonnement*, of debates in which various viewpoints are put forth until one viewpoint finally emerges victorious and the opponents are merely subdued rather than convinced.

According to an American monograph (Frazier and Gaziano, 1979), his work on the dissertation left Park exhausted and disappointed. In this mood, he turned down an offer to teach at the University of Chicago after returning to the United States. Even today, a similar fate probably awaits authors who try to equate public opinion and rationality.

The method normally used to examine the concept of public opinion is exemplified by Francis G. Wilson's article in the *American Political Science Review* of 1993, "Concepts of public opinion" (Wilson 1933, 371–91). The term is divided into the components "public" and "opinion"; then "the relation of opinion and the public, the relation of the public and government, and the relation of opinion and government" are analyzed (ibid., 382). These relations are characterized by the idea of *participation*. The meaning of "public" is restricted to "the body of persons having the right of participation in government" (390). The pressure of this public opinion is seen as a burden upon government.

A similar approach was pursued about thirty years later by Childs in *Public Opinion*, in the chapter on definitions cited above. Childs subdivides the chapter into a study of "Publics," "Opinions" and "Degree of uniformity"; this is followed by "Process of opinion formation," "Quality of opinions," "Who holds the opinions?" and "The subject matter of opinions." He then proceeds to sketch the historical background and to characterize each decade of the twentieth century with regard to topics of public opinion and techniques of influencing it. Finally, he describes how, since the thirties, it has become more and more feasible and common to measure public opinion at regular intervals by means of public opinion polls. At this point, the essay ends.

About half of the fifty definitions of public opinion compiled by Childs are rooted in the rational concept of public opinion. James T. Young (1923, 577–78) calls public opinion "the social judgment of a self-conscious community on a question of general import after rational, public discussion" (Young 1923, 577–78). A. W. Halcombe (1923, 36) defines it as "[opinions which are based on] a substantial part of the facts required for a rational decision." And J. A. Sauerwein (1933, 29) comments, "It is rather exaggerated to pretend that there exists, at the present time, a public opinion, in the intellectual sense, outside of the elite." At the same time, however, an underlying note of resignation can be heard: "Perhaps it sounds a bit harsh, but there is no such thing as a public opinion, and it requires only a moderate understanding of human nature to show that such a thing as an intelligent public opinion is not possible" (Jordan 1930, 339).

The great esteem in which rationality is held by Western civilization certainly explains why the concept of public opinion as rationality has survived. It also explains why some feel that taking apart the concept like a machine and defining the parts and their relationship to one another will enable them to grasp the nature of public opinion.

Basically, the concept of public opinion has been, and still is, subjected to rather high-handed treatment, as if an arbitrary decision could be made on whether to retain or discard the concept or on the role it should be allotted in a democracy in the future. This tendency was apparent even in the first systematic paper on the subject, A. Lawrence Lowell's "Public Opinion and Popular Government" (1913). Lowell establishes what he feels is "true" public opinion and thus ought to be heeded by the government: opinions that have been formed following thorough discussion. Under his definition, only the opinions of individuals who have given thought to the matter carry any weight. And he further limits his definition by applying it only to those issues that fall under the jurisdiction of the government; thus religion, for example, is excluded.

In the early 1930s, with the emergence of the representative survey method, the term "public opinion" gained wider currency. People had no qualms about speaking about "public opinion polls" or "public opinion research," or about giving the new journal founded in 1937 the title *Public Opinion Quarterly.* But were the findings obtained from surveys really what is called "public opinion?" Both then and now, researchers have often equated public opinion with the results of opinion polls. The strategy was to create a technical definition of public opinion, based on the tools and raw products of survey research, for example: "Public opinion consists of people's reactions to definitely worded statements and questions under interview conditions" (Warner 1937, 377). "Public opinion is not the name of a something, but a classification of a number of somethings, which, on statistical arrangement in a frequency distribution, present modes or frequencies that command attention and interest" (Beyle 1931, 183). "Now that we have the reality of public opinion polls we will undoubtedly keep on calling public opinion a well analyzed distribution of attitudes" (Lazarsfeld 1957, 43). In an article written on the occasion of the fiftieth anniversary of the *Public Opinion Quarterly,* James Beniger refers to Albert Gollin's "now ubiquitous definition of public opinion as the aggregation of the individual attitudes by pollsters" (Beniger 1987, 54; Gollin 1980, 448).

The first researcher to take a critical view of this situation was Herbert Blumer. In his 1948 article "Public Opinion and Public Opinion Polling," he sharply criticizes "a paucity, if not a complete absence, of generalizations about public opinion despite the voluminous amount of polling studies of public opinion."

> What impresses me is the apparent absence of effort or sincere interest on the part of students of public opinion polling to move in the direction of identifying the object which they are supposedly seeking to study, to record, and to measure. . . . They are not concerned with independent analysis of the nature of public opinion in order to judge whether the application of their technique fits that nature.
>
> A few words are in order here on an approach that consciously excuses itself from any consideration of such a problem. I refer to the narrow operationalist position that public opinion consists of what public opinion polls poll. Here, curiously, the findings resulting from an operation, or use of an instrument, are regarded as constituting the object of study

> instead of being some contributory addition to knowledge of the object of study. The operation ceases to be a guided procedure on behalf of an object of inquiry; instead, the operation determines intrinsically its own objective. . . . All that I wish to note is that the results of narrow operationalism, as above specified, merely leave or raise the question of what the results mean. (Blumer [1948] 1953)

Following this strong rebuff, Blumer turns to the investigation of the contents, formation and function of public opinion within a democracy, masterfully outlining the concept of a rational public opinion with its manifest function of informing politicians in a democracy about the attitudes of the functional groups that constitute a society's organizations. His primary focus is on interest groups—unions, business associations, chambers of agriculture, and ethnic groups. Blumer does not say why these interest groups, and the pressure they exert on politicians, may be termed "public opinion." However, he does convincingly portray the part these groups play in the formation of politicians' opinions. At the same time, he demonstrates how politicians must take heed of the pressure exerted by these groups. Naturally, not all individuals in a society exert the same level of influence in the opinion-formation process. Many individuals enjoy high status, prestige, a high level of expertise; they are very interested and involved, and they have considerable influence on a number of other persons. On the other hand, there are also individuals who display none of these qualities. Yet in representative surveys these different people, whose judgment and influence do not carry the same weight, are treated equally. From the arguments presented, it is clear that Blumer does not consider surveys to be a suitable method for ascertaining public opinion.

Thirty years later, Pierre Bourdieu advanced essentially the same arguments in his essay "Public Opinion Does Not Exist" (Bourdieu 1979; Herbst, 1992). At the 1991 conference of the American Midwest Association of Public Opinion Research (MAPOR) in Chicago, a session was held on the topic of European concepts of public opinion, as described in a series of articles published subsequently in the *International Journal of Public Opinion Research* (Beniger 1992). The theories of public opinion developed by Foucault, Habermas, and Bourdieu were presented. All three are based on the assumption that opinion formation is a rational process.

Along with the growing interest in rational choice theories in the field of political science and the increasing fascination with cognitive processes among psychologists, the idea of public opinion as rationality seems to be becoming even more entrenched toward the end of this century. James Beniger, for example (1987, 58–59), expects a new paradigm to emerge along these lines: "If attitudes can be allowed to depend on cognition (knowledge and schemata) as well as affect, however, and possibly also on behavioral predispositions, then communication that changes 'only' cognitions may be just as important to attitudinal change as communication with affective components. Indeed, public opinion research has a venerable literature suggesting that credible information can have a more lasting impact on public opinion than mere persuasive appeals. Further elaboration of the process paradigm toward the better understanding of this type of public opinion formation and change might be expected to play a central role in the pages of POQ during its second half-century."

Public opinion as a latent function: Social control

At the twenty-fifth annual conference of the American Association for Public Opinion research in 1970, in the session titled "Toward a Theory of Public Opinion," Brewster Smith, a psychologist at the University of Chicago, stated that research had "not yet faced the problem of how opinions of individuals articulate to produce social and political consequences" (Smith 1970, 454).

The problem could not be solved because nobody was looking for a public opinion capable of exerting pressure. The rational concept of public opinion does not explain the pressure that public opinion must exert if it is to have any influence on the government and the citizens. *Raisonnement* is enlightening, stimulating, and interesting, but it is not able to exert the kind of pressure from which—as John Locke said—not one in ten thousand remains invulnerable. Or as Aristotle expressed it, he who loses the support of the people is a king no longer. Or as David Hume wrote, "it is . . . on opinion only that government is founded; and this maxim extends to the most despotic and most military governments, as well as to the most free and most popular" ([1741/1742] 1963, 29). If public opinion is viewed as social control, its power is easy to explain. In a letter written by Cicero in 50 B.C., Cicero tells his friend Atticus that he had taken on a false opinion due to the influence of public opinion (*publicam opinionem*). Even in this first instance of the use of the term found to date, "public opinion" is not used to designate good and rational judgment, but rather the opposite.

The concept of public opinion shaped by rationality is based on the notion of the well-informed citizen capable of advancing sensible arguments and making sound judgments. This concept focuses on *political* life and *political* controversies. Most authors who use this concept do admit that only a small group of informed and interested citizens actually participate in such arguments and judgments. Yet the concept of "public opinion as social control" affects *all* members of society. Since participation in the process that threatens isolation and prompts fears of isolation is not voluntary, social control exerts pressure both on the individual, who fears isolation, and on the government—it too will be isolated and eventually toppled without the support of public opinion. The example of South Africa shows that nowadays an entire country can be isolated by world opinion until it is compelled to concede.

The concept of public opinion as social control is not concerned with the quality of the arguments. The decisive factor is which of the two camps in a controversy is strong enough to threaten the opposing camp with isolation, rejection, and ostracism. The significance of people's notions of the other side's strength was described at the beginning of this book, exemplified by the last-minute swing in the German federal elections of 1965 and 1972. The similar phenomenon observed by Lazarsfeld in the American presidential election of 1940, which he explains in terms of individual psychology as the bandwagon effect—everyone wants to be on the winning side—is interpreted by the theory of public opinion in social psychological terms. No one wants to be isolated. Both the bandwagon mechanism and the spiral of silence rest on the common assumption that individuals monitor the signals in their environment with regard to the strength and weakness of the various camps. The difference lies in the motive for these observations. Moreover, the spiral of silence theory emphasizes gradual, incremental changes that result from an ongoing social process, while the bandwagon suggests a more sudden jump from one position to another based on new information as to who's ahead. Both could be operating at the same time (Davison 1958).

Many writers have intuitively recognized that victory or defeat in the process of public opinion does not depend on what is right or wrong. Thus, the disapproval with which deviant behavior is punished does not, as noted by the German scholar of jurisprudence Ihering in 1883, have a rational character like the disapproval of "an incorrect logical conclusion, a mistake in solving an arithmetic problem, or an unsuccessful work of art." Rather, it is expressed as the "conscious or unconscious practical reaction of the community to injury of its interests, a defense for the purposes of common security" (Ihering 1883, 242, cf. 325). In other words, it is a matter of cohesion and a consensus on values in a society. This can only involve moral values—good and bad—or aesthetic values—beautiful and ugly—as only these have the emotional component capable of triggering the threat of isolation and the fear of isolation.

The two concepts of public opinion compared

In comparing the two different concepts of public opinion, it must be emphasized that they are based on quite different assumptions about the function of public opinion. Public opinion as a rational process focuses on democratic participation and the exchange of different viewpoints in public matters, along with the demand that these ideas be heeded by the government, and concern that the opinion-formation process may be manipulated by the power of the state and capital, by the mass media and modern technology (Habermas 1962).

Public opinion as social control is centered on ensuring a sufficient level of consensus within society on the community's values and goals. According to this concept, the power of public opinion is so great that it cannot be ignored by either the government or the individual members of society. This power stems from the threat of isolation that society directs at deviant individuals and governments, and from the fear of isolation, which results from man's social nature.

Constantly monitoring one's environment *and* observing the reactions of others, as expressed by the willingness to speak up or the tendency to remain silent, creates a link between the individual and society. This interaction lends power to the common consciousness, common values and common goals, along with the accompanying threats directed at those who deviate from these values and goals. The fear of isolation experienced in cases of deviation is a derivative of the exhilaration felt during shared group experiences. Researchers assume that these reactions evolved in the course of human development in order to ensure sufficient cohesion of human societies. Empirical evidence in support of this assumption is provided by the "experience sampling method," or EMS, which shows that being alone is connected with depression and low spirits for most people (Csikszentmihalyi 1992).

One of the major differences between the rational concept of public opinion and the concept of public opinion as social control lies in the interpretation of the word "public." According to the democratic-theoretical concept of public opinion as the product of *raisonnement,* "public" is viewed in terms of the content of the themes of public opinion, which are political contents. The concept of public opinion as social control interprets "public" in the sense of the "public eye" (Burke 1791): "for all eyes to see," "visible to all," *coram publico.* The public eye is the tribunal at which judgment is passed on the government and each individual as well.

The two concepts also diverge when it comes to the interpretation of the word "opinion." According to the democratic-theoretical concept, opinion is primarily a matter of individual views and arguments, whereas the concept of public opinion as social control applies it to a much greater area, in fact to everything that visibly expresses a value-related opinion in public, which may be directly in the form of expressed convictions, but also indirectly in the form of buttons and badges, flags, gestures, hairstyles and beards, publicly visible symbols, and publicly visible, morally loaded behavior. This concept of public opinion may even be applied to the area of embarrassment (Goffman 1956; Hallemann 1989). Its relevance extends from all rules of a moral nature ("political correctness") to taboos: areas of severe, unresolved conflict that may not be addressed in public, lest social cohesion be threatened.

From the perspective of the democratic-theoretical concept of public opinion, one must be critical of the use of the term "public opinion research" as a designation for representative surveys, as Herbert Blumer, Bourdieu, and many other supporters of this concept have been, for such surveys treat the opinions of informed persons and those of uninformed persons as carrying equal weight. That cannot reflect reality.

From the perspective of public opinion as social control, all members of society participate in the process of public opinion, in the conflict over values and goals aimed in part at reinforcing traditional values and in part at doing away with old values and replacing them with new values and goals. It is possible to observe this process with the tools of representative surveys. For the most part, however, the questions needed are different from those included in conventional public opinion polls. Along with questions designed to ascertain the respondent's opinion, questions on the climate of opinion are required. Respondents must be asked how they perceive their environment: What do most people think? What is increasing or decreasing? They must be asked questions about the threat of isolation—which views and modes of behavior are unpopular—and questions about the willingness to speak out and the tendency to remain silent.

According to this concept of public opinion, many questions included in polls today do not ascertain "public opinion." Questions must address value-laden opinions and modes of behavior, by which the individual isolates or may isolate himself in public.

Since the mid 1960s, attempts to revive the concept of public opinion as social control have met with little success (Noelle 1966). One possible explanation is offered by Mary Douglas in her book, *How Institutions Think* (1986, 76): "First, on the principle of cognitive coherence, a theory that is going to gain a permanent place in the public repertoire of what is known will need to interlock with the procedures that guarantee other kinds of theories." In this respect, there are no difficulties with the concept of public opinion as rationality: it can be linked to existing theories of democracy, to the fascination with rational choice and collective action theories, and to cognitive models of psychology. The social-psychological dynamic concept of public opinion, on the other hand, has drawbacks. As Douglas notes (ibid., 82), "there is a professional dislike [among sociologists] of control models."

Theorists in the philosophy of science have developed a number of criteria for testing the quality of competing concepts. For example:

1. Empirical applicability
2. Which findings are explained by the concept? How great is the potential for clarification?
3. Degree of complexity, i.e. the magnitude of the areas included, or the number of variables included
4. Compatibility with other theories

The concept of public opinion as social control appears superior when judged by at least three of these criteria. First, it can be empirically tested. Provided that certain requirements of the theory are fulfilled—for example, topicality, the moral or aesthetic component, and the position of the mass media—it is possible to make valid forecasts of individual behavior (for example, the tendency to speak out or remain silent) and on the distribution of opinions in society (Noelle-Neumann 1991).

Second, this concept has explanatory power. The theory of the spiral of silence results in if-then statements; that is, it connects observable phenomena to other phenomena, by asserting and proving that there are certain social rules. Using the rational concept of public opinion, it would be very difficult to explain the phenomenon first observed in 1965, when the stable distribution of individual opinions was accompanied by a completely independent development of the climate of opinion and a last-minute change in voting intentions (see p. 2, above). It would also be difficult with the rational concept of public opinion to explain why the differences in the distribution of opinions among various population segments (divided according to age, social class, etc.) are so much greater than the estimates made by the various groups about the perceived climate of opinion ("How most people think"). And finally, with the rational concept of public opinion, it would be especially difficult to explain why those individuals who are the best informed about a certain topic, in other words the experts, often find themselves alone in their opinion, confronted by the representatives of public opinion, journalists, and the population in general, who together take a position that is diametrically opposed to that of the experts. Empirical evidence on this situation has been presented by Stanley Rothman and other researchers (for example, Snyderman and Rothman 1988).

Third, the social-control concept of public opinion has a higher degree of complexity. It links the individual level with the social level, and pertains to many more areas than just politics.

The concept does encounter difficulties when it comes to compatibility with other theories, as previously indicated. But it can be connected with social-psychological findings on group dynamics (Sherif 1936, 1965; Asch 1951, 1952) and also with Ervin Goffman's social-psychological theories on embarrassment and stigmatization.

Although the capabilities of the two concepts of public opinion have been compared in this paper, this does not mean that one must necessarily choose between them. The rational exchange of arguments, or *raisonnement*, unquestionably plays a role in the process of public opinion, although there has been too little empirical research on this subject. For even morally-loaded values need cognitive support in order to assert themselves in public opinion.

If we seek an image to explain the relationship between public debate and public opinion as social control, public debate might be seen as an inlay, set into the dynamic social psychological process and sometimes guiding and articulating it, but often remaining at an intellectual level and thus having no effect on moral emotions, where the pressure of public opinion originates. As defined by Merton, the manifest function of public debate—bringing about a decision by presenting arguments in public—is conscious, intended, and approved of. Often, however, the population is not convinced on an emotional level—not electrified—and the decision function thus lacks the strength required to create and defend the social consensus needed. The only opinion that can fullfill the latent function of maintaining social cohesion is opinion that is emotionally accepted and approved of by the population. In this view, public debates often make up part, but not all, of the public opinion process.

The manifest function might also be termed the apparent function, while the latent function is the real function. Merton illustrates this using the famous example of Hopi rain dances, which have the stated function of inducing rain in times of drought but the latent, and thus real, function of providing the Hopi tribe with cohesion in times of need.

Because the latent function of public opinion as social control, with its aim of integrating society and ensuring a sufficient level of consensus, is neither intentional nor consciously recognized, there are often misapprehensions about the concept. Perhaps it will be possible someday to reconcile the intellectuals with the idea that public opinion exerts pressure on the individual to conform. This would turn the latent function of public opinion into a manifest function. It would, in other words, come to be seen as a necessary force in society.

In the first edition of this book I did not touch either on the rational concept of public opinion or on research findings on reference groups and group dynamics. My primary goal was to describe the new perspective that arose from the rediscovery of the role of public opinion as social control, a role of which we are only now becoming fully aware. In this second edition I have not only included discussion of some of the important commentators on public opinion, such as Robert Park, Herbert Blumer, and Pierre Bourdieu, but have attempted to clarify the relationship between the social-psychological dynamic concept of public opinion as social control and the democratic-theoretical concept of public opinion as *raisonnement* in the public sphere. The task of investigating the interaction between reference groups, group dynamics, mass psychology and public opinion as social control still lies ahead.

Afterword, to Express Thanks

I do not gladly bid my readers goodbye. I hope to meet them again once the relations between public opinion and politics, public opinion and the economy, public opinion and art, science and religion are investigated, and when it has been shown that the way public opinion has been described in this book leads to a better understanding than before, allowing both diagnosis and prediction.

Much of what has for so long accompanied me belongs to me no longer. I used to think of myself, in relation to my subject, as a solitary stroller in a park. Nevertheless, I was really not solitary. Among those who have helped me I want to thank above all Helmtrud Seaton in the Allensbach Institute, who discharged simultaneously the tasks of scientific assistant and secretary; I do not believe that I could have written the book without her.

Many colleagues from the Institut für Demoskopie Allensbach have helped me, often with genuine enthusiasm, even when my requests came in the middle of the obligatory program of contract research and involved what seemed to be ludicrous questionnaire requests or tabulations—in connection with the train test, for example. As one who was particularly involved in the work, I want to mention the staff member responsible for the archives of the Institute, Werner Süsslin, and, functioning simultaneously as the reader for French texts and a stimulating commentator, Gertrud Vallon.

I have also received assistance at the Institut für Publizistik of the Johannes Gutenberg University of Mainz: from master's theses by Christine Gerber on Rousseau, Angelika Tischer née Balven on Tocqueville, and Dieter Petzolt on "the public eye as consciousness," of which the sections on Luther were of particular importance to me. At the University of Chicago, Frank Rusciano's master's thesis on Machiavelli has been helpful.

I would like to thank Professor Jean Stoetzel of the University of Paris V —René Descartes for having provided me with his unpublished notes for a lecture on public opinion and for having put me in touch with his Ph.D. candidate Colette Ganochaud, who was writing her dissertation about Rousseau's concept of public opinion.

I would like to thank my colleague in Mainz, Hans Mathias Kepplinger, for his equanimity in discussing my topic and the stimulation he always provided. And I thank Imogen Seger-Coulborn, who was the only one to read the manuscript chapter by chapter as it was written; I hope this demonstrates how highly I value her critical commentary. She has had my interest in public opinion in mind for many years while conducting her own research in the social sciences and has sent me many messages on the subject. In thanking her I also thank the many friends and colleagues who have helped me by pointing out sources. Imogen's notes often were quite brief but always contained a meticulous reference, for example: Henry David Thoreau in his journal of 1840, when he was twenty-three. And Thoreau's entry: "It is always easy to break the law but even the bedouins in the desert find it impossible to resist public opinion."

At the turn of the year 1979–80   E.N.N.

Afterword to the Second Edition

*F*or the translation of the new parts of this edition into English, I would like to thank the staff members of the English Department at the Allensbach Institute, Maria Marzahl and Patty McGurty. For his help in revising the translation, I am grateful to Matthew Levie, who, as a student from Harvard University, completed an internship at the Allensbach Institute in the summer of 1991. In addition, I want to express my thanks to Jamie Kalven, who edited the manuscript and so eradicated any last traces of German linguistic peculiarities, and I am especially thankful to Mihaly Csikszentmihalyi, professor of psychology at the University of Chicago, who has once again taken away precious time from his work as a scholar and author in order to compare the translation with the original German text, as he did with the first English edition. For their wise and persevering work, I would like to thank Erich Lamp and Anne Niedermann (née Jäckel), authors whom the reader will encounter in the new chapters 25 to 27, and finally, Helmtrud Seaton, my assistant for many years, without whose help it would have been impossible to complete this edition while also fulfilling my obligations at the Allensbach Institute and the University of Mainz.

We have of course continued our research; here is a report on our most recent discoveries and developments.

Not long ago, we came across another surprising discovery in our seminar at the University of Mainz: Sir William Temple (1628–99) had something to say about public opinion (Frentiu 1990). Temple divided his life's work between political and diplomatic missions on the one hand, and the pursuit of philosophical and literary studies in the private seclusion of the library on his country estate on the other, as Montaigne had done, who lived a century earlier. Impressed by Jonathan Swift, who was almost forty years his junior, Temple hired the twenty-two-year-old as his secretary; their work together was to span two decades, and Swift published a four-volume collection of Temple's works.

In the works of Sir William Temple, who preceded David Hume by more than fifty years, we discovered Hume's major theme: toppling governments when they no longer possess authority or the confidence of the people, which, according to Temple, amounted to the same thing. And one hundred years before

Madison, we find in Temple's works the central tenet of the spiral of silence: man "will hardly hope, or venture to introduce opinions wherein he knows none, or few of his mind, and thinks all others will defend those already received" (Temple [1672] 1964, 58–59).

I have been gently chided by a former student for giving too much prominence to the sources of my ideas and too little to my own work. The reason I have cited other writers with such zeal is that, as a scientist, I regard all of those I encounter along with way toward the discovery of a particular truth—at another time, in another part of the world—as my friends. This is also why I am so grateful to graduate students like Sabine Mathes, who, using the case of nuclear energy, enthusiastically investigated the connection between the various factors involved in the interaction of mass media and public opinion until it was finally possible to envision the part played by the different elements in the process of public opinion in chronological terms. The tenor of the media, or a change in the tenor of the media, precedes a change in the assessment of the climate of opinion. A change in the assessment of the climate of opinion precedes a change in one's own attitudes. Behavior—the willingness to speak out—is adjusted to the assessment of the climate of opinion but, conversely, also influences assessments of the climate of opinion in a feedback process that sets off a spiraling process.

It seemed like a gift when Hans Zetterberg called my attention to Plato's *Pythagoras*. In this dialogue, the myth is discussed in which Zeus declared that talents should be divided up among the people, with each person being given a different talent—for example, one received the gift of craftsmanship, the other of making music, or the gift of healing. Finally, Hermes was to distribute political gifts, the sense of justice (*dike*) and the sense of shame (*aidos*). Hermes asked, Should I distribute these gifts just as I did the others, or should I distribute them to everyone? "To everyone," said Zeus, "everyone is to share in them; for cities could not arise if only a few shared in these gifts, as they do in the others."

"Aidos is . . . a difficult idea," say the editors of an English edition of *Pythagoras*. "It is useless to agree on a code of behavior if the members of the community do not abide by it. One way in which such conventions are enforced is by public opinion. Members of a community tend to be seriously concerned about the feelings of other members of that community toward them. Aidos represents that fear of public disapproval which ensures that in general we shall follow society's conventions" (Hubbard and Karnofsky 1982, 96). This is the answer to Protagoras' question: "Does there not have to be something which all citizens share in if there is to be a nation at all?"

Appendix

Studies of Literature on Public Opinion
A Guide to Text Analysis

The literature is to be studied with the following questions in mind:

1. Does the publication contain one or more definitions of public opinion? If it is not a collective publication about definitions, which definition or definitions of public opinion does it take as its point of departure?

2. Does the publication continue the work of other authors—whether contemporary or from the past—and does it do so simply by way of casual citations or does it establish a sense of continuity? Which authors?

3. Which classical authors are quoted on the subject of public opinion, explicitly or even casually?

4. Does part of the publication or the entire work focus on the content of public opinion (at a certain time, on certain subjects, supported by or fought against by certain groups or institutions), or is the content of public opinion simply used to exemplify the workings of public opinion?

5a. Does part or all of the work focus on the workings of public opinion? Does it do so from the perspective of social psychology, or is the perspective political or cultural, or from yet another field?

5b. Or are the workings of public opinion outlined wherever the context allows, even though it does not constitute the focus of the publication?

6. Is public opinion dealt with as a critical, intellectual, highly valued power of judgment (the elite concept) or as a means of integration, pressure for conformity, social control (the integration concept)?

7. Does the author present public opinion as being wise or foolish, or as alternately wise and foolish? What characteristics are ascribed to public opinion? Or does the author forgo making a value judgment?

8. Is conformity mentioned in connection with public opinion? Is the fear of isolation mentioned as a cause of conformity? Does the publication mention the concept of "social fear" (or synonymous terms) in connection with conformity?

9. Is the individual's fear of isolation particularly emphasized as a factor in the process of public opinion?

10. How does the individual perceive the approval or disapproval of the environment (signals from the environment)?

11. Is David Hume's principle "It is . . . on opinion only that government is founded" treated, or is a more general position taken on the idea that every government must take public opinion into account?

12. Is it explicitly stated or, at least, implied in the publication that public opinion/climate of opinion is morally loaded, is connected with moral judgment?

13. Does the author explicitly or implicitly distinguish between rational and moral positions? How is the relationship between the two described? Is a distinction made between phases when moral positions dominate and others when rational positions dominate?

14. Does the work make an explicit or an implicit distinction between public opinion (a specific subject, short-term) and the climate of opinion (tendency to be diffuse, long-term)? On the basis of this work, is there a possibility of applying the concept of public opinion as the embodiment of the climate of opinion?

15. Does the publication contain a discussion of the term "public"? Is "public" construed legally, politically, or in terms of social psychology (tribunal, public eye)?

16. What is described as an expression of public opinion: media content, election returns, symbols, rituals (celebrations), institutions, fashion, rumors, gossip, people's reactions to behavior, patterns of speech, or other?

17. How is the relationship between journalism, the mass media, and public opinion viewed?
    a) Is published opinion identified with public opinion, or are they clearly distinguished?
    b) Are the mass media viewed as having strong or limited influence on the formation of public opinion, or is this question not dealt with?
    c) Does the work describe other factors that influence public opinion? Which ones?

18. Does the work deal with the effect of public opinion on certain areas, such as law, religion, the economy, science, the arts/aesthetics (pop culture)?

19. Does the publication distinguish between an individual's perception of opinion and fear of isolation in his or her family, in his or her wider circle of friends, acquaintances, neighbors, and co-workers, and, finally, in the anonymous public?

20. Is it possible to draw conclusions about the author's personal views

on the phenomenon of public opinion or on the concept of "public" or the public eye by examining the zeitgeist, the cultural and social conditions or the circumstances under which the author lived?

21. Where has this questionnaire fallen short? Where in the publication were there explicit or implicit statements about public opinion or the term "public" which you were unable to include using these questions?

Bibliography

Albig, William. 1939. *Public Opinion*. New York: McGraw-Hill Book Co.

Altschuler, Bruce E. 1990. "Review of 'Political Culture and Public Opinion. Edited by Arthur Asa Berger.'" *American Political Science Review* 84:1369–70.

Albertini, Rudolf von. 1951. *Das politische Denken in Frankreich zur Zeit Richelieus*. Beihefte zum Archiv für Kulturgeschichte, no. 1. Marburg: Simons Verlag.

Albrecht, Angelika. 1983. "Lachen und Lächeln—Isolation oder Integration?" Master's thesis, Johannes Gutenberg-Universität, Mainz.

Allport, Floyd H. 1937. "Toward a Science of Public Opinion." *Public Opinion Quarterly* 1, no. 1:7–23.

Alverdes, Friedrich Wilhelm. 1925. *Tiersoziologie; Forschungen zur Völkerpsychologie und -soziologie*. Ed. Richard Thurn. Vol. 1. Leipzig: Hirschfeld.

Aristotle. 1986. *Politik*. Ed. and trans. Olof Gigon. Munich: Deutscher Taschenbuch Verlag. English: 1959. *Politics*. Trans. H. Rackham. London: Heinemann.

Asch, Solomon E. 1951. "Effects of Group Pressure upon the Modification and Distortion of Judgments." In *Groups, Leadership, and Men*, ed. H. Guetzkow. Pittsburgh: Carnegie. Reprinted 1953 in *Group Dynamics: Research and Theory*, ed. Dorwin Cartwright and Alvin Zander, 151–62. Evanston, Ill., and New York: Row, Peterson and Co.

———. 1952. "Group Forces in the Modification and Distortion of Judgments." In *Social Psychology*, 450–73. New York: Prentice Hall, Inc.

Bader-Weiss, G., and K. S. Bader. 1935. *Der Pranger: Ein Strafwerkzeug und Rechtswahrzeichen des Mittelalters*. Freiburg: Jos. Waibel'sche Verlagsbuchhandlung.

Bandura, Albert. 1968. "Imitation." In *International Encyclopedia of the Social Sciences*, ed. David L. Sills, 7:96–101. New York: Macmillan Co. & Free Press.

Barber, Bernard, and Lyle S. Lobel. 1953. "Fashion in Women's Clothes and the American Social System." In *Class, Status, and Power: A Reader in Social Stratification*, ed. Reinhard Bendix and Seymour Martin Lipset, 323–32. Glencoe, Ill.: Free Press.

Bauer, Wilhelm. 1914. *Die öffentliche Meinung und ihre geschichtlichen Grundlagen*. Tübingen: J. C. B. Mohr (Paul Siebeck).

———. 1920. "Das Schlagwort als sozialpsychische und geistesgeschichtliche Erscheinung." *Historische Zeitschrift* 122:189–240.

———. 1930. *Die öffentliche Meinung in der Weltgeschichte*. Wildpark-Potsdam: Akademische Verlagsgesellschaft Athenaion.

Beniger, James R. 1978. "Media Content as Social Indicators: The Greenfield Index of Agenda-Setting." *Communication Research* 5:437–53.

———. (1987). "Toward an Old New Paradigm. The Half-Century Flirtation with Mass Society." In *Public Opinion Quarterly* 51:46–66.

———. 1992. "The Impact of Polling on Public Opinion: Reconciling Foucault, Habermas and Bourdieu." *International Journal of Public Opinion Research* 4, no. 3.

Bentham, Jeremy. [1838–43] 1962. "The Constitutional Code." In *The Works of Jeremy Bentham*, ed. J. Bowring, vol. 9, bk. 1, chap. 8, "Public Opinion Tribunal," pp. 41–46. New York: Russell & Russell.

Berger, Arthur Asa. 1989. *Political Culture and Public Opinion*. New Brunswick and Oxford: Transaction Publishers.

Berlyne, D. E. 1969. "Laughter, Humor, and Play." In *Handbook of Social Psychology*, 2d ed., ed. Gardner Lindzey and Elliot Aronson, vol. 3, 795–852. Reading, Mass.: Addison-Wesley Publishing Company.

Beyle, Herman C. 1931. *Identification and Analysis of Attribute-Cluster-Blocs*. Chicago: University of Chicago Press.

Blake, Robert R., and Jane Suygley Mouton. 1954. "Present and Future Implications of Social Psychology for Law and Lawyers." *Journal of Public Law* 3:352–69.

Blumer, Herbert. 1948. "Public Opinion and Public Opinion Polling." *American Sociological Review* 13:542–47.

Boas, George. 1969. *Vox Populi: Essays in the History of an Idea*. Baltimore: The Johns Hopkins Press.

Bourdieu, Pierre. 1979. "Public Opinion Does Not Exist." In *Communication and Class Struggle*, ed. A. Mattelart and S. Siegelaub. New York: International General.

Braatz, Kurt. 1988. *Friedrich Nietzsche—Eine Studie zur Theorie der öffentlichen Meinung*. Monographien und Texte zur Nietzsche Forschung, no. 18. Berlin and New York: de Gruyter.

Bryce, James. 1888–89. *The American Commonwealth*. 2 vols. London: Macmillan.

Bucher, Lothar. 1887. "Über politische Kunstausdrücke." *Deutsche Revue*, no. 12:67–80.

Burke, Edmund. [1791] 1826. "An Appeal From the New to the Old Whigs." In *The Works of the Right Honourable Edmund Burke*, a New Edition, vol. 6, 73–267. London: Printed for C. and J. Rivington.

Carson, Rachel. 1962. *Silent Spring*. Boston: Houghton Mifflin Co. Reprinted 1977, New York: Fawcett.

Cartwright, Dorwin, and Alvin Zander, eds. [1953] 1968. *Group Dynamics: Research and Theory*. 3d ed. New York: Evanston, and London: Harper & Row.

Cicero, 1980. *Atticus-Briefe*. Ed. H. Kasten. Munich and Zürich: Artemis.

Childs, Harwood L. 1965. *Public Opinion: Nature, Formation, and Role.* Princeton, N.J., Toronto, New York, and London: D. van Nostrand.

Choderlos de Laclos, Pierre A. [1782] 1926. *Les liaisons dangereuses.* 2 vols. Paris: Les Editions G. Crès.

Chuliá-Rodrigo, Maria Elisa. 1989. "Die öffentliche Meinung in Cervantes' Roman 'Don Quijote von der Mancha.'" Master's thesis, Johannes Gutenberg-Universität, Mainz.

Conradt, David P. 1978. "The 1976 Campaign and Election: An Overview." In *Germany at the Polls: The Bundestag Election of 1976,* ed. Karl H. Cerny, 29–56. Washington, D.C.: American Enterprise Institute for Public Policy Research.

Csikszentmihalyi, Mihaly. 1992. "Public Opinion and the Psychology of Solitude." Paper presented at the Johannes Gutenberg University of Mainz, January 22, 1992.

Darwin, Charles. 1873. *The Expression of the Emotions in Man and Animals.* London: Murray.

Davison, W. Phillips. 1958. "The Public Opinion Process." *Public Opinion Quarterly* 22:91–106.

———. 1968, "Public Opinion: Introduction." In *International Encyclopedia of the Social Sciences,* ed. David L. Sills, 13:188–97. New York: Macmillan Co. & Free Press.

Descartes, René. [1641] 1964. "Meditationes de Prima Philosophia." In *Oeuvres,* ed. Charles Adam and Paul Tannery, vol. 7. Paris: Librairie Philosophique J. Vrin, English: 1931. "Meditations on First Philosophy." In *The Philosophical Works,* trans. Elizabeth S. Haldane and G. R. T. Ross, 2d rev. ed. Cambridge: At the University Press.

Dicey, Albert V. 1905. *Lectures on the Relations Between Law and Public Opinion in England During the Nineteenth Century.* London: Macmillan.

———. [1905]. 1962. *Law and Public Opinion in England.* London: Macmillan.

Dietze, Jörn. 1992. "Symbolischer Interaktionismus und öffentliche Meinung." Forthcoming Master's thesis, Johannes Gutenberg-Universität, Mainz.

Donsbach, Wolfgang, and Robert L. Stevenson. 1986. "Herausforderungen, Probleme und empirische Evidenzen der Theorie der Schweigespirale." *Publizistik* 31:7–34.

Douglas, Mary. 1986. *How Institutions Think.* Syracuse, N.Y.: Syracuse University Press.

Dovifat, Emil. [1937] 1962. *Zeitungslehre.* Vol. 1. Berlin: Walter de Gruyter & Co. (Sammlung Göschen. no. 1039).

Draper, Theodore. 1982. "Hume and Madison: The Secrets of Federalist Paper No. 10." *Encounter* 58. no. 2 (February).

Dulmen, Richard van. 1977. *Reformation als Revolution: Soziale Be-*

wegung und religiöser Radikalismus. Munich: Deutscher Taschenbuchverlag (dtv-Wissensch. Reihe 4273).

Durkheim, Emile. [1895] 1958. *The Rules of Sociological Method.* Glencoe, Ill.: The Free Press.

Eckert, Werner. 1985. "Zur öffentlichen Meinung bei Machiavelli—Mensch, Masse und die Macht der Meinung." Master's thesis, Johannes Gutenberg-Universität, Mainz.

Eckstein, Harry. 1966. *Division and Cohesion in Democracy: A Study of Norway.* Princeton, N.J.: Princeton University Press.

Elder Seneca. 1974. *Controversae.* Trans. M. Winterbottom. Vol. 1. Cambridge, Mass.: Harvard University Press.

Erasmus of Rotterdam. [1516] 1968. *Fürstenerziehung. Institutio Principis Christiani. Die Erziehung eines christlichen Fürsten.* Ed. Anton J. Gail. Paderborn: Schöningh. English: 1986. "The Education of a Christian Prince. Institutio Principis Christiani." Trans. Neil M. Cheshire and Michael J. Heath. In *Collected Works of Erasmus,* ed. A. H. T. Levi, 199–288. Toronto and London: University of Toronto Press.

Ewen, Wolfgang, Wolfgang Heininger. Sabine Holicki, Axel Hopbach and Elmar Schlüter. 1981/82. "Selbstexperiment: Isolationsdrohung." Term paper, Johannes Gutenberg-Universität, Mainz.

Festinger, Leon. 1957. *A Theory of Cognitive Dissonance.* Evanston, Ill.: Row, Peterson.

Fields, James M., and Howard Schuman. 1976. "Public Beliefs about the Beliefs of the Public." *Public Opinion Quarterly* 40:427–48.

Frame, Donald M. 1965. *Montaigne: A Biography.* New York: Harcourt, Brace & World.

Frazier, Jean P., and Cecile Gaziano. 1979. *Robert Ezra Park's Theory of News, Public Opinion and Social Control.* Journalism Monographs 64.

Frentiu, Carmen. 1990. "Die öffentliche Meinung in den Essays 'Upon the Original and Nature of Government' (1672) and 'Of Popular Discontents' (1685) von Sir William Temple." Term paper, Johannes Gutenberg-Universität, Mainz.

Frey, Siegfried, H.-P. Hirsbrunner, J. Pool, and W. Daw. 1981. "Das Berner System zur Untersuchung nonverbaler Interaktion." In *Methoden der Analyse von Face-to-Face-Situationen,* ed. Peter Winkler. Stuttgart: Metzler.

Frisch, Max. [1967] 1979. *Öffentlichkeit als Partner.* 6th ed. Frankfurt/Main: Suhrkamp.

Fromm, Erich. 1980. *Greatness and Limitations of Freud's Thought.* New York: Harper & Row.

Funkhouser, G. R. 1973. "The Issues of the Sixties: An Exploratory Study in the Dynamics of Public Opinion." *Public Opinion Quarterly* 37:62–73.

Gallacher, S. A. 1945. "Vox Populi—Vox Dei." *Philological Quarterly* 24 (January).

Ganochaud, Colette. 1977–78. "L'opinion publique chez Jean-Jacques Rousseau." 2 vols. Doctoral diss. Université de Paris V, René Descartes. Sciences Humaines, Sorbonne.

Gehlen, Arnold. 1965. *Zeit-Bilder: Zur Soziologie und Ästhetik der modernen Malerei*. Frankfurt and Bonn: Athenäum.

Geldner, Ferdinand. 1930. "Die Staatsauffassung und Fürstenlehre des Erasmus von Rotterdam." *Historische Studien* (Berlin) 191.

Gerber, Christine. 1975. "Der Begriff der öffentlichen Meinung im Werk Rousseaus." Master's thesis. Johannes Gutenberg-Universität, Mainz.

Gersdorff, Carl Ernst August von. 1846. *Über den Begriff und das Wesen der oeffentlichen Meinung: Ein Versuch*. Jena: J. G. Schreiber.

Glanvill, Joseph. 1661. *The Vanity of Dogmatizing: or Confidence in Opinions: Manifested in a Discourse of the Shortness and Uncertainty of our Knowledge, And its Causes; With Some Reflexions on Peripateticism; and An Apology for Philosophy*. London: E. C. for Henry Eversden at the Grey-Hound in St. Pauls-Church-Yard.

Glynn, Carroll J., and Jack M. McLeod. 1985. "Implications of the Spiral of Silence Theory for Communication and Public Opinion Research." In *Political Communication Yearbook 1984*, ed. Keith R. Sanders, Linda Lee Kaid, and Dan Nimmo, 43–65. Carbondale, Edwardsville: Southern Illinois University Press.

Goethe, Johann Wolfang von. 1964. *Werke, Briefe und Gespräche*. Commemorative edition, ed. Ernst Beutler. Vol. 14, *Schriften zur Literatur*, "Weltliteratur, Homer noch einmal." Zurich and Stuttgart: Artemis.

Goffman, Erving. 1956. "Embarrassment and Social Organization." *American Journal of Sociology* 62:264–71.

———. 1963a. *Behavior in Public Places: Notes on the Social Organization of Gatherings*. New York: The Free Press.

———. 1963b. *Stigma: Notes on the Management of Spoiled Identity*. Englewood Cliffs, N.J.: Prentice-Hall.

Gollin, Albert E. 1980. "Exploring the Liaison between Polling and the Press." *Public Opinion Quarterly* 44:445–61.

Goodnight, Thomas. 1992. "Habermas, The Public Sphere and Controversy." *International Journal of Public Opinion Research* 4, no. 3.

Habermas, Jürgen. 1962. *Strukturwandel der Öffentlichkeit: Untersuchungen zu einer Kategorie der bürgerlichen Gesellschaft*. Neuwied: Hermann Luchterhand.

Hallemann, Michael. 1984. "Peinlichkeit als Indikator. Theorie der Peinlichkeit—demoskopische Analyse—Bezüge zur Publizistikwissenschaft unter besonderer Berücksichtigung des Phänomens Öffentlichkeit." Master's thesis, Johannes Gutenberg-Universität, Mainz.

———. 1986. "Peinlichkeit und öffentliche Meinung." *Publizistik* 31:249–61.

———. 1989. "Peinlichkeit: Ein Ansatz zur Operationalisierung von Isolationsfurcht im sozialpsychologischen Konzept öffentlicher Meinung." Dissertation, Johannes Gutenberg-Universität, Mainz.

Haller, William. 1965. *Tracts on Liberty in the Puritan Revolution 1638–1647.* Vol. 1, Commentary. New York: Octagon Books.

Harig, Ludwig. 1978. "Rousseau sieht das Weisse im Auge des Königs: Ein literaturhistorischer Rückblick." *Die Welt,* no. 71 (25 March).

Haviland, John Beard. 1977. *Gossip: Reputation, and Knowledge in Zinacantan.* Chicago: University of Chicago Press.

Hegel, Georg Wilhelm Friedrich. [1821] 1970. *Werke.* Vol. 7, *Grundlinien der Philosophie des Rechts.* Frankfurt/Main: Suhrkamp.

Heider, Fritz. 1946. "Attitudes and Cognitive Organization." *Journal of Psychology* 21:107–12.

Hennis, Wilhelm. 1957a. *Meinungsforschung und repräsentative Demokratie: Zur Kritik politischer Umfragen.* Recht und Staat in Geschichte und Gegenwart, no. 200/201. Tübingen: J. C. B. Mohr (Paul Siebeck).

―――. 1957b. "Der Begriff der öffentlichen Meinung bei Rousseau." *Archiv für Rechts- und Sozialphilosophie* 43: 111–15.

Hentig, Hans von. 1954–55. *Die Strafe: Frühformen und kulturgeschichtliche Zusammenhänge.* Berlin, Göttingen, and Heidelberg: Springer.

Herbst, Susan. 1992. "Surveys in the Public Sphere: Applying Bourdieu's Critique of Opinion Polls." *International Journal of Public Opinion Research* 4, no. 3.

Hesiod. 1959. "Works and Days." In *The Homeric Hymns and Homerica,* trans. G. Evelyn-White, ed. T. E. Page et al. 2–65. Loeb Classical Library, 2d rev. ed. London: William Heinemann.

Hobbes, Thomas. [1650, 1889] 1969. *The Elements of Law: Natural and Politic.* London: Frank Cass & Co.

Hofstätter, Peter R. 1949. *Die Psychologie der öffentlichen Meinung.* Vienna: Wilhelm Braumüller.

Holcombe, A. W. 1923. *The Foundations of the Modern Commonwealth.* New York: Harpers.

Holicki, Sabine. 1984. "Isolationsdrohung—Sozialpsychologische Aspekte eines publizistikwissenschaftlichen Konzepts." Master's thesis, Johannes Gutenberg-Universität, Mainz.

Holtzendorff, Franz von. 1879, 1880. *Wesen und Werth der öffentlichen Meinung.* Munich: M. Rieger'sche Universitäts-Buchhandlung (Gustav Himmer).

Homer. 1951. *The Iliad of Homer.* Trans. with an Introduction by Richmond Lattimore. Chicago and London: The University of Chicago Press.

Hubbard, B. A. F., and E. S. Karnofsky. 1982. *Plato's Protagoras: A Socratic Commentary,* with a Foreword by M. F. Burnyeat. London: The Trinity Press.

Hume, David. [1739/1740] 1896. *A Treatise of Human Nature.* Reprinted from the original edition in three volumes. Ed. L. A. Selby-Bigge. Oxford: At the Clarendon Press.

———. [1751] 1962. *Enquiries Concerning the Human Understanding and Concerning the Principles of Morals*. Ed. L. A. Selby-Bigge. 2d ed. Oxford: At the Clarendon Press.

———. [1741/1742] 1963. *Essays Moral, Political, and Literary*. London: Oxford University Press.

Hyman, Herbert. 1957. "Toward a Theory of Public Opinion." *Public Opinion Quarterly* 21:54–60.

Ihering, Rudolph von. 1883. *Der Zweck im Recht*. Vol. 2. Leipzig: Breitkopf and Härtel.

Institut für Demoskopie Allensbach. 1952. "Die Stimmung im Bundesgebiet." October. Graph.

International Encyclopedia of Communications. New York, Oxford: Oxford University Press, 1989.

International Encyclopedia of the Social Sciences, ed. David L. Sills. New York: Macmillan Co. & Free Press, 1968.

Jäckel, Anne. 1988. "Ungeschriebene Gesetze im Lichte der sozialpsychologischen Theorie öffentlicher Meinung." Master's thesis, Johannes Gutenberg-Universität, Mainz.

Jahoda, Marie. 1959. "Conformity and Independence: A Psychological Analysis." *Human Relations* 12:99–120.

John of Salisbury [1159] 1927. *The Statesman's Book of John of Salisbury. Being the Fourth, Fifth, and Sixth Books, and Selections from the Seventh and Eighth Books, of the Policraticus*. Trans. and with an Intro. by John Dickinson. New York: Russell & Russell.

Jordan, E. 1930. *Theory of Legislation*. Indianapolis: Progress Publishing Company.

Kaiser, Joseph H. 1975. "Sozialauffassung, Lebenserfahrung und Sachverstand in der Rechtsfindung." *Neue Juristische Wochenschrift*, no. 49.

Kant, Immanuel. 1893. *Critique of Pure Reason*. Trans. J. M. D. Meiklejohn. London: George Bell & Sons.

Katz, Elihu. 1981. "Publicity and Pluralistic Ignorance: Notes on 'The Spiral of Silence.'" In *Öffentliche Meinung und Sozialer Wandel/ Public Opinion and Social Change*. Festschrift for Elisabeth Noelle-Neumann, ed. Horst Baier, Hans Mathias Kepplinger, and Kurt Reumann, 28–38. Opladen: Westdeutscher Verlag.

Kepplinger, Hans Mathias. 1975. *Realkultur und Medienkultur: Literarische Karrieren in der Bundesrepublik*. Alber-Broschur Kommunikation, vol. 1. Freiburg and Munich: Karl Alber.

———. 1979. "Ausgewogen bis zur Selbstaufgabe? Die Fernsehberichterstattung über die Bundestagswahl 1976 als Fallstudie eines kommunikationspolitischen Problems." *Media Perspektiven*, no. 11:750–55.

———. 1980a. "Optische Kommentierung in der Fernsehberichterstattung über den Bundestagswahlkampf 1976." In *Politikfeld-Forschung 1979*, ed. Thomas Ellwein. Opladen: Westdeutscher Verlag.

———. 1980b. "Kommunikation im Konflikt. Gesellschaftliche Bedingungen kollektiver Gewalt." *Mainzer Universitätsgespräche*, Mainz.

———. 1983. "Visual Biases in Television Campaign Coverage." In *Mass Communication Review Yearbook*, ed. Ellen Wartella, D. Charles Whitney, and Sven Windahl, 3:391–405. Beverly Hills: Sage.

———. 1987. *Darstellungseffekte: Experimentelle Untersuchungen zur Wirkung von Pressefotos und Fernsehfilmen*. Alber-Broschur Kommunikation, vol. 15. Freiburg and Munich: Karl Alber.

———. 1988. "Die Kernenergie in der Presse: Eine Analyse zum Einfluß subjektiver Faktoren auf die Konstruktion von Realität." *Kölner Zeitschrift für Soziologie und Sozialpsychologie* 40:659–83.

———. 1989a. *Künstliche Horizonte. Folgen, Darstellung und Akzeptanz von Technik in der Bundesrepublik Deutschland*. Frankfurt/Main: Campus.

———. 1989b. "Nonverbale Kommunikation: Darstellungseffekte." In *Fischer Lexikon Publizistik—Massenkommunikation*, ed. Elisabeth Noelle-Neumann, Winfried Schulz, Jürgen Wilke, 241–255. Frankfurt/Main: Fischer Taschenbuch-Verlag.

Kepplinger, Hans Mathias, and W. Donsbach. 1982. "The Influence of Camera Angles and Political Consistency on the Perception of a Party Speaker." Paper presented to the 5th International Conference on Experimental Research in TV Instruction, St. Johns, Canada, 28–30 June.

Kepplinger, Hans Mathias, and Michael Hachenberg. 1979. "The Challenging Minority: A Study in Social Change." Lecture at the annual conference of the International Communication Association, Philadelphia, May 1979.

Kepplinger, Hans Mathias, and Herbert Roth. 1979. "Creating a Crisis: German Mass Media and Oil Supply in 1973/74. *Public Opinion Quarterly* 43:285–96.

Klapp, Orrin E. 1954. "Heroes, Villains, and Fools as Agents of Social Control." *American Sociological Review* 19, no. 1:56–62.

König, René. 1967. "Das Recht im Zusammenhang der sozialen Normensysteme." *Kölner Zeitschrift für Soziologie und Sozialpsychologie*, special issue 11, Studien und Materialien zur Rechtssoziologie, 36–53.

Lamp, Erich. 1988. "Öffentliche Meinung im Alten Testament: Eine Untersuchung der sozialpsychologischen Wirkungsmechanismen öffentlicher Meinung in Texten alttestamentlicher Überlieferung von den Anfängen bis in babylonische Zeit." Dissertation, Johannes Gutenberg-Universität, Mainz.

Landecker, Werner S. 1950. "Types of Integration and Their Measurement." *American Journal of Sociology* 56:332–40. Reprinted 1955 in Paul F. Lazarsfeld and Morris Rosenberg, eds., *The Language of So-*

cial Research: A Reader in the Methodology of Social Research, 19–27. New York and London: Free Press and Collier-Macmillan.

LaPiere, Richard T. 1954. *A Theory of Social Control.* New York, London, and Toronto: McGraw-Hill.

Lawick-Goodall, Jane van. 1971. *In the Shadow of Man.* Boston: Houghton Mifflin.

Lazarsfeld, Paul F. 1957. "Public Opinion and the Classical Tradition." *Public Opinion Quarterly* 21, no. 1:39–53.

Lazarsfeld, Paul, Bernard Berelson and Hazel Gaudet. [1944] 1948, 1968. *The People's Choice: How the Voter Makes Up His Mind in a Presidential Campaign.* 2d ed. 1948; 3d ed. 1968. New York: Columbia University Press.

LeGoff, Jacques. 1989. "Kann denn Lachen Sünde sein? Die mittelalterliche Geschichte einer sozialen Verhaltensweise." *Frankfurter Allgemeine Zeitung,* no. 102 (3 May 1989): N3.

Lenau, Nikolaus. 1954. *Stundenbuch für Letternfreunde: Besinnliches und Spitziges über Schreiber und Schrift, Leser und Buch.* Ed. Horst Kliemann. Berlin and Frankfurt.

Leonhardt. R. W. 1965. "Der Kampf der Meinungsforscher. Elisabeth Noelle-Neumann: 'Ich würde mich gar nicht wundern, wenn die SPD gewänne.'" *Die Zeit,* 17 September.

Lersch, Philipp. 1951. *Gesicht und Seele: Grundlinien einer mimischen Diagnostik.* Munich and Basel: Reinhardt.

Lewin, Kurt. 1947. "Group Decision and Social Change." In *Readings in Social Psychology,* ed. Theodore M. Newcomb and Eugene L. Hartley, 330–44. New York: Henry Holt and Company.

———. (1935–1946) 1948. *Resolving Social Conflicts: Selected Papers on Group Dynamics.* A Publication of the University of Michigan Research Center for Group Dynamics, ed. Gertrud W. Lewin. New York: Harper.

Limmer, Wolfgang. 1976. "Wem schrei ich um Hilfe?" *Der Spiegel,* no. 41:236–39.

Lippmann, Walter. [1922, 1954] 1965. *Public Opinion.* New York: Macmillan—Paperback edition 1965, New York: Free Press.

Locke, John. 1824. *The Works of John Locke.* Frederic Ives Carpenter Memorial Collection, 12th ed.

———. [1690] 1894. *An Essay Concerning Human Understanding.* Drafted in 1671. Historical-critical edition. Ed. Alexander Campbell Fraser. 2 vols. Oxford: At the Clarendon Press.

Lorenz, Konrad. 1966. *On Aggression.* Trans. Marjorie Kerr Wilson. New York: Harcourt, Brace & World.

Lowell, A. Lawrence. 1913. *Public Opinion and Popular Government.* New York.

Luhmann, Niklas. 1971. "Öffentliche Meinung." In *Politische Planung:*

Aufsätze zur Soziologie von Politik und Verwaltung, 9–34. Opladen: Westdeutscher Verlag. First published in 1970 in *Politische Viertel- jahresschrift* 11, no. 1:2–28; reprinted 1974 in *Zur Theorie der poli- tischen Kommunikation,* ed. Wolfgang R. Langenbucher, 27–54, 311– 17; Munich: R. Piper & Co.; and 1979 in *Politik und Kommunikation: Über die öffentliche Meinungsbildung,* ed. Wolfgang R. Langen- bucher, 29–61. Munich and Zurich: R. Piper & Co.

Machiavelli, Niccolò. [1532] 1971. "Il Principe." In *Tutte le Opere,* ed. Mario Martelli. Florence: Sansoni. English: 1950. *The Prince and the Discourses.* Trans.: Luigi Ricci, E. R. P. Vincent, and Christian Det- mold. New York: Random House.

Madison, James. [1788] 1961. "The Federalist No. 49." In *The Federalist,* ed. Jacob E. Cooke, 338–47. Middletown, Conn.: Wesleyan University Press.

Malraux, André. 1972. *Felled Oaks: Conversation with DeGaulle,* Trans. Irene Clephane. New York: Holt Rinehart & Winston.

Mathes, Sabine. 1989. "Die Einschätzung des Meinungsklimas im Kon- flikt um die Kernenergie durch Personen mit viel und wenig Fern- sehnutzung." Master's thesis, Johannes Gutenberg-Universität, Mainz.

McCombs, M. E., and D. L. Shaw. 1972. "The Agenda-Setting Function of Mass Media." *Public Opinion Quarterly* 36:176–87.

McDougall, William. 1920, 1921. *The Group Mind.* Cambridge: At the University Press.

McLeod, J. M., L. B. Becker and J. E. Byrnes. 1974. "Another Look at the Agenda-Setting Function of the Press." *Communication Research,* no. 1:131–66.

Mead, George Herbert. 1934. *Mind, Self, and Society: From the Stand- point of a Social Behaviorist.* Chicago: University of Chicago Press.
———. 1982. "1927 Class Lectures in Social Psychology." In *The Individ- ual and the Social Self,* ed. David L. Miller. Chicago: University of Chicago Press.

Mead, Margaret. 1937. "Public Opinion Mechanisms among Primitive Peoples." *Public Opinion Quarterly* 1 (July): 5–16.

Merton, Robert K. [1949] 1957. *Social Theory and Social Structure: To- ward the Codification of Theory and Research.* New York: Free Press.

Milgram, Stanley. 1961. "Nationality and Conformity." *Scientific Ameri- can* 205:45–51.

Molcho, Samy. 1983. *Körpersprache.* Munich: Mosaik-Verlag.

Montaigne, Michel de. [1588] 1962. "Essais." In Oeuvres complètes, ed. Maurice Rat and Albert Thibaut. Paris: Gallimard. English, 1908. *The Essayes of Michael Lord of Montaigne.* Trans. John Florio. 3 vols. London: Grant Richards.

Moores, Kaaren Marita. 1990. "Die öffentliche Meinung im Werk Montes- quieus." Master's thesis, Johannes Gutenberg-Universität, Mainz.

Moreno, Jacob L. [1934] 1953. *Who Shall Survive? Foundations of Socio-metry, Group Psychotherapy and Sociodrama.* Rev. ed. Beacon, N.Y.: Beacon House.

Moscovici, Serge. 1991. "Silent Majorities and Loud Minorities. Commentary on Noelle-Neumann." In *Communication Yearbook* 14, ed. James A. Anderson. Newbury Park: Sage.

Mreschar, Renate I. 1979. "Schmidt war besser im Bild als Kohl: Universität analysierte Kameraarbeit bei der TV-Berichterstattung vor der Bundestagswahl 76." *Frankfurter Rundschau,* no. 255 (1 November 1979): 26.

Müller, Johannes von. [1777] 1819. "Zuschrift an alle Eidgenossen." In *Sämmtliche Werke,* ed. Johann Georg Müller, pt. 27, 24–50. Tübingen: J. G. Cotta'sche Buchhandlung.

Murie Adolph. 1944. *The Wolves of Mount McKinley.* Washington: U.S. National Park Service, Fauna Series, no. 5.

Nagler, Johannes [1918] 1970. *Die Strafe: Eine juristisch-empirische Untersuchung.* Aalen: Scientia. Reprint of the Leipzig edition of 1918.

Neumann, Erich Peter, and Elisabeth Noelle. 1961. *Umfragen über Adenauer: Ein Portät in Zahlen.* Allensbach and Bonn: Verlag für Demoskopie.

Neumann, Gerd-Heinrich. 1981. *Normatives Verhalten und aggressive Aussenseiterreaktionen bei geselliglebenden Vögeln und Säugern.* Opladen: Westdeutscher Verlag.

Newcomb, Theodore. 1950. *Social Psychology.* New York: Dryden.

Nibelungenlied, Das. 1965. Trans. Felix Genzmer. Stuttgart: Reclam.

Niedermann, Anne. 1991. "Ungeschriebene Gesetze: Ein sozialpsychologischer Ansatz zur Beschreibung des Spannungsfeldes zwischen öffentlicher Meinung und Recht." Dissertation, Johannes Gutenberg-Universität, Mainz.

Niedermann, Bernd. 1991. "Öffentliche Meinung und Herrschaft am Beispiel des erfolgreichen Politikers Kardinal Richelieu." Master's thesis. Johannes Gutenberg-Universität Mainz.

Nietzsche, Friedrich. 1967. "Zur Genealogie der Moral. Dritte Abhandlung: was bedeuten asketische Ideale?" In *Werke.* Kritische Gesamtausgabe, vol. 6, pt. 2, ed. Giorgio Colli and Mazzino Montinari. Berlin and New York: de Gruyter.

Noelle, Elisabeth. 1966. *Öffentliche Meinung und Soziale Kontrolle.* Recht und Staat, no. 329. Tübingen: J. C. B. Mohr (Paul Siebeck).

Noelle-Neumann, Elisabeth. 1971. "Öffentliche Meinung." In *Publizistik: Das Fischer Lexikon,* ed. Elisabeth Noelle-Neumann and Winfried Schulz. Frankfurt/Main: Fischer.

―――. 1973. "Return to the Concept of Powerful Mass Media." *Studies of Broadcasting,* no. 9 (March 1973): 67–112.

―――. 1974. "Die Schweigespirale: Über die Entstehung der öffentlichen Meinung." In *Standorte im Zeitstrom: Festschrift für Arnold Gehlen zum 70. Geburtstag am 29. Januar 1974,* ed. Ernst Forsthoff and Reinhard Hörstel, 229–30. Frankfurt/Main: Athenäum. Reprinted 1977, 1979, in Elisabeth Noelle-Neumann, *Öffentlichkeit als Bedrohung: Beiträge zur empirischen Kommunikationsforschung,* 169–203. Alber-Broschur Kommunikation, vol. 6. Freiburg and Munich: Karl Alber. English: 1974. "The Spiral of Silence: A Theory of Public Opinion." *Journal of Communication* 24:43–51.

———. 1977a. "Turbulences in the Climate of Opinion: Methodological Applications of the Spiral of Silence Theory." *Public Opinion Quarterly* 41:143–58.

———. 1977b. "Das doppelte Meinungsklima: Der Einfluss des Fernsehens im Wahlkampf 1976." *Politische Vierteljahresschrift* 18, nos. 2–3:408–51. English: 1978. "The Dual Climate of Opinion: The Influence of Television in the 1976 West German Federal Election." In *Elections and Parties,* ed. Max Kaase and Klaus von Beyme, 137–69. German Political Studies, vol. 3. Beverly Hills: Sage.

———. 1978. "Kampf um die öffentliche Meinung: Eine vergleichende sozialpsychologische Analyse der Bundestagswahlen 1972 und 1976." In *Entscheidung ohne Klarheit: Anmerkungen und Materialien zur Bundestagswahl 1976,* ed. Dieter Just and Peter Röhrig, 125–67. Bonn: Schriftenreihe der Bundeszentrale für politische Bildung, vol. 127.

———. 1979. "Die Führungskrise der CDU im Spiegel einer Wahl: Analyse eines dramatischen Meinungsumschwungs." *Frankfurter Allgemeine Zeitung,* no. 72 (26 March 1979): 10.

———. 1981. "Das Bundesverfassungsgericht und die ungeschriebenen Gesetze—Antwort an Ernst Benda." *Die Öffentliche Verwaltung* 35:883–88.

———. 1984. *The Spiral of Silence: Public Opinion—Our Social Skin.* Chicago/London: University of Chicago Press. German edition (1980): *Die Schweigespirale: Öffentliche Meinung—unsere soziale Haut.* Munich/Zurich: Piper. Revised and enlarged edition (1989): *Öffentliche Meinung: Die Entdeckung der Schweigespirale.* Frankfurt/Main/Wien/Berlin: Ullstein.

———. 1985. "The Spiral of Silence: A Response." In *Political Communication Yearbook 1984,* ed. Keith R. Sanders, Linda Lee Kaid, and Dan Nimmo, 66–94. Carbondale, Edwardsville: Southern Illinois University Press.

———. 1989a. "Advances in Spiral of Silence Research." *KEIO Communication Review* 10:3–34.

———. 1989b. "Die Theorie der Schweigespirale als Instrument der Medienwirkungsforschung." *Kölner Zeitschrift für Soziologie und Sozialpsychologie,* special issue 30, Massenkommunikation, 418–40.

———. 1991. "The Theory of Public Opinion: The Concept of the Spiral of Silence." In *Communication Yearbook 14,* ed. James A. Anderson, 256–87. Newbury Park: Sage.

Nosanchuk, T. A., and Jack Lightstone. 1974. "Canned Laughter and Public and Private Conformity." *Journal of Personality and Social Psychology* 29:153–56.

O'Gorman, Hubert, and Stephen L. Garry. 1976. "Pluralistic Ignorance—A Replication and Extension." *Public Opinion Quarterly* 40: 449–58.

Oncken, Hermann, 1914. "Politik, Geschichtsschreibung und öffentliche Meinung." In *Historisch-politische Aufsätze und Reden* 1:203–43. Munich and Berlin: R. Oldenbourg.

Osgood, Charles E., George J. Suci, and Percy H. Tannenbaum. [1957] 1964. *The Measurement of Meaning*. Urbana, Ill.: University of Illinois Press.

Ostertag, Michael. 1992. "Zum Wirkungspotential nichtsprachlicher Äußerungen in politischen Sendungen. Der Einfluß offensiver und defensiver Verhaltensstrategien auf das Erscheinungsbild von Politikern und Journalisten in Fernsehinterviews." Dissertation, Johannes Gutenberg-Universität, Mainz.

Palmer, Paul A. [1936] 1950. "The Concept of Public Opinion in Political Theory." In *Reader in Public Opinion and Communication,* ed. Bernard Berelson and Morris Janowitz, 3–13. Glencoe: Free Press.

Park, Robert E. [1972] 1975. *The Crowd and the Public and Other Essays*. ed. Henry Elsner, Jr., and trans. Charlotte Elsner. Heritage of Sociology series. Chicago: University of Chicago Press.

Peer, Limor. 1992. "The Practice of Opinion Polling as a Disciplinary Mechanism: A Foucauldian Perspective." *International Journal of Public Opinion Research* 4, no. 3.

Petzolt, Dieter. 1979. "Öffentlichkeit als Bewusstseinszustand: Versuch einer Klärung der psychologischen Bedeutung." Master's thesis, Johannes Gutenberg-Universität, Mainz.

Plato. 1900. "The Republic" In *Works,* vol. 2, trans. Henry Davis. London: George Bell & Sons.

Pound, Roscoe. 1930. "Public Opinion and Social Control." *Proceedings of the National Conference of Social Work*. 57th annual session held in Boston, Mass., June 8–14, 1930. Chicago: University of Chicago Press.

Pribram, Karl. 1979. "Sehen, Hören, Lesen—und die Folgen im Kopf: Informationsverarbeitung im Gehirn." Lecture given at the joint meeting of specialists of the German Society for Reading, the foundation In Medias Res, and the German Society for Communication Research: "The Ecology of the Media—a Future Problem of Our Society: On the Way Toward Cable-Connected Illiterates?" on 27 April 1979, in Mainz.

Priscillianus. 1889. *Opera. Priscilliani quae supersunt*. Maximem partem nuper detexit adiectisque commentariis criticis et indicibus primus edidit Georgius Schepss. Pragae, Vindobonae: F. Tempsky. Lipsiae: G. Freytag.

Rabelais, François. 1955. *Œuvres complètes*. Texte établi et annoté par Jacques Boulenger. Rev. ed., ed. Lucien Scheler. Paris: Gallimard.

Raffel, Michael. 1984. "Der Schöpfer des Begriffs *öffentliche Meinung*: Michel de Montaigne." *Publizistik* 29, no. 1.

————. 1985. "Michel de Montaigne und die Dimension Öffentlichkeit: Ein Beitrag zur Theorie der öffentlichen Meinung." Dissertation, Johannes Gutenberg-Universität, Mainz.

Reiwald, Paul. 1948. *Vom Geist der Massen: Handbuch der Massenpsychologie*. Internationale Bibliothek für Psychologie und Soziologie, vol. 1. Zurich: Pan Verlag.

Renaudet, Augustin. 1954. *Erasme et l'Italie*. Geneva: Librairie E. Droz.

Richelieu, Armand du Plessis Cardinal de. [1688] 1947. *Testament Politique*. Ed. Louis André; preface by Leon Noel. Paris: Robert Lafont.

Richter, Horst E. 1976. *Flüchten oder Standhalten*. Hamburg: Rowohlt.

Roegele, Otto, B. 1979. "Massenmedien und Regierbarkeit." In *Regierbarkeit: Studien zu ihrer Problematisierung*, vol. 2, ed. Wilhelm Hennis, Peter Graf Kielmansegg, and Ulrich Matz, 177–210. Stuttgart: Klett-Cotta.

Ross, Edward Alsworth. [1901, 1929] 1969. *Social Control: A Survey of the Foundations of Order*. With an introduction by Julius Weinberg, Gisela J. Hinkle, and Roscoe C. Hinkle. Cleveland and London: The Press of Case Western Reserve University. First published by Macmillan in 1901.

Rossow, Kenneth. "Sociodemographic Characteristics, Perceived Normative Threat, and Response Falsification for Survey Topics with High Social Desirability." Lecture presented at AAPOR annual meeting, May 1983.

Rousseau, Jean-Jacques. [1762] 1953. "The Social Contract." In *Political Writings*, ed. and trans. Frederick Watkins. London: Nelson.

————. [1762] 1962a. "Du Contrat Social." In *Du Contrat Social ou Principes du Droit Politique*. Paris: Garnier.

————. [1762] 1962b. "Lettre à M. D'Alembert." In *Du Contrat Social ou Principes du Droit Politique*. Paris: Garnier.

————. [1744] 1964a. "Depêches de Venise. XCI." In *Oeuvres complètes*, vol. 3. La Pléiade. Paris: Gallimard.

————. [1750/55] 1964b. "Discours sur l'origine et les foundements de l'inégalité parmi les hommes." In *Oeuvres complètes*, vol. 3. La Pléiade. Paris: Gallimard. English: 1964. *The First and Second Discourses*. Ed. Roger D. Masters, trans. Roger D. and Judith R. Masters. New York: St. Martin's Press.

————. [1761] 1964c. "La nouvelle Héloise." In *Oeuvres complètes*, vol. 2. La Pléiade. Paris: Gallimard.

————. [1762] 1964d. "Émile ou de l'éducation." In *Oeuvres complètes*, vol. 4. La Pléiade. Paris: Gallimard. English: 1957. *Émile*. Trans. Barbara Foxley. London: J. M. Dent & Sons.

———. [1762] 1967. *Lettre à d'Alembert sur les Spectacles.* Paris: Garnier-Flammariche. English: 1960. *Politics and the Arts.* Trans. Allan Bloom. Glencoe, Ill.: Free Press.

———. [1766–70] 1968. *Les Confessions.* Paris: Garnier-Flammarion. English: 1945. *The Confessions of Jean Jacques Rousseau.* New York: Random House.

Rusciano, Frank L. [n.d.] "Passing Brave: Elite Perspectives on the Machiavellian Tradition." Master's thesis, Department of Political Science, University of Chicago.

Rusciano, Frank L., and Roberta Fiske-Rusciano. 1990. "Towards a Notion of 'World Opinion.'" *International Journal of Public Opinion Research* 2, no. 4:305–22.

Salmon, Charles T., and F. Gerald Kline. 1985. "The Spiral of Silence Ten Years Later: An Examination and Evaluation." In *Political Communication Yearbook 1984,* ed. Keith R. Sanders, Linda Lee Kaid, and Dan Nimmo, 3–30. Carbondale, Edwardsville: Southern Illinois University Press.

Sauerwein, J. A. 1933. "The Moulders of Public Opinion." In: *Public Opinion and World Politics,* ed. Quincy Wright. Chicago: University of Chicago Press.

Schanck, R. L. 1932. "A Study of a Community and Its Groups and Institutions Conceived of as Behaviors of Individuals. *Psychological Monographs* 43.

Schlarb, Armin. 1984/85. "Die Beziehung zwischen öffentlicher Meinung und symbolischem Interaktionismus." Term paper, Johannes Gutenberg-Universität, Mainz.

Schlegel, Friedrich. 1799. *Lucinde.* Berlin: Heinrich Frölich.

Schöne, Walter, 1939. *Der Aviso des Jahres 1609.* Published in facsimile with an afterword. Leipzig: Otto Harrassowitz.

Schulman, Gary I. 1968. "The Popularity of Viewpoints and Resistance to Attitude Change." *Journalism Quarterly* 45:86–90.

Schulz, Winfried. 1976. *Die Konstruktion von Realität in den Nachrichtenmedien: Eine Analyse der aktuellen Berichterstattung.* Alber Broschur Kommunikation, vol. 4. Freiburg: Karl Alber.

Sherif, Muzafer. [1936] 1965. *The Psychology of Social Norms.* New York: Octagon Books.

Smend, Rudolf. 1928. *Verfassung und Verfassungsrecht.* Munich: Duncker & Humblot.

———. 1956. "Integrationslehre." In *Handwörterbuch der Sozialwissenschaften,* 5:299–302. Stuttgart, Tübingen, and Göttingen: Gustav Fischer, J. C. B. Mohr (Paul Siebeck), and Vandenhoeck & Ruprecht.

Smith, Brewster M. 1970. "Some Psychological Perspectives on the Theory of Public Opinion." *Public Opinion Quarterly* 34:454–55.

Snyderman, Mark, and Stanley Rothman. 1988. *The IQ Controversy: The Media and Public Policy.* New Brunswick: Transaction Books.

Speier, Hans. 1950. "Historical Development of Public Opinion." *American Journal of Sociology* 55, no. 4:376–88.

Spencer, Herbert. (1879) 1966. "The Data of Ethics.: In *The Works of Herbert Spencer*, vol. 9, *The Principles of Ethics*, part 1, 1–303. Osnabrück: Otto Zeller.

Staatslexikon. Recht—Wirtschaft—Gesellschaft. Freiburg, Basel, Vienna: Verlag Herder, 1988.

Streller, Siegfried, ed. 1978. *Hutten—Müntzer—Luther: Werke in zwei Bänden*. 3d ed. Vol. 1. Berlin and Weimar: Aufbau-Verlag.

Stross, Brian. 1978. "Gossip in Ethnography." *Reviews in Anthropology*, 181–88.

Sturm, Hertha, Ruth von Haebler and Reinhard Helmreich. 1972. *Medienspezifische Lerneffekte: Eine empirische Studie zu Wirkungen von Fernsehen und Rundfunk*. Schriftenreihe des Internationalen Zentralinstituts für das Jugend- und Bildungsfernsehen, no. 5. Munich: TR-Verlagsunion.

Swift, Jonathan. [1706] 1965. "Thoughts on Various Subjects." In *Prose Works*, vol. 1, *A Tale of a Tub*. Oxford: Basil Blackwell.

Taine, Hippolyte. [1877] 1916. *Les origines de la France contemporaine, III. La Révolution l'Anarchie*. Vol. 1. Paris: Hachette.

Tarde, Gabriel. 1890. *Les lois de l'imitation*. Paris. English: 1903. *The Laws of Imitation*. New York: Holt.

———. 1898. "Le public et la foule." *La Revue de Paris*, vol. 4.

———. 1969. *Gabriel Tarde on Communication and Social Influence: Selected Papers*. Ed. with intro. by Terry N. Clark. Chicago and London: University of Chicago Press.

Taylor, Garth. 1982. "Pluralistic Ignorance and the Spiral of Silence: A Formal Analysis." *Public Opinion Quarterly* 46:311–35.

Temple, Sir William. [1672] 1964. *An Essay Upon the Original and Nature of Government*. The Augustan Reprint Society, Publication no. 109. Los Angeles: University of California.

T'Hart, Harm. 1981. "People's Perceptions of Public Opinion." Paper presented to the International Society of Political Psychology. Mannheim.

Thucidides. 1981. *Geschichte des Peleponnesischen Krieges*. Ed. and trans. Georg Peter Landmann. Munich: Deutscher Taschenbuch Verlag. English: 1881. *The History of the Peleponnesian War*. Trans. B. Jowett. Oxford: At the Clarendon Press.

Tischer, Angelika. 1979. "Der Begriff 'Öffentliche Meinung' bei Tocqueville." Master's thesis, Johannes Gutenberg-Universität, Mainz.

Tocqueville, Alexis de. [1835/40] 1948. *Democracy in America*. Ed. Phillips Bradley, trans. Henry Reeve. 2 vols. New York: Alfred A. Knopf.

———. [1856] 1952. "L'Ancien régime et la révolution." In *Oeuvres complètes*, vol. 2. Paris: Gallimard, English: 1955. *The Old Régime and the*

French Revolution. Trans. Stuart Gilbert. New York: Doubleday, Anchor.

Tönnies, Ferdinand. 1922. *Kritik der öffentlichen Meinung*. Berlin: Julius Springer.

Trotter, Wilfred. 1916. *Instincts of the Herd in War and Peace*. London: T. Fisher Unwin.

Tucholsky, Kurt. 1975. *Schnipsel*. Ed. Mary Gerold-Tucholsky and Fritz J. Raddatz. Reinbek: Rowohlt.

Turnbull, Colin M. 1961. *The Forest People: A Study of the Pygmies of the Congo*. New York: Simon and Schuster.

Uexküll, Thure von. 1963, 1964. *Grundfragen der psychosomatischen Medizin*. Reinbek: Rowohlt.

Van Zuuren, Florence J. 1983. "The Experience of Breaking the Rules." Paper presented at the "Symposium on Qualitative Research in Psychology" in Perugia, Italy, August 1983. Department of Psychology, University of Amsterdam, Revesz Report no. 47.

Veblen, Thorstein, [1899] 1970. *The Theory of the Leisure Class: An Economic Study of Institutions*. London: Unwin Books.

Verba, Sidney. 1970. "The Impact of the Public on Policy." *Public Opinion Quarterly* 34:455.

Warner, Lucien. 1939. "The Reliability of Public Opinion Survey." *Public Opinion Quarterly* 3:376–90.

Weiland, Jan Sperna, et al., eds. 1988. *Erasmus von Rotterdam: Die Aktualität seines Denkens*. Hamburg: Wittig.

Wiese, Leopold von. [1924–28] 1955. *System der Allgemeinen Soziologie als Lehre von den sozialen Prozessen und den sozialen Gebilden der Menschen (Beziehungslehre)*. Berlin: Duncker & Humblot.

Wilson, Francis. G. 1933. "Concepts of Public Opinion." *American Political Science Review* 27:371–91.

———. 1939. "James Bryce on Public Opinion: Fifty Years Later." *Public Opinion Quarterly* 3, no. 3:420–35.

Yavetz, Zvi. 1979. *Caesar in der öffentlichen Meinung*. Schriftenreihe des Instituts für Deutsche Geschichte, Unversität Tel Aviv, no. 3. Düsseldorf: Droste.

Young, James T. 1923. *The New American Government and Its Work*. New York: Macmilllan Co.

Zimen, Erik. 1981. *The Wolf: A Species in Danger*. Trans. Eric Mosbacher New York: Delacorte Press.

Zimmermann, Tassilo. 1988. "Das Bewußtsein von Öffentlichkeit bei Homer." Master's thesis, Johannes Gutenberg-Universität, Mainz.

Zippelius, Reinhold. 1978. "Verlust der Orientierungsgewissheit?" In *Recht und Gesellschaft: Festschrift für Helmut Schelsky zum 65. Geburtstag,* ed. Friedrich Kaulbach and Werner Krawietz. Berlin: Duncker & Humblot.

Index